BEYOND DETERRENCE

BEYOND DETERRENCE

Britain, Germany and the New European Security Debate

Oliver Ramsbotham
Research Fellow, School of Peace Studies,
University of Bradford, and Member of the Oxford Research Group

and

Hugh Miall
Member of the Oxford Research Group

in association with the
OXFORD RESEARCH GROUP

First published by
MACMILLAN PRESS LTD
Houndmills, Basingstoke, Hampshire RG21 6XS
and London
Companies and representatives
throughout the world

ISBN 0–333–55038–2

A catalogue record for this book is available
from the British Library.

This book is printed on paper suitable for recycling and
made from fully managed and sustained forest sources.

Transferred to digital printing 1999

Printed in Great Britain by
Antony Rowe Ltd, Chippenham, Wiltshire

Contents

v

List of Boxes

List of Tables

List of Figures

Acknowledgements

Hugh Miall and Oliver Ramsbotham are grateful to Betty Booth, Judith Fay, John Hamwee, Rosie Houldsworth, Paul Ingram, Erica Parra, Anne Piper, Tony Thomson and Tony Voss of the Oxford Research Group for support given, including reading and commenting on the text. Scilla Elworthy, Director of the Group, has provided constant inspiration. Jacquie Hope has given invaluable help in translation and advice on German left wing politics. Particular thanks are due to Lothar Gutjahr of the Institut für Friedensforschung und Sicherheitspolitik an der Universität Hamburg for organising the interviews with leading spokespersons from the political parties in the Bundestag on which Chapter 5 is based. His own analysis of West German conservative outlooks on foreign and defence policy between 1986 and 1990 is the finest available study of the subject and we hope to arrange to have it published in Britain as soon as possible. The contribution made by the Media Transcription Service should also be acknowledged.

Additional thanks for comments on passages adapted for an Institute for Public Policy Research paper go to Ken Booth, Michael Clarke, Ronald Higgins, Mary Kaldor, Catherine Kelleher, Patricia Lewis, Robert Neild, Jane Sharp and the Director of the Institute, James Cornford.

The authors are especially grateful to the Barrow and Geraldine S Cadbury Trust, the Network Trust, the Joseph Rowntree Charitable Trust, the Woodstock Trust, the Howard Cheney Peace Settlement and Dr Hector Cameron who made the work possible.

Introduction and Summary of Main Argument

This book begins with the remarkable events of 1989 and 1990. The collapse of communism in Central and Eastern Europe, the Soviet acceptance of the unification of Germany, the signing of the highly asymmetrical Conventional Forces in Europe (CFE) agreement, the announced withdrawal of all Soviet troops based on foreign territory, the unanimous United Nations Security Council condemnation of Iraqi aggression and subsequent endorsement of economic sanctions and military action – these unprecedented developments convinced even hard-headed pragmatists that a critical turning-point in world affairs had now been reached. NATO's London Declaration of 6 July 1990 stated officially that the two alliances 'are no longer adversaries'. The Paris Charter of 21 November 1990 proclaimed 'a new era of peace and cooperation in Europe'. In the wake of the Iraqi invasion of Kuwait the US Secretary of State referred to 'a critical juncture in history',[1] the British Foreign Secretary to 'a defining moment' in which 'the international community through the United Nations' could create a 'new world order' if the Iraqi challenge to the UN/ CSCE principle of border inviolability was crushed.[2] In his 1991 new year message to the America people the Soviet President said

> 'the most important thing now, at this crucial period of history, is firmly to understand that the nations of the world may achieve progress and security for all, and consequently for themselves, only through common efforts, cooperation and acknowledgement of interdependence of interests'.[3]

This amounted to nothing less than a blueprint for a transition from confrontation to cooperation in Europe. The age of great power war had ended in 1945, since when the Cold War era of mutual deterrence associated with superpower domination and the bloc system had supervened. As is amplified in the text, this was by its nature a highly ambiguous transitional phase, and, at any rate so far as the 1989 British Statement on the Defence Estimates was concerned, the declared aim now was to move beyond it to create a system of 'mutually assured security' in which:

'the total neutralisation of war becomes so sure, accepted and permanent that, even when interests may differ widely, nations of East and West can conduct their business together by means in which the thought of armed conflict simply plays no part'.[4]

As 'democracy and the rule of law are extended far and wide', the military dimension would be progressively marginalised, and attention would be concentrated instead on tackling the great common challenges that confronted all CSCE countries, indeed the whole world. For example:

'Our ability to come together to stop or limit damage to the world's environment will be the greatest test of how far we can act as a world community.'[5]

To this extent by the end of 1990 there can be said at government level to have been an unprecedented measure of declared agreement about ends in Europe. But this needs to be qualified in two ways.

First, in the Soviet Union mounting economic chaos and nationalist separatism have eroded the centre ground that Mikhail Gorbachev has been trying to build on. By the beginning of 1991 the strength of the reactionary backlash has become painfully evident. Unable, or perhaps as a Leninist unwilling, to take the radical path at home, the President seems to be attempting to placate domestic conservative opinion (the crushing of the Baltic Republics and the appointment of Boris Pugo as interior minister) while still preserving the 'new thinking' that has transformed the international scene abroad (continued commitment to the 'common European home' and the appointment of Alexandr Bessmertnykh as foreign minister). It is doubtful if this can be sustained.

Second, in the West, despite the declared agreement about ends, there remains deep and at times bitter disagreement about means. This disagreement covers almost every aspect of the security question and reaches out to embrace the whole of politics. Indeed it involves the definition of security itself. Beneath it lie two poles to the debate, found in various forms in most countries. One is described here as a realist 'view from within', which interprets international affairs as a

maelstrom of competing state interests and defines threats to security
as threats to the interests of particular countries or alliances. From this
perspective the emphasis in the West is on collective alliance security
and deterrence. The other pole is described as a transformationist
'view from above', which sees the main threats now as common threats
throughout the region and the remedies therefore as common
remedies. Here the emphasis is on common security and disarmament. The realist view is stronger towards the 'right' end of the
political spectrum (or in the Soviet Union among the 'conservatives'),
the transformationist view towards the 'left' (or in the Soviet Union
among the 'reformers').

What is the significance of this realist/transformationist debate? Its
significance lies in the way it relates to the transitional age of mutual
deterrence at great power level that Europe is passing through. This
era looks both ways – forward to a future age of mutually assured
security if war is indeed to be permanently prevented; back to a past
age of great power war in case deterrence fails. The realist and
transformationist poles recognise different aspects of this hybrid
epoch. The realists accurately acknowledge the fact of unregenerate
political interests, military capabilities and multiple power centres
inherited from the past age of war in Europe. The transformationists
recognise the overriding imperatives of mutual vulnerability which
now impel all responsible decision-makers forward to a future age of
mutually assured security. Neither has a monopoly of the truth. Both
must be taken account of in the formulation of policy throughout the
continent. But two asymmetries further complicate the situation and
give the debate its final significance.

The first asymmetry strongly favours the realist position. It is the
fact that, for obvious reasons, realist thinking is entrenched in existing
centres of power. This makes realist positions mutually reinforcing.
For example, between 1985 and 1990 the extraordinary transformationist initiatives of Soviet Perestroika undermined realist orthodoxy
in the West and greatly strengthened transformationist thinking. But
the revival of conservative realism in the Soviet Union is likely to have
the opposite effect. Realists in the West say that the conservative
backlash in the Soviet Union proves how wise they were to insist that
the West should keep its guard up. Transformationists say that one
contributory reason for this backlash has been the West's inexcusable
reluctance to reciprocate Soviet gestures adequately. Whichever view is
accepted, it is undoubtedly the case that realists in positions of power
are able to appeal to potent particular interests at times of tension, to

cite rival power centres as justification for their policies, and to manipulate the machinery of state secrecy to stifle opposition and protect themselves from outside challenge. This is becoming increasingly prevalent again in the Soviet Union, where centralised powers of repression are very great, but it is also evident in a different form in the West. Where dissidence is suppressed, in the East or in the West, it is invariably the transformationist voice that is silenced.

The second asymmetry, however, favours the transformationist position. At least, it should do. The logic of mutual vulnerability in the nuclear age now extends to include growing political, economic and cultural interdependence and universal exposure to overarching environmental threats. By determining the penalty of failure, it impels responsible leaders to transcend inherited realist instincts and to embrace the transformationist agenda. In the long term this can only be achieved to the extent that the realist 'view from within' is progressively replaced in centres of power throughout the region by a transformationist 'view from above'. It remains fundamentally important that this should continue to be the case in the Soviet Union, where recent transformationist policies now seem gravely threatened. But for their part Western countries like Britain have so far shown few signs of the necessary imaginative reciprocation, or awareness of the fundamental nature of the transformation that the logic of their own declared long-term policies themselves demand.

In short, both realist and transformationist perspectives play essential roles in the transitional era of mutual deterrence. But, whereas it is the transformationist perspective which eventually needs to prevail, realist instincts throughout the region are still successfully stifling it.

That is why the striking absence of defence/security debate in Britain is to be deplored. The insularity of the British defence debate of the 1980s as projected through the media, with its emphasis on 'independent' deterrence and 'unilateral' disarmament, was marked. Even this came to an end with the abandonment of unilateralism at the Labour Party conference in October 1989. Since then there has been silence. In 1990 British politics all of a sudden woke up to the fact that the days of 'splendid isolation' were over and the future lay in Europe. In the economic and monetary fields the evolution of Western Europe became a major theme of domestic politics. But the security dimension remained a lacuna. Inherited realist instincts, in the form of nationalist suspicion of European neighbours and Atlanticist yearning for a continuing world role, remained dominant, strongly reinforced by the experience of the Gulf war. Questions about the future of Europe, which can only be settled through cooperation with European partners, were drowned out.

This book aims to redress the balance. Despite recent suggestions to the contrary, even from a realist perspective British interests now largely coincide with those of other Western European (and increasingly Central and Eastern European) countries. If attention is focused below the level of national stereotype, a comparable spread of party political opinion can be discerned in most European countries, including Britain. It is a pan-European debate. And it is not so much a case of a simple 'either/or' as of variety of emphasis within a broad overall consensus ranged around the realist and transformationist poles. Unfortunately adversarial two-party British politics obscures this. It gives the impression that there must either be a choice between black-and-white diametric opposites or no debate at all.

Part I outlines the main security questions confronting European decision-makers and describes the two poles to the debate. Part II presents the German debate for purposes of comparison, because, for geographical and historical reasons, the transformationist agenda has been well developed there for many years. Part III analyses the British debate. On the surface it appears as if there have been two different debates going on in Germany and Britain. But closer scrutiny shows that this is not the case. There is now a comparable spread of party political opinion, as is to be expected in two West European democracies which belong to the same alliance (NATO) and community (the EC) and share the same basic interests and concerns. The conclusion to this part of the book (pp. 177–81) is that this should now be explicitly recognised and built on as both countries cooperate in the joint task of shaping a common European future. Part IV returns to the broad theme of Part I and the book ends by stressing the wider significance of the great realist-transformationist debate of which the German and British debates are part.

NOTES

1. James Baker, testimony to Congress, 5 September 1990.
2. Douglas Hurd, address to the United Nations, 26 September 1990.
3. Mikhail Gorbachev, *Soviet News*, 2 January 1991, no. 6559.

4. *Statement on the Defence Estimates* 1989, vol. 1, HMSO, pp. 11–12.
5. Margaret Thatcher, speech at Aspen, Colorado, 5 August 1990.

Part I
The Setting

1 9 November 1989: Five Anomalies in the Post-War European Security System Exposed

'On leaving church that evening a French journalist tells me a strange piece of news: Schabowski, the Communist Party boss in Berlin and Egon Krenz have hinted at the possibility that the border might be opened. I find Konstanze, my twenty-year old daughter, and her friend Astrid, who is twenty-one. Rapidly we jump into the car and drive at great speed to the nearest crossing: Bornholmer Strasse. We are among the very first to get there.

Dream and reality become confused. To our amazement the guards let us through. The girls cry. They cling together tightly on the back seat, as if they're expecting an air raid. We are crossing the strip that for twenty-eight years has been a death zone.

And suddenly we see West Berliners. They wave, cheer, shout. We look back. Hundreds, thousands are pouring out behind us. Now the news has spread like wildfire. There are people who recognise me. They pull open the car door. Kisses and tears. We are in a trance. All around us people are beating their fists on my car with joy. The dents will remain, souvenirs of that night. Then Astrid suddenly begs me to stop the car. She has never been in the West before. She longs to put her foot down on the street just once. Actually to touch the ground. Armstrong taking that very first step on the surface of the moon.'[1]

The breaching of the Berlin Wall on 9 November 1989 was a catalyst. Although historians teach us not to make too much of single events, it seemed evident to the millions who watched with astonishment on television throughout Europe that a watershed had been reached. This was a turning-point from which there could be no going back. The post-war order in Europe was disappearing fast and a new order was being created.

In Europe the security debate, which had begun in the late 1970s and gathered momentum during the second half of the 1980s in response to the advent of Mikhail Gorbachev, came to a head. Fundamental questions were now being asked about the whole future of European security. Party political opinion in different Western European countries coincided to create a truly international debate. Christian Democrats, Social Democrats and other parliamentary groupings developed coordinated alternative programmes. The issues were by definition transnational, so it was natural that the politics should be transnational too.[2]

In Britain, however, by an extraordinary irony of timing, political commentators had just decided that the 'defence debate' was over. They referred to the private British debate of the 1980s, which, so far as they were concerned, ended at the Labour Party conference in October 1989. That was when the main opposition party abandoned its commitment to scrap British nuclear weapons and get rid of American nuclear weapons from Britain no matter what happened elsewhere. Political commentators in Britain seemed to think that this was all there was to it. In their eyes the new issues raised by the collapse of the Berlin Wall did not connect with British politics at all. To the incomprehension of foreign observers, the British defence debate had been conducted in a foreign policy vacuum. When 'defence' dropped out of the political agenda after October 1989, all that was left was the vacuum. At exactly the moment when the European security debate entered its decisive phase, British politicians fell silent.

Why was the breaching of the Berlin Wall such a significant event?

Right through to the second half of 1989 there had been a near consensus among NATO and Warsaw Pact leaders that German unification must come last in what was expected to be the long process of European 'normalisation'. Years, if not decades, must pass while the initiatives of Yuri Andropov and Mikhail Gorbachev worked themselves out. Politicians from all the parties represented in the West German parliament agreed. Yet when the Berlin Wall fell it immediately became plain that German unification was going to come, not last, but first. Nothing could stop it. This was not a process initiated from above, as Soviet Perestroika had been. It was an irresistible popular movement fuelled from below.

And the fact that German unification was coming first, rather than last, altered almost everything else. It is hard to exaggerate its implications. The whole of the post-war European security system had been built on the premise of a divided Germany. Now that this premise had been removed, a series of anomalies that had until then been developing unobtrusively within the European security system were exposed. They could no longer be ignored. However reluctant a number of political leaders, particularly in the West, may have been to confront them, there was now no alternative but to do so.

1 CONTINUED MILITARY CONFRONTATION ACROSS A POLITICALLY NON-EXISTENT FRONTIER

The German anomaly itself was dramatic, if not absurd.

Militarily the two Germanies were still members of hostile alliances. Indeed, they were the front-line states. Even in peacetime the boundary between them, the inner German border, was called the Central Front. To the north and south the two alliances were separated by a belt of neutral countries. So it was along the Central Front that the decisive engagements were expected if war broke out. This was the axis around which the two gigantic blocs were locked.

In the 1980s, 380 000 of the 627 000 Soviet troops in Eastern Europe had been permanently stationed in East Germany together with great masses of equipment. They were linked to the vast reserves held ready in the Soviet Union by the 58 000 Soviet troops in Poland together with their communication, engineering and other support units.[3] For decades in the eyes of Western planners it had been these Russian troops in East Germany, maintained in a higher state of readiness than other Soviet forces, that had posed the most immediate threat to the West. 8000 tanks, 3300 heavy artillery pieces and 1530 warplanes seemed poised for a Blitzkrieg assault.[4] In contrast, the 70 000 Soviet troops in Czechoslovakia were not deployed against the West German border, but back behind the Prague–Brno–Bratislava line. The NVA (East German army) numbered 180 000. Other than Iceland (which has no forces) East Germany was the only European country in which foreign troops outnumbered its own.

Ranged against the NVA and the Soviet forces in East Germany were the bulk of NATO's European land forces. Most of the 330 000 American troops in Western Europe were permanently stationed in West Germany, as were British, Belgian, Dutch, Canadian and French

troops. The Bundeswehr was 440 000 strong. One in 54 of the
population living in Germany East and West was in the armed forces.[5]

So it was that easily the greatest armed confrontation in history
hinged along the 300-mile inner German border. Either side of the
frontier tanks ploughed backwards and forwards through the fields
and low-flying aircraft screamed across the skies. West Germany
hosted about 5 000 military exercises, 85 large field exercises, 580 000
aircraft sorties and 110 000 low-altitude practice flights a year.[6] Some
150 primary NATO nuclear units and 30 primary Warsaw Pact nuclear
units were stationed on German territory together with over 4000
warheads for missiles, shells and bombs. Nowhere else on earth were
nuclear weapons so numerous and so densely deployed (see Figure
1.1).[7]

Yet on 9 November 1989 the inner German border, militarily still
the key sector of the Central Front between the two greatest armed
alliances in the world, had politically ceased to exist.

2 A SECURITY SYSTEM DOMINATED BY OPPOSING BLOCS NO LONGER CORRESPONDING TO POLITICAL AND ECONOMIC REALITIES

Germany was not the only area where the inherited bloc system no
longer related to underlying realities.

Although attempts had been made to turn the Eastern bloc into a
viable economic and political entity, its cohesion was always essentially
military. The Warsaw Pact was a defensive glacis or a springboard for
further advance, depending upon one's point of view. Yet it became
increasingly plain that what counted in the modern world at great
power level was economic strength, not military might. Under
Brezhnev the Soviet Union had finally achieved military parity with
the United States as a global power. By the mid-1980s strategic nuclear
weapons systems proliferated, tanks were reported to be coming off
the production lines at the rate of 3000 a year, a submarine a month to
be slipping off the launchways.[8] But this was being achieved from an
economic base perhaps half the size of that of the United States. A
number of Western economists now calculate that the Soviet economy
stopped growing in the late 1970s and actually began to contract
during the 1980s. The same conclusion was probably reached some
years earlier in the Soviet Union. By the autumn of 1989, 243 of the

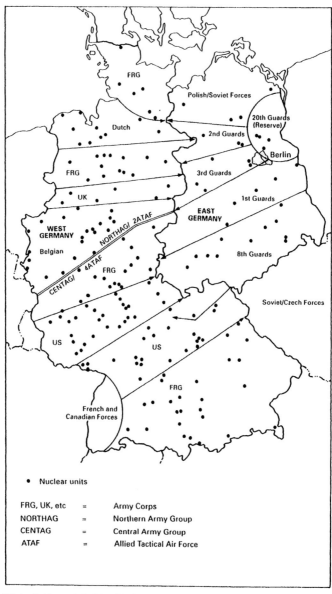

Source: W. A. Arkin and R. W. Fieldhouse, *Nuclear Battlefields*, Ballinger, 1985.

FIGURE 1.1 *The central-front in the 1980s: the greatest concentration of nuclear weapons in the world*

273 main consumer items were no longer regularly available on shop shelves. For the first time since the 1920s large-scale famine had been predicted for the winter of 1990–1.[9] The combination was unsustainable and catastrophic. It undermined the whole fabric of Soviet society:

> 'Squandering a quarter of our budget on military expenditure, we have ruined our country. As a ruined country we shall have no need of defence. An impoverished people have no need for an army.'[10]

Military power did not compensate the Soviet Union for loss of economic and cultural influence. For example, East Germans, whose standard of living was up to three times as high as that prevailing in the Soviet Union, had come to pity and despise rather than fear the ill-paid and dispirited Soviet conscripts marooned in their midst. It was the economically successful West Germany, which, without any military forces beyond its own borders, was rapidly gaining in influence and power. Nor had the giant Warsaw Pact military establishment even provided security for the Soviet Union. On the contrary, it had only helped to stimulate the renewed arms race of the Thatcher–Reagan years.

Bowing to this logic, in January 1986 Mikhail Gorbachev launched the Soviet Union on what has been called his 'diplomacy of decline'. In his address to the parliament of the Council of Europe on 6 July 1989 he repudiated the 1968 Brezhnev doctrine which had claimed the right to intervene when socialism was threatened in the 'Socialist Commonwealth'. The communist regimes in Eastern Europe were doomed the moment it became clear that there would be no Soviet intervention, and, with the fall of those regimes, the political basis on which the old Warsaw Pact had rested was gone. So it was that the Russian troops in East Germany, precisely those highly feared forces whose threatened drive to the Channel had for years dictated the main thrust of the whole of the defence planning of the Western powers, watched impotently as, in their own backyard, the Soviet Union's front-line ally was carried by unarmed citizens into the waiting embrace of NATO.

What about the Western bloc? 'We have taken away your enemy', said the Soviet spokesman Gennadi Gerasimov. Could NATO survive after the demise of the Warsaw Pact? This is a question to be taken up in the next chapter. What is being highlighted here is the growing anomaly that had developed independently within the Western alliance. The political bases on which the two blocs rested were entirely different, but in both cases a growing discrepancy between military and economic realities could be discerned.

On 4 April 1949, when the North Atlantic Treaty was signed in Washington by its original twelve member states, the situation had been relatively simple. Faced with post-war economic dislocation and large Soviet armies, the smaller countries of Western Europe had chosen to rely on both the economic and military protection of the United States. American capital rescued the Western European economies through the Marshall Plan and American armed forces guaranteed their security through NATO.

By 1989, however, the situation had changed dramatically. On the surface the military dimension of NATO remained much the same. It was still seen to depend on forward deployed American ground troops and the American strategic nuclear deterrent. The Supreme Allied Commander was still an American, and, as his unexpected initiative at the May NATO Summit demonstrated, the US President still retained undisputed leadership of the alliance. But the economic balance of power had shifted decisively. Instead of the impoverished and divided Europe of 1949, an increasingly powerful economic community had been built. The prospect of the single European market in 1992 filled many Americans with apprehension. An annual overall trade deficit of $120 billion a year, with 5.8 per cent GDP being spent on defence, seemed to symbolise the scale of their country's relative decline.[11] Behind the 'burden-sharing' controversies of 1988 had lurked a resentment at the continuing cost to the United States of protecting ungrateful allies who were rapidly becoming dangerous economic rivals. The parallel idea that the economic challenge from Japan (trade surplus $85 billion; defence spending below 1 per cent GDP) was a greater threat than the vanishing military threat from the Soviet Union gained ground. In Europe this shift of economic power was translated into a shift of political power. Within NATO the influence of European allies, particularly West Germany, became greater. And the importance of NATO as a whole waned as the European Community's economic strength grew.

So it was that in the West as in the East the events of 1989 highlighted the deeper discrepancies that had by then developed between the old system of military blocs and the new political realities of Europe. The removal of the inner German border left the gigantic bloc confrontation suspended in mid-air across a politically non-existent 'Central Front'. Vast armed forces on either side were stranded in central Europe. While still possessing overwhelming military power, the two superpowers no longer dominated the continent. Mounting disintegration and disunion in Eastern Europe shattered one bloc. Growing cohesion and strength in Western Europe forced a transformation in the other. Between the two, multiplying relations between European states across the former Iron Curtain grew more significant than comparable relations on either side with their respective superpowers.

3   THE MUTUAL DEPENDENCE AND MUTUAL INCOMPATIBILITY OF DETERRENCE AND DEFENCE IN THE NUCLEAR AGE

The fall of the Berlin Wall finally convinced even the most determined Western sceptics that Soviet policy was not a carefully disguised plot to further traditional Soviet aims – the denuclearisation of Europe, the neutralisation of Germany and the withdrawal of US troops. The Soviet leader meant what he said when he declared:

'The fundamental principle of the new political outlook is very simple: nuclear war cannot be a means of achieving political, economic, ideological or any other goals. And military technology has developed to such an extent that even a non-nuclear war would now be comparable to a nuclear war in its destructive effect. This conclusion is truly revolutionary. It means discarding a way of thinking and acting which has formed over centuries, even millennia. It is the political function of war that has always been the justification for war, a "rational" explanation. But now Clausewitz's dictum that war is the continuation of policy only by different means has grown hopelessly out of date. It belongs to the libraries. In today's world such war is senseless; it is irrational. There would be neither winners nor losers. World civilization would inevitably perish. It would be suicide rather than war in any conventional sense of the word.'[12]

Western leaders agreed:

'In the nuclear age war between the great powers can never be won and must never be fought.'

In the Helsinki Final Act, signed on 1 August 1975 by all 35 members of the Conference on Security and Cooperation in Europe (CSCE), every country in Europe from the Atlantic to the Urals, with the exception of Albania but including the United States and Canada, pledged itself in all circumstances to uphold the overarching priority of the non-use of force and the inviolability of frontiers from external military attack. On 29 May 1987 the Political Consultative Committee of the Warsaw Pact laid down as the essence of its military doctrine that:

'Never, and under no circumstances, shall we begin hostilities against any state or any alliance of states.'[13]

At almost exactly the same time the British Secretary of State for Defence, commenting on NATO's strategy of keeping open the option of a first use of nuclear weapons in order to deter Soviet conventional attack, emphasised:

'The fundamental fact is that NATO is a purely defensive alliance – we have made the only significant declaration: that we will on no account use *any* weapon first.'[14]

All of this, taken together, amounted to an historic landmark. Up to 1945 war had been seen as a normal and in many cases early recourse for great powers in their dealings with one another. It was the ultimate sanction of policy. Now for the first time governments in both alliances genuinely subscribed to the thesis that the mutual maximum use of force, no matter how just the cause, would be mutually disastrous. The prevention of war became an overarching common priority, eclipsing sectional interest. Leaders of all twenty-three countries in both alliances agreed that they must turn their backs on what all hoped was a past *age of war*, and build towards what all hoped would be a future *age of mutually assured security*.

But, no matter what these governments might say and genuinely believe about the necessity of avoiding great power war, preparations for fighting precisely such a war were still going on. In the tradition of the nineteenth-century German Schlieffen Plan the Soviet General Staff continued to plan holding operations in the East along the Chinese frontier and massive counter-attacks in the West in case of war. NATO commanders continued to develop deep strike concepts. Nuclear weapon laboratories, missile manufacturers, silo crews, targeters, in the United States and in the Soviet Union, went on preparing for strategic strikes against each other in the full intention of carrying them out if the orders came. In March 1989, eight months before the collapse of the Berlin Wall, NATO's biennial WINTEX-CIMEX command post exercise simulated a release by NATO of scores of nuclear weapons against targets in East Germany and Eastern Europe with average yields ten times that of the Hiroshima bomb in response to a Warsaw Pact conventional advance. There was no simulation of what would happen if, as was generally seen to be likely, the Soviet Union responded in kind.[15]

What was happening? The transformation symbolised by the breaching of the Berlin Wall exposed the underlying paradoxes inherent in all military strategy at great power level in the nuclear era. In what all hoped was the past *age of war*, usable military force had served political ends. In what all hoped would be a future *age of mutually assured security*, political arrangements would reduce the function of military forces to little more than policing operations. But in the present era the great powers were in a transition phase, the *age of mutual deterrence*. In this age the role of military force was deeply paradoxical. At maximum force levels deterrent threats were effective to the extent that use was seen to be irrational (here the *age of deterrence* looks ahead to an *age of mutually assured security*); yet the only way to make such threats credible was to plan for possible use (here the *age of deterrence* looks back to the *age of war*). This contradiction, deliberately translated down to lower force levels by military doctrine on both sides, was unavoidable. It was characteristic of the hybrid age of mutual deterrence itself. Some saw this as creative ambivalence, others as dangerous schizophrenia. Either way, Lawrence Freedman's conclusion, suitably broadened to refer in general to a mutual maximum use of force at great power level, applies:

'At the end of over 40 years of attempts at constructing nuclear strategies one is forced to the conclusion that . . . strategic thought . . . may have reached a dead end. For the position we have reached is one where stability depends on something that is more the antithesis of strategy than its apotheosis – on threats that things will get out of hand, that we might act irrationally, that possibly through inadvertence we could set in motion a process that in its development and conclusion would be beyond human control and comprehension.'[16]

BOX 1.1   FLEXIBLE RESPONSE: WATERSHED
BETWEEN DETERRENCE AND DEFENCE

For more than twenty years NATO's doctrine for a possible use
of nuclear weapons in Europe had been 'flexible response'.

'Flexible response depends on conventional forces of sufficient size and quality to prevent an aggressor achieving a
quick and easy conventional victory; second, on sub-strategic
nuclear weapons which enhance deterrence by providing a
range of nuclear options short of a strategic nuclear exchange;
and, thirdly, on strategic nuclear forces which remain the
ultimate deterrent.'[17]

The three levels of response were to be 'direct defence' at the
enemy's chosen level of conflict, 'deliberate escalation' which
aimed unilaterally to intensify the conflict to a level where cost
and risk were perceived by the enemy to be disproportionate to
expected gains, and the final sanction of 'general nuclear
response'. An option of first use of sub-strategic nuclear
weapons was kept open at level 2.

Flexible response was a politically controversial strategy in
the West, controversy once again hinging around the distinction
between deterrence (the psychological manipulation of enemy
intentions so that there was no need for defence) and defence
(the repulsion of invading enemy forces once deterrence had
failed). As originally defined in NATO's Military Committee
document MC14/3 of January 1968, flexible response was a
military defence doctrine. It determined criteria for the use of
nuclear weapons in case deterrence failed. But the primary
political purpose was deterrent. It was to prevent war in the
first place. The aim was to restore credibility to the Western
deterrent at a time when Soviet counter-deployment of strategic
nuclear weapons had made a threat of first use of American
strategic nuclear weapons in response to a conventional attack
unconvincing. The trouble was that Soviet counter-deployment
of sub-strategic systems tended in turn to undermine the
credibility of the sub-strategic component in flexible response
as well.

The result was a progressive dilution of the defence function
of theatre nuclear weapons in NATO rationales from 'war-

14

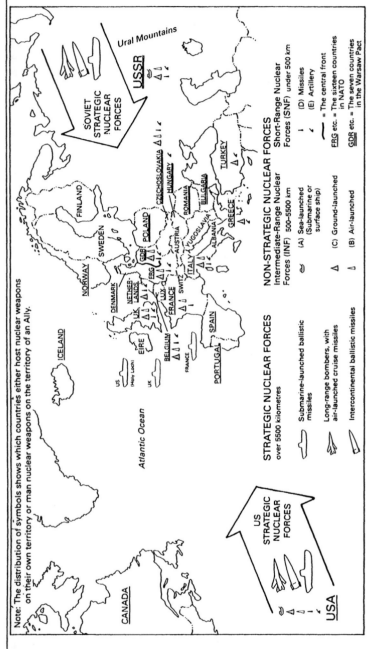

FIGURE 1.2 *The age of deterrence: strategic and sub-strategic nuclear weapons in Europe in the 1980s*

fighting'[18], to the restoration of 'intra-war deterrence'[19], to 'political signalling'[20], to 'assuring and stabilising a system of reciprocal security in Europe'.[21] Yet the fact remained that, like all weapons, nuclear weapons could only deter by evident capability for effective use. While official rationales played down the defence function, weapons laboratories and military planning staffs still saw it as paramount. A 'follow-on to Lance' was needed as a 'corps-support weapon system'.[22] A 'tactical air to surface missile' was needed 'to allow tactical aircraft to strike heavily defended, hardened and relocatable targets at a range of 250 kilometers or more'.[23] In fact flexible response meant different things to different people.[24] The United States favoured use of shorter-range systems to support US ground troops without necessarily involving a strategic exchange with the Soviet Union. West Germany, on the other hand, favoured use of longer-range systems against the Soviet Union to maximise early involvement of the US deterrent and minimise danger of limited nuclear war being confined to Europe. To military planners theatre nuclear systems were weapons, to civilian planners they were political instruments to deter the enemy and reassure allies.[25]

The controversy about flexible response was polarised either side of this deterrent/defence watershed. On one side were critics who emphasised the *defence* function. They began from the apprehension that a 'first use' of nuclear weapons would be irrational or immoral or both:

> 'The facts of the matter are that, if NATO initiated the use of nuclear weapons, it would suffer proportionately much more damage than the Warsaw Pact.'[26]

Under any plausible scenario first use of short-range nuclear artillery and missiles was seen to be suicidal, and, in view of the risk of escalation, irresponsible. At the other end of the spectrum the ultimate sanction of the third level of flexible response – 'general nuclear response' – was considered lunatic. Critical academic studies of nuclear war planning,[27] party political argument against 'first use' options,[28] attacks on current strategy by former military and civilian leaders,[29] objections on moral grounds[30] – all started from a preoccupation with the implications of use.

On the other side of the watershed were official rationales for flexible response which emphasised the *deterrent* function:

'Although conventional parity would bring important benefits for stability, only the nuclear element can confront a potential aggressor with an unacceptable risk. Therefore, for the foreseeable future, deterrence will continue to require an adequate mix of nuclear as well as conventional weapons.'[31]

An option of first use of nuclear weapons had to be kept open, otherwise they could not fulfil their primary function which was to deter conventional war. A complete spectrum of survivable, responsive and effective nuclear capabilities had to be maintained for the same reason. The horror of the prospect of use, which appalled critics, was here invoked as a blessing:

'Conventional weapons are not really a deterrent to war. They never have been if you look at history. The real deterrent to war is the horror of nuclear weapons . . . They deter from all major wars because we are all so frightened of what might happen. It's as simple as that.'[32]

So critics, alarmed at plans for use in defence, rejected flexible response as a deterrent strategy; supporters, confident of the efficacy of deterrence, ignored warnings about the implications of defence. The unresolved debate between the two reflected the paradoxical tensions inherent in great power military planning at both theatre and strategic levels in the transitional mutual deterrent age.

4 THE LAVISHING OF SCARCE RESOURCES ON MILITARY FORCES WHOSE MAIN DECLARED FUNCTION IS TO PREVENT THEIR OWN USE

By the autumn of 1989 rapidly decreasing public perceptions of military threat in Europe and mounting concern about economic development, social welfare and the environment, led to a growing demand for a massive transfer of resources from the military to the civilian sectors. The discrepancy between continuing high levels of military spending and the desperate need for resources elsewhere became glaring.

In November 1989 over 7 million full-time active-duty troops, 90 000 main battle tanks, 125 000 armoured vehicles, 16 000 combat aircraft, 8 000 helicopters, 128 000 artillery pieces and 2 500 major ships still faced each other across the European divide. To put this in perspective, Hitler defeated France and invaded Russia with 3 000 tanks. In addition there were more than 7 000 nuclear armed missiles in the Atlantic-to-Urals area and 10 000 nuclear charges for artillery and aircraft, as well as the vast strategic nuclear arsenals held in reserve by the two superpowers and built in to alliance strategic planning on both sides. A single submarine armed with Trident D-5 missiles could deliver warheads with a yield twenty times greater than that of all the munitions fired by all belligerents during the whole course of the Second World War.[33]

By 1989 the total cost of this enormous effort had climbed to over $600 billion – two-thirds of global military expenditure. This staggering figure was what was being spent annually by both alliances on their military establishments in Europe. It compares with the total of $35–45 billion given every year throughout the world in economic aid.[34] In addition, these countries were also responsible for the bulk of arms exports to the rest of the world – including, of course, Iraq. Nine out of the top twelve arms exporters were CSCE countries.

In the United Kingdom defence expenditure was running at £21 ($35) billion a year. Defence accounted for over 10 per cent of overall government spending and half government spending on research and development. A million jobs depended on defence contracts. In the 1989 *Statement on the Defence Estimates* Britain was described as the 'world's third largest defence exporter'.[35] France was still trying to 'go it alone', maintaining a complete strategic nuclear triad as well as a full range of indigenous weapons programmes and pushing arms exports with greater vigour and fewer scruples than Britain.[36]

Although seen as eminently justified, indeed necessary, when looked at from the perspective of individual countries and alliances taken singly, the situation appeared to many to be irrational if not immoral when viewed as a whole. Remaining perceived threats from outside Europe could hardly justify continued military spending on anything like this scale.

How else could the money be spent? A number of studies offered comparisons. It was suggested that a phased programme of 50 per cent defence cuts in real terms by the year 2000 in Britain would save $80

billion (1990 prices), comparable to the North Sea oil bonanza. One
estimate concluded that a switch of resources on this scale, properly
invested, would result in an increase of 1.8 per cent in British GDP
above what it would otherwise have been.[37] As for the resources now
desperately needed in Eastern Europe and the Soviet Union, some idea
of the scale of the problem can be gained from the estimate that about
DM 500 billion will have to be invested in the former East Germany to
put the area back on its feet.[38] Finally, on a global scale, according to
one estimate a quarter of current NATO and Warsaw Pact annual
military spending could fund massive forest-planting programmes to
begin to halt global warming, promote energy conservation and
develop renewable energy sources worldwide, slow population
growth, reduce Third World debt and help create the conditions
necessary for renewed economic progress in the poorer countries.[39]

'Progress on disarmament could pay huge dividends. For example, a
mere 5 per cent reduction in current military outlays of $1 trillion a
year, if allocated instead to health care, could double public
expenditures for the health care of the 4 billion people in the Third
World, providing enough resources to immunize every baby and to
bring fresh water and basic sanitation within ten years to every
village.'[40]

5   THE ENDING OF THE COLD WAR TO BE MANAGED THROUGH THE DEFENCE ESTABLISHMENTS CREATED BY IT

The final anomaly was shown up in the reaction of defence establishments, East and West, to the galloping pace of political events. Once
again, what appeared rational when looked at from each side
separately looked irrational when viewed as a whole. Traditional
worst case analysis and response to capabilities rather than intentions
on both sides meant that more attention was paid to on-going weapons
programmes than to statements by political leaders. The inertia of the
two juggernauts reinforced each other so that Soviet and Western
military planners were seen to be trying to minimise reductions and
resist change. Many, not only in the Soviet Union, looked back with

nostalgia to the certainties of the Brezhnev era. Not a few greeted the Iraqi invasion of Kuwait with a measure of relief:

'Self-evident villains like Saddam have a very useful function in providing justification for not reducing military spending, without the need for too much propaganda by our governments.'[41]

In the East the vast vested interests of the Soviet military complex were not enough to deflect a determined, even desperate, leadership. But signs of mounting resistance were detected from the early months of 1990 and by the end of the year threatened to overwhelm the reform movement. Conservative pressure from within the military establishment became increasingly evident as large numbers of tanks were transferred to naval units or transported across the Urals to evade CFE restrictions and the resignation of Eduard Shevardnadze in December 1990 revived fears that agreements already reached might begin to unravel.

In the West Mikhail Gorbachev's initiatives were met with scepticism. His unexpected acceptance of the INF zero option in 1987 was greeted with public pleasure but private consternation (Manfred Wörner warned that he would crawl from Stuttgart to Ulm if the Treaty was signed[42]). The announcement of substantial unilateral cuts in December 1988 was played down. Force-to-space ratios were treated as sacrosanct. The French defence establishment struggled to maintain planned weapon programmes. The British Ministry of Defence resisted a defence review. The Pentagon fought to protect the defence budget.[43] Despite unprecedented Soviet concessions for the opening of the CFE talks in Vienna on 6 March 1989, Western defence establishments clung to past positions until President Bush boldly cut the Gordian knot with an imaginative package of measures hastily put together at the last minute for the NATO summit in May.

The fall of the Berlin Wall made even the CFE negotiations, proceeding at breakneck speed in negotiators' eyes, seem ponderous if not irrelevant.[44] By the time of NATO's London Declaration of 6 July 1990 it had become plain that political leaders in the West would have to sketch out an even bolder vision for the future if the gap between public perceptions and institutional instincts was to be closed. The Soviet leadership conceded a united Germany locked into the NATO Alliance; Soviet forces looked set to leave Eastern Europe by 1994 if not sooner; Soviet policy supported Western aims in the Gulf crisis against its former ally, Iraq; the Soviet Union itself seemed destined to disintegrate. Yet on 25 September 1990 the Pentagon's annual assessment of Soviet capabilities warned of Moscow's 'enormous military might' and advised strenuously against a premature change in America's military posture.[45]

In short, it became clear to many that if Cold War confrontation was indeed to be transcended in Europe then the vast military establishments on both sides, programmed to react to worst-case analyses of each others' capabilities, would have to be overborne. There was a demand for statesmanship able to envisage commonly desired goals and capable of working effectively towards them.

NOTES

1. Werner Krätschell in *New Europe*, Granta/Penguin, 1990, p. 144 [edited].
2. See, for example, the joint policy statements agreed by all socialist/social democratic parties in European NATO countries in Bonn (November 1985), Oslo (September 1986), etc.
3. Figures given 13 December 1989 by Soviet Deputy Foreign Minister Vladimir Petrovsky, *Soviet News*.
4. 1987 figures from Warschauer Pakt Streitkräftepotential, pp. 5, 9, cited in *Soviet Military Withdrawal from Eastern Europe*, Vojtech Mastny, Council for Arms Control, 1989.
5. This calculation is made in The Comprehensive Concept of Defence and Disarmament for NATO from Flexible Response To Mutual Defensive Superiority, BASIC (UK), ASWG (UK), CNS (US), 1989, p. 4.
6. *New Directions for NATO*, IRSS/IPIS Report, December 1988, p. 12.
7. William Arkin and Richard Fieldhouse, *Nuclear Battlefields*, Ballinger, 1985, p. 196.
8. Statistics often cited by Western leaders at the time, for example Margaret Thatcher at the Brussels NATO summit, 2 March 1988.
9. Academician Aganbegyan, cited in *Strategic Survey 1989–1990*, IISS, p. 17.
10. Eduard Shevardnadze, speech at 28th Party Congress, 3 July 1990, Soviet News, no. 6534.
11. 1989 defence expenditure figure from *The North Atlantic Treaty Organization: Facts and Figures*, NATO Information Service, 1990.
12. *Perestroika*, Collins, 1987, pp. 140–1 [edited].
13. *On the Military Doctrine of the Warsaw Pact Member Countries*, Berlin, 29 May 1987.
14. George Younger in *Choices: Nuclear and Non-Nuclear Defence Options*, Brasseys, 1987, p. 459.

15. For the political storm that this provoked, particularly in West Germany, see Elizabeth Pond, 'War games brought NATO rift into the open', *Boston Globe*, 4 June 1989.
16. *The Evolution of Nuclear Strategy*, 2nd edn, Macmillan, 1989, p. 433.
17. *Statement on the Defence Estimates 1990*, vol. I, HMSO.

    The role of theatre nuclear weapons at the second level of response ('deliberate escalation') was 'to support NATO's doctrine of flexible response' by keeping open the option that 'conflict in Europe could be escalated in a controlled way to seek its termination on terms favourable to the Alliance', *Fiscal Year 1982 Arms Control Impact Statement* submitted to Congress by the President, February 1981, US Government Printing Office, p. 239. Such uses were politically defined from 1962 through an elaborate series of compromises between the competing interests and perceptions of NATO members. Latterly these were coordinated through NATO's Nuclear Planning Group of defence ministers, notably in the 1969 Provisional Political Guidelines, the 1970 General Release Guidelines and the 1986 General Political Guidelines.
18. As described in Jane E. Stromseth, *The Origins of Flexible Response*, Macmillan, 1988.
19. 'The fundamental objective of maintaining the capability for selective sub-strategic use of theatre nuclear weapons is political – to demonstrate in advance that NATO has the capability and will to use its nuclear weapons in a deliberate politically controlled way with the objective of restoring deterrence by inducing the aggressor to make the decision to terminate his aggression and withdraw', *Nuclear Deterrence Post INF*, Ministry of Defence paper presented to the House of Commons All Party Foreign Affairs Select Committee, January 1988.
20. For example Wolfgang Altenburg, Chief of NATO's Military Committee, 'the danger is one of war through miscalculation . . . so this must be corrected by sending a nuclear signal through the use of a nuclear weapon outside our territory', *Der Spiegel*, 24 July 1990.
21. Gerhard Stoltenberg, German Defence Minister, *Washington Post*, 1 May 1990.

    When the rationale reaches this stage, not only has the 'military' defence function been entirely subsumed under the 'political' deterrent function, it has moved on beyond deterrence altogether. The full quotation is: 'in the future nuclear forces will serve not so much for deterring an expressly designated political opponent, but rather to assure and stabilise a system of reciprocal security in Europe cemented by treaty.'
22. This is made clear in almost every specification for the follow-on to Lance from the late 1970s through to early 1990. For example, 'The Corps Support Weapon System (CSWS) is an army programme in the concept design phase to explore development of a corps level replacement for the Lance missile system. The CSWS will be targeted against enemy second echelon formations, installations and fixed targets', *Fiscal Year 1982 Arms Control Impact Statement*, US Government Printing Office, p. 245.

23. This is, for example, how 'US field commanders', who have made the capability a 'top priority since 1987', are described as seeing the weapon in *Aviation Week and Space Technology*, 29 January 1990.

24. Again Jane E. Stromseth, *The Origins of Flexible Response*, is illuminating here.

25. Although it could be the other way round. Compare:

    'The fundamental NATO strategy of reliance on nuclear weapons and the possibility always of using them hasn't changed. You must never let down your armed forces by not letting them have the most up-to-date equipment, first, sufficient to deter, second, to fight and win over the adversary' (Margaret Thatcher, interview after NATO summit, BBC Television, 6 July 1990, Media Transcription Service)

    and

    'In my judgement the years 1983 to 1987 were those in which the military ceased, for all practical purposes, to think of nuclear weapons as a conceivable war-fighting option' (General Sir Hugh Beach in correspondence).

26. Field Marshal Lord Carver in *Choices*, p. 177.

27. Including those by Paul Bracken, *The Command and Control of Nuclear Forces*, Yale University Press, New Haven, 1983; Desmond Ball, *Targeting for Strategic Deterrence*, Adelphi Paper 185 IISS, London, 1983, and *Controlling Theatre Nuclear War*, Strategic and Defence Studies Centre, Australian National University, Canberra, 1987; William Arkin and Richard Fieldhouse, *Nuclear Battlefields*.

28. For example, the rejection of flexible response because a first use of sub-strategic nuclear weapons would 'risk a rapid escalation of nuclear war' (British Liberal Democrats), 'precipitate a nuclear holocaust' (British Labour Party), etc. For references see Ch. 8.

29. For example, Lord Carver above, and Robert McNamara here:

    'Most Americans are simply unaware that NATO strategy calls for early initiation of the use of nuclear weapons in a conflict with the Soviets. Eighty per cent of them believe we would not use such weapons unless the Soviets used them first. They would be shocked to learn they are mistaken. And they would be horrified to be told that senior military commanders themselves believe that to carry out our present strategy would lead to the destruction of our society. Yet those are the facts' (*Choices*, pp. 355–6).

    This is particularly striking because it was Robert McNamara himself as American defense secretary who instituted flexible response in the first place. Robert McNamara's aim had been to replace the strategy of massive retaliation in which conventional forces were seen as little more than a tripwire so that the West would launch its full strategic nuclear force at the first sign of conventional conflict. The idea was to build up conventional forces so that the nuclear threshold would be raised. What in fact happened was that strategy instead came to depend on an early first use of sub-strategic nuclear systems. This was not part of the original thinking: 'I never suggested using a nuclear artillery shell of ten-mile range to launch from German soil and land also on German soil', Robert McNamara interviewed on BBC Radio 4, 'Analysis', 6 October 1989, Media Transcription Service, ref. no. 567.

30. For example the degree of probability that deterrence will succeed is considered irrelevant to the central moral issue by John Finnis, Joseph Boyle and Germain Grisez in *Nuclear Deterrence, Morality and Realism*, Clarendon Press, 1987. So long as there is a possibility that deterrence might fail, the intention to use nuclear weapons in the way threatened is already complete. And since what is thereby threatened necessarily includes an impermissible destruction of innocents, deterrence based on such threat is not permitted either: 'whoever chooses to make the deterrent threat intends, conditionally but really, what is threatened. If what is threatened includes the killing of innocent persons, the threat includes an intention prohibited by common morality', p. 86.

31. Paragraph 5 of the NATO communiqué, 'Conventional Arms Control: The Way Ahead', 2 March 1988, NATO Press Service, and innumerable similar examples.

32. Lord Carrington, Secretary-General of NATO, interviewed on BBC Radio 4, 20 February 1988.

33. Higher estimates from NATO and WTO equivalent force figures (1988), cited in Jonathan Dean, *Meeting Gorbachev's Challenge*, Macmillan, 1989, pp. 37–8.

34. Figures from Ruth Leger Sivard, *World Military and Social Expenditures 1989–90*, World Priorities Inc, 1990.

35. *Statement on the Defence Estimates*, 1989, vol. 1, HMSO, p. 33.

36. See, for example, François Heisbourg, evidence to House of Commons Defence Select Committee, *Defence Implications of Recent Events*, July 1990, HMSO.

37. *The Peace Dividend and the UK Economy*, Paul Dunne and Ron Smith, Cambridge Econometrics, Spring Report 1990.

38. *Financial Times*, 12 January 1990.

39. *State of the World 1988*, Worldwatch Institute, W. W. Norton, 1988.

40. Ruth Leger Sivard, *World Military and Social Expenditures*.

41. Manfred Sadlowski, *Military Technology*, August 1990, quoted by Terry Jones, *Guardian* 29 September 1990.

42. Cited in Clay Clemens, *Beyond INF: West Germany's Centre Right Party and Arms Control in the 1990s*, International Affairs, Winter 1988/9.

43. The Pentagon's long-range planning paper *Defense Policy Guidance* of January 1990 was still based on the premise of a 14-day warning time of Soviet frontal attack.

44. Note the section 'Is CFE Still Relevant?' in *Strategic Survey 1989–1990*, IISS, p. 206.

45. US Department of Defense, *Soviet Military Power*, 1990.

2 The New Agenda: What are the Big Questions Now?

The anomalies that had developed within the post-war European security system by the end of the 1980s were so deep that to address them adequately was to have to rethink security policy from the ground up. This was not just a case of revising national or even alliance strategy. It was a case of managing a transition to an entirely different phase of international relations. Opinions might differ about the pace of change and about the nature of specific steps to be taken, but not, it will be argued here, about the ultimate goal of policy. This was an unprecedented state of affairs.

So far as concerned relations among themselves, the leaders of all 35 CSCE countries (soon to be 34 after the unification of Germany) were being asked to carry Europe safely but purposefully through the age of deterrence, decisively away from the past era of inter-state war and towards a future era of mutually assured security. In the NATO London Declaration of 6 July 1990 this was heralded as an epoch in which the two alliances 'are no longer adversaries'. In the Paris Charter of 20 November 1990 it was described as 'a new era of democracy, peace and cooperation' in Europe.[1]

So far as the rest of the world went, CSCE governments had to work out how this evolving European 'peace order' could coexist with other regions in which these political, economic and cultural preconditions were missing. Much of the world was still living in an age of war.[2]

The tension between these two requirements was well illustrated when President Saddam Hussein of Iraq invaded Kuwait on 2 August 1990. On the one hand the invasion showed how in the Middle East the use or threat of use of military force was still seen to bring political gain. Governments did not subscribe to the principle of border

24

inviolability. On the other hand the united condemnation of the Iraqi action by all CSCE countries underlined how in Europe the UN/CSCE principle of border inviolability was now said to be universally upheld. The Gulf crisis was described as a 'critical juncture in history', a 'defining moment' in the evolution of a 'new world order'. That is to say, superpower collaboration in the United Nations was seen to open the way to the real possibility of the evolution of some kind of future global security system.[3]

By the beginning of 1991 this programme had reached a critical point. Which paradigm would predominate? Would the remarkable transformation in Europe be further consolidated, and, after the immediate Gulf crisis was resolved, a comparable process be initiated in the Middle East? Or, triggered by upheaval in the Soviet Union, would the kind of unregenerate forces so dramatically exposed in the Gulf subsequently revive in Europe and threaten to drag the continent back to confrontation if not war?

All political leaders in Europe say that the future in Europe must lie in the first of these two directions. To that extent there is overall agreement about ends. But there is continuing profound, and at times bitter, disagreement about means. The disagreement is in the deepest sense political. It concerns the whole nature of the new European order that is emerging from the dissolution of the Yalta system. It involves judgements about the past, assessments of the present and recommendations for the future. The party political debate is complex and varies from country to country. Nevertheless broad patterns can be discerned. Those to the right of the political spectrum in Western European countries tend to begin from one set of assumptions; those to the left from another. As a result they see the problems in different ways and come to different conclusions about what should be done about them. There is comparable debate going on in the Soviet Union.

It is possible to isolate six fundamental questions around which the new security debate now hinges. Five of them are generated by the five anomalies examined in Chapter 1. But there is a prior question which has to be considered first.

1 WHERE DOES THE THREAT TO SECURITY LIE?

The nature of any security policy is conditioned by the nature of the perceived threat or threats that it is there to meet. So the first task is to define where the risk and danger is seen to come from.

Here we immediately confront a problem. From whose perspective is the threat to be defined? Clearly there are innumerable perspectives, national and international. Not only will different countries and alliances have different perspectives, but so will different peoples, regions, interest groups, parties. Moreover, these perspectives will not coexist as distinctly defined alternatives. They will mutually contradict one another. Considering the extraordinary economic, political and cultural variety in Europe, the overall picture will be impossible to draw. Wherever we try to begin, our description will turn out to rest on assumptions which are themselves in question.

As some readers will have realised, this book has already been caught up in this. Chapter 1 purported to be descriptive. But the anomalies described there only become evident when the situation is looked at independently of particular governments, countries and alliances, as if 'from above'. For example the present level of defence spending in Europe seems outrageously high when it is taken *in toto* in a context where all relevant governments are saying that these forces should never be used against each other. But that does not correspond to reality as seen 'from within' individual national and alliance defence establishments. From this perspective, a perspective reinforced by centuries of history and the whole paraphernalia of inherited power, the palpable danger comes from the perceived capabilities of potentially hostile states. Capabilities endure, political circumstances and intentions may change. Planners must, therefore, retain forces sufficient to ensure against all possible future contingencies. Not to do so would be the height of irresponsibility.

We have reached a fundamental distinction which will be further developed in what follows. At the outset we refer to it as the distinction between a 'view from within' and a 'view from above'. We ask what the perceived threats are, first, inside Europe, second, to European countries from outside, and, third, at a global level as affecting Europe, when viewed both 'from within' existing power structures and as if 'from above'. To make this distinction complicates things but carries us to the heart of the debate.

(i) Threats from within Europe

If the 'view from within' is that of the defence communities in the Western alliance, there are two main preoccupations in addition to specific national concerns. The first is the nature of the residual threat from the Soviet Union. The second is the situation in the non-Soviet countries of Central and Eastern Europe.

Since, as Chapter 1 showed, NATO's entire existing defence structures are a function of the perceived Soviet military threat, assessment of the potential danger from the current Soviet upheaval remains fundamental. This is the great imponderable which hangs over Europe. The last of the nineteenth-century polyglot empires is seen to be convulsed in terminal crisis. The Communist Party of the Soviet Union still clings to power but is effectively paralysed. The economy has collapsed and the subject populations face near starvation in many areas. Over a hundred different nationalities in the fifteen republics spread across eleven time zones from desert pastoralists to Arctic herdsmen, Christian Ukrainians to Muslim Tadzhiks, Western Slavs to Eastern Aleuts find themselves facing an increasingly uncertain and violent future as central control disintegrates. Russians make up barely half the population. Nearly a quarter of Soviet citizens live in republics and autonomous regions predominantly peopled by races and cultures other than their own. Nationalist, ethnic and religious antagonisms are thought to be coming rapidly to the boil. Scores of Lebanons or potential Northern Irelands are thought to be brewing. Against a background of mounting political chaos, inter-sectarian hatred and economic despair the entire mixture is seen to be about to explode.

Such is the worst-case judgement now being made by a number of Western planners. What conclusions are drawn about potential threats to the West? The disintegration of the Soviet Union is regarded as in many ways more dangerous than previously perceived Soviet strength. Both anarchy and reactive authoritarianism are feared. What would happen to the vast Soviet nuclear forces? Might they fall into unscrupulous hands, or become involved in civil war? Might a break-away country like Ukraine (which already has a seat in the United Nations) become a de facto nuclear power? More immediately, what about existing conventional forces? Could there be an attempted military coup? Although the CFE agreement signed in Paris on 19 November 1990 appears favourable to the West, because non-Soviet Warsaw Pact forces which were originally counted in on the Soviet side to balance the numbers are now no longer a Soviet asset (see Box 2.1), there is a time-lag while the treaty is being implemented and huge amounts of equipment are being transported East of the Urals instead of being destroyed. Even if the Soviet Union did fall apart, the Russian Republic (RSFSR) on its own, stretching nearly five thousand miles

---

BOX 2.1   FORCE HOLDINGS AGREED IN THE PARIS CFE TREATY, 19 NOVEMBER 1990

By 1994 holdings of weapon systems identified as the key to mounting surprise attack, initiating large-scale offensive action and seizing and holding territory will be as follows in the Atlantic to the Urals area:

	NATO	*Soviet Union*
Tanks	20 000	13 300
Artillery	20 000	13 700
Armoured Combat Vehicles	30 000	20 000
Combat Aircraft	6 800	5 150
Attack Helicopters	2 000	1 500

---

from Leningrad in the West to Vladivostock in the East, would remain easily the most potent military power in Europe (see Figure 2.1). NATO analysts are sceptical about claims that Soviet forces are being 'defensively' restructured.[4]

Nevertheless it is generally acknowledged that whatever the nature of future regimes in the Soviet Union, there would be little incentive for the mounting of a direct conventional assault on the West, and, given the de facto belt of neutral countries which now separates NATO from the Soviet Union in Central and Eastern Europe, little capacity either. Warning time of surprise attack is seen to be the crucial factor here. It used to be calculated as 10 to 14 days. In December 1989 the US National Intelligence Estimate was 33 to 44 days. An intelligence assessment presented to President Bush in August 1990 suggested that once Soviet troops are out of Eastern Europe it would take Moscow two years to mount a conventional attack.[5]

Turning to the situation in Eastern and South-Eastern Europe, there is concern about increasing instability in the region. With the dissolution of the Eastern bloc, old ethnic and nationalist tensions are re-emerging, exacerbated by unresolved border disputes going back half a century or more. Figure 2.2 shows how Poland has in effect been 'shunted' a couple of hundred of kilometres to the West since the

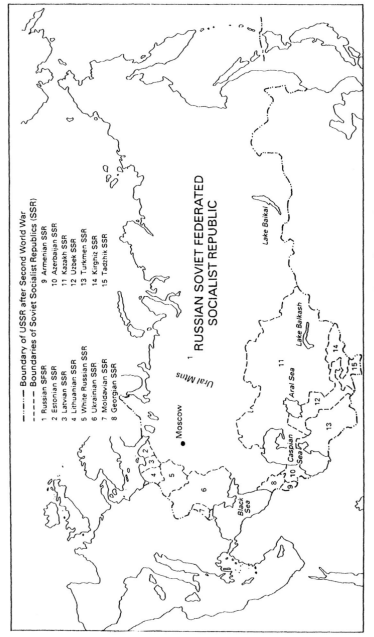

----- Boundary of USSR after Second World War
---- Boundaries of Soviet Socialist Republics (SSR)

1 Russian SFSR
2 Estonian SSR
3 Latvian SSR
4 Lithuanian SSR
5 White Russian SSR
6 Ukrainian SSR
7 Moldavian SSR
8 Georgian SSR

9 Armenian SSR
10 Azerbaijan SSR
11 Kazakh SSR
12 Uzbek SSR
13 Turkmen SSR
14 Kirghiz SSR
15 Tadzhik SSR

RUSSIAN SOVIET FEDERATED
SOCIALIST REPUBLIC

Moscow

Ural Mtns

Lake Baikal

Lake Balkash

Aral Sea

Caspian Sea

Black Sea

FIGURE 2.1   *The fifteen republics of the USSR*

----- Frontiers after the First World War

1 Finnish border dispute with Soviet Union
2 Finnish minority in Soviet Union
3 Estonian independence movement, including Russian minority
4 Latvian independence movement, including Russian minority
5 Lithuanian independence movement, including Russian minority
6 Polish minority in Lithuania
7 German minority in Soviet Union
8 German minority in Poland
9 Byelorussian minority in Poland
10 Polish minority in Byelorussia
11 Byelorussian independence movement
12 Polish minority in Ukraine
13 Ukrainian independence movement
14 Hungarian minority in Slovakia
15 Romanian border dispute with Soviet Union
16 Soviet Moldavians want union with Romania
17 Hungarian minority in Romania
18 Slovene minority in Austria
19 Slovenian independence movement
20 Hungarian minority in Yugoslavia
21 Albanian-Serb conflict: Kosovo
22 Romania-Bulgaria border dispute
23 Turkish minority in Greece
24 Macedonia claimed by Bulgaria, Greece, Yugoslavia
25 Turkish minority in Bulgaria
26 Aegean Islands: Greco-Turkish dispute
27 Cyprus: Greco-Turkish dispute

FIGURE 2.2   *Ethnic and nationalist disputes in Central and Eastern Europe*

beginning of the century. Hungary was drastically pruned after the First World War leaving Magyar minorities stranded across the borders in neighbouring countries. Yugoslavia seems to be facing disintegration. The closer the situation is looked at the more complex it is seen to be. Minority groups are rarely confined to distinct areas, and nearly always themselves have problems with smaller alien enclaves within what they regard as their own territory. All of this is made worse by the severe difficulties now gripping most of these countries as the old system of command economies officially coordinated through the Council for Mutual Economic Assistance (CMEA) breaks down and new market economies integrated into the West have hardly as yet begun to replace them. In this climate political extremism may thrive and the search for scapegoats intensify.

In what ways could this constitute a threat to the wealthier countries of the West? A direct military threat is not envisaged. Nor, since less than 4 per cent of imports to the West come from this region, should economic repercussions necessarily be serious in the first instance. But there is apprehension that disorder might become contagious, concern about cross-border pollution from archaic Central and East European industry, and, above all, fear of a potential 'human flood' of economic refugees pouring West in search of a better standard of living.[6]

What has been said so far represents a 'view from within' the defence establishments of the West. What about the 'view from within' equivalent communities in the East?

Here, although the demise of the Warsaw Pact and the imminent withdrawal of Soviet forces is welcomed, there is great uncertainty about the future. In Central and Eastern Europe the resulting security vacuum increases nervousness about a renationalisation of local armed forces at a time of mounting pressure from ethnically displaced peoples. And there are two-hundred-year-old fears of Russian military power on one side and German revanchism on the other. The increasing economic power of Germany arouses deep apprehension – a fear, it must be said, also shared by some observers in the West.[7]

As for reactions from within the Soviet defence establishment, criticism of current policy is sometimes trenchant and outspoken. From this perspective what has happened since 1989 has been an unmitigated disaster. There is alarm that 'we have returned to the 1939 situation' and 'the West is building up its own security at our expense'.[8] There is passionate feeling against the Gorbachev/Shevard-nadze reforms:

'At a stroke it has torn down the whole geopolitical architecture of Eastern Europe which our country had paid a huge price to establish. The internal European balance of power has been destroyed, with unpredictable results. The sentimental theory of "our common European home" has led to the ruin of the East European Communist parties, changes in sovereignty and the inevitable reunification of Germany . . . The political map of Europe will change its colours and configurations, and the bones of Russian infantrymen will rattle in their forgotten graves.'[9]

In contrast to all this, what happens if an attempt is made to see the situation, not from the point of view of particular countries, peoples and alliances, but as if 'from above'? Those who adopt such a vantage-point claim that this is the only perspective from which the deep problems can be discerned and the lasting remedies therefore discovered.

From this outlook the whole landscape appears in a different light. Military-political problems, for example, are no longer described in terms of threat from distinct defence establishments taken singly, but are seen to be constituted by structural interaction between all such establishments taken together. The dangers are said to lie in continuing militarisation of political relations, with high defence budgets and mutually reinforcing offensive strategies which have hardly as yet begun to be addressed. Agreed reductions are expected to be confined to older equipment and competitive military research and development and ongoing qualitative nuclear and non-nuclear weapons programmes to continue unabated. This is all seen to be part of the inherited tradition of state-centred and military-dominated definitions of security. The result is an interacting network of policies, practices and strategies in which attempts to strengthen individual states or alliances thereby increase perceived threats to others. Institutionalised juggernauts, bolstered by psychological projection, bureaucratic habit and vested interest, mutually reinforce each other and perpetuate the system.[10]

But the main result of the shift to a 'view from above' is seen to be the broadening of the whole concept of security. Military dispositions are regarded as symptoms of deeper political and economic imbalances. The emphasis in security thinking is displaced from states to peoples, and from physical defence to social relations and material well-being. From this perspective what is most striking in Europe at the moment is the dramatic discontinuity in security as we travel from

West to East. On one side of the divide are NATO, EC and EFTA countries moving rapidly towards closer integration within an already achieved security community in which inter-state violence is precluded and economic achievement apparently assured. On the other side are some hundreds of millions of people whose security is directly threatened in the most immediate way by political dislocation, environmental degradation and economic collapse. Fears expressed in the West about contagious political instability, the spread of pollution, floods of economic refugees from the East, and so on, are seen to be quite out of place. The danger is, on the contrary, that the rich West will continue to protect its own interests, turn itself into a fortress, defend its frontiers, reduce the Eastern hinterland to economic dependency and effectively replace the old iron curtain with a new golden one. The iron curtain kept the peoples of Central and Eastern Europe in. The golden curtain will keep them out. This would be a recipe for instability and disaster. The greatest European security challenge from the perspective of the 'view from above', therefore, is the overcoming of this new version of the old East–West divide.[11]

(ii) Threats to Europe from the Outside

Here we turn first to a 'view from within' Europe as a whole. What dangers can be said to confront European countries from regions outside?

From a Soviet perspective (considering the view from Moscow as 'European'), there is the immense border with China, and the threat from Islamic fundamentalism in Afghanistan and Iran poised to spill over and infect the 60 million Muslims in the Soviet Union from the Volga Tartars in the West to the Kirghiz, Uzbeks and Kazakhs in the East.

Elsewhere, with the exception of the Turkish border, Europe is surrounded by sea, and, given the wealth and military strength of the Western European countries, it might not seem that there could be much of a direct threat to the physical safety of Europeans from outside powers.

Nevertheless, in direct proportion as perceived Cold War dangers subside, threats from other areas, like North Africa and the Middle East, appear to replace them – at any rate in the public rationales of a number of European governments.

Islamic rivalry with Christendom, and Arab resentment at European colonialism and imperialism provide rich historical soil for hostility. Britain and France in particular are held responsible for many of the inherited problems – such as the creation of Israel, the existence of Kuwait, the artificial borders of Jordan, and so on. Arab culture and religion are widely seen to have been scorned and violated by the West, the economic interests of the bulk of the Arab populations to have been thwarted by the unholy alliance between Western capitalists and oil-rich sheiks. This is fertile soil for the seizing of Western hostages and the mounting of terrorist attacks against Western interests. Spreading missile technologies might enable a Gaddafi or a Saddam Hussein to threaten direct strikes against European countries. Developing nuclear capabilities might make such strikes potentially devastating. An attack on Turkey would automatically trigger the NATO alliance. An attack on Saudi Arabia would threaten oil supplies on which European countries are increasingly dependent, and a sharp raising of prices would be equally devastating. An attack on Israel might prompt American pressure for European intervention. Above all, a rapid increase in population against a background of economic failure, political instability and Islamic fundamentalism in areas like the North African Maghreb is seen to threaten an uncontrollable flood of refugees across the Mediterranean.[12]

But a 'view from above' in this case embraces both Europe and the areas around it. Once again, the result is to see the situation as an interactive whole. From this perspective Islamic Arab and Christian European interests and views have to be reconciled if there is to be stability and mutual security. The problem of oil supplies involves Arab resentment at perceived Western economic imperialism as well as European anxiety about perceived Arab attempts to use oil as a political weapon. The problem of spreading missile technologies and nuclear weapon proliferation involves Arab perceptions of the Western attempt to preserve a nuclear monopoly as well as Western perceptions of the Arab attempt to break it. In this interpretation the problem of the Iraqi arms build-up, for example, is inseparable from the problem of the European arms export drive. Common problems require common solutions.

(iii) Global Threats

Finally we reach the apotheosis of the 'view from above'. Here the world community is taken as a whole and the overwhelming problems are seen to be those which confront the entire human family. In 1978 Ronald Higgins identified these threats as population growth, food crisis, resource scarcity, environmental degradation, nuclear abuse and the tendency of science and technology to run beyond human control. These were compounded by the 'seventh enemy', our own blindness and apathy to all of this. He saw these threats as converging within an unstable global arena of economic underdevelopment and ill-relieved poverty. The fundamental problem is how to overcome the gross disparity in levels of development in the world without thereby making the environmental problems far worse.[13]

According to one version of the 'view from above', developed economies like those of the United States, West Europe and Japan have achieved their levels of growth by exploiting less developed regions and by disproportionate consumption of the earth's irreplaceable resources. The greenhouse effect, depletion of the ozone layer, deforestation, soil erosion, accumulation of toxic waste – these are seen as consequences of the industrialised world's climb up the development ladder. But now an increasing proportion of the world's exploding population finds itself stranded at the bottom of the ladder. As it looks up it sees the small club of rich nations, predominantly white northerners, trying to preserve its control of international capital in the name of fiscal stability, retain an indefinite monopoly of nuclear weapons in the name of non-proliferation, and pull the ladder of development up after it in the name of environmental protection.[14]

In short, these converging global problems are seen to dwarf the dwindling military threats that continue to preoccupy defence establishments in Europe, East and West. Here it is not a case of we in the rich North or West protecting ourselves from enemies somewhere else. It is the affluent nations who are if anything the greatest culprits. And failure to address these interconnected problems of development and sustainability will spell disaster for us all.

2 WHAT IS THE APPROPRIATE RESPONSE?

With this question we enter a whirlpool of uncertainty. To the extent that threats are now no longer clearly defined, responses are no longer clearly determined. In the absence of adequate threat analysis, planners, advisers and critics tend to be thrown back on more instinctive reactions: 'wait and see' or 'now is the time for bold initiatives'. Advocates of both the 'view from within' and the 'view from above' are caught up in this.

Beginning with perceptions from within the Western defence establishments, what is now the best way to respond to the residual Soviet threat? The basic principle of alliance collective security underpinned by nuclear deterrence is still seen to be essential. But this is now interpreted in different ways. The 'wait and see' approach (exemplified at Alliance level through to the end of 1990 by the British government) argues that it is easy to wind down defences and hard to rebuild them, so the West should retain 'tried and tested means' while waiting to see what happens to Soviet capabilities over the next few years. The 'we must now plan for a new Europe' approach (exemplified to 1990 by the German government) argues that German unification and the likely withdrawal of Soviet troops from Eastern Europe by 1994 transforms the situation and demands an entirely different NATO response. Because reorganisation in an alliance like NATO is so complicated and lead times for new weapons are so long, we must begin planning now. If we do not, the wrong signals will be given to Moscow (here is the beginning of a 'view from above'). Central to this rethinking will be how doctrines like the American AirLand battle, developed during the 1980s to harness technological advances to deep-strike offensive strategies (albeit within an overall defensive posture), are adapted in the new circumstances. These concepts are often seen as the antithesis of the non-offensive defence principles characteristic of the 'view from above'. The restructuring of the Central Region horizontal 'layercake' into vertical covering, rapid reaction, and manoeuvre forces will be difficult, but perhaps not as difficult as agreeing the political objectives.[15]

As for responses to Eastern European instability and out of area threats, these are as yet underdetermined. The problem is how to adapt a force structure up to now almost entirely geared to repelling a massive frontal Soviet assault through the Fulda Gap to completely different contingencies. Neither 'forward defence' nor 'flexible response' as previously conceived are relevant to, say, border clashes in disputed Macedonia between Bulgaria, Greece and Yugoslavia, or to an advance into Saudi Arabia by Iraq.[16]

Turning to a 'view from above', this is found in moderate form in the rapidly expanding 'arms control' dimension to Western defence planning. Formally focused on the strategic nuclear weapon (START), chemical weapon (CW), conventional force (CFE), and confidence and security building (CSBM) talks, it extends to include fundamental questions about whether emphasis should shift from what opponents see as 'offensive' postures like forward deployed main battle tanks, strike aircraft, aircraft carriers to 'defensive' systems employing barriers, certain types of smart weapons, and mobile reserves. Exchange of information about evolving Soviet concepts of 'reasonable defence sufficiency' is central here, as is careful consideration of alternative strategy in the direction of 'mutual defensive superiority'. Should allied troops stay in Germany if and when Soviet troops leave? If so, in which direction should they be orientated? Should there be role specialisation? Should national capabilities be merged in multinational forces? Fundamental to all this is the whole relationship between unilateral modernisation and multilateral arms control.[17]

These considerations lead on to the central concept of common security, as developed in countries like Sweden and Germany over the last decade, and to the newer variants now evolving in the wake of the revolutionary changes that are transforming Central and Eastern Europe. Just as NATO and Warsaw Pact strategies were developed against the background of bloc-to-bloc confrontation, so were alternative 'common security' concepts in the 1970s and 1980s. They assumed that the problem was one of achieving an overall mutual security relationship between two integrated command structures locked across a clearly defined border. The ending of this simple confrontation removes the original context and forces some radical rethinking. Is it possible to coordinate military forces of all kinds in Europe within a single overarching collective security system? If so, how does this relate to what is likely to be going on in adjacent areas?[18]

Proposed studies and models for possible future force structures in Europe are varied and complicated. Details of national and alliance planning are kept hidden behind official secrets barriers. Nevertheless it is once again the distinction between a 'view from within' and a 'view from above' which is found to lie at the heart of the current debate. And beyond this again lies the whole transformationist response to the United Nations Palme, Brandt and Brundtland commissions, insofar as this affects Europe. It involves defining the requirements for peaceful conflict resolution, for the building of a new economic order, for the creation of an ecologically sustainable future. Is the inherited 'nation-state' system adequate to the task? This leads on to the next question.[19]

3   WHAT SHOULD THE FUTURE SECURITY ARCHITECTURE IN EUROPE BE?

With this question we move from strategies to structures. The two most potent surviving structures are NATO and the European Community, both in the West. The divorce between the defence monopoly of the one and the growing economic and political strength of the other poses the first main problem. How can the growing integration of Western Europe not include a security and defence component? Will the pressure in this direction not grow as American and European security interests diverge? On the other hand at the moment the only integrated military command is NATO's, forged in the face of a perceived massive Soviet threat. Is it likely that the European nations will be able to create anything comparable when there is no such threat, and, as response to the Gulf crisis showed, divergence is still so great? The second question concerns how and whether other countries, particularly to the East, will come to be included in some form of pan-European security system. Is it not a structure of this kind that must eventually replace the blocs, rather than a new (West) European superstate? Will not anything less be dangerously regressive and represent an inexcusable failure to rise to the real challenges of the late twentieth century?

Table 2.1 and Figure 2.3 give an idea of the untidiness of the 'Europlethora', the present multiplicity of overlapping institutions. It is liable to be outpaced by events as EFTA countries apply to join the EC, Central and Eastern European countries apply to join the Council of Europe, etc.[20]

The question here is not so much one of clear-cut alternatives. Institutions rarely vanish, and varying inherited national security interests and levels of economic and political development are bound to complicate the situation for some time to come. It is more a question of emphasis, timing and what the long-term preferred goals may be. What follows is an attempt to simplify a complicated situation by highlighting four groups of institutions that tend to given greater or lesser emphasis as movement takes place across the political spectrum. For example, those towards the 'right' end of the spectrum tend to emphasise NATO (i), and those towards the 'left' to emphasise CSCE (iv). In broad terms the former tends to be associated with a 'view from within' and the latter with a 'view from above'. In addition there is the separate possibility, welcome or unwelcome, of fragmentation into a more or less loose association of 'sovereign nation states'.[21]

TABLE 2.1 Membership of European institutions

Membership of European institutions 1991

· Members
A Applied for membership

Institution	No. of Members	USSR	Poland	Czechoslovakia	Hungary	Romania	Bulgaria	United States	Canada	United Kingdom	Germany	Belgium	Netherlands	Luxembourg	Italy	France	Spain	Portugal	Norway	Denmark	Iceland	Greece	Turkey	Finland	Sweden	Ireland	Switzerland	Austria	Liechtenstein	Holy See	Malta	Cyprus	Monaco	San Marino	Yugoslavia	Albania
North Atlantic Treaty Organisation	16							·	·	·	·	·	·	·	·	·	·	·	·	·	·	·	·													
Independent European Programme Group	13									·	·	·	·	·	·	·	·	·	·	·		·	·													
Western European Union	9									·	·	·	·	·	·	·	·	·																		
European Community	12									·	·	·	·	·	·	·	·	·		·		·	A			·		A			A	A				
European Free Trade Association	7																		·		·			·	·		·	·	·							
Council of Europe	24		A	A	·					·	·	·	·	·	·	·	·	·	·	·	·	·	·	·	·	·	·	·	·		·	·		·	A	
Warsaw Treaty Organisation	6	·	·	·	·	·	·																													
Conventional Forces in Europe Negotiations	22	·	·	·	·	·	·	·	·	·	·	·	·	·	·	·	·	·	·	·	·	·	·													
Conference on Security and Cooperation in Europe	34	·	·	·	·	·	·	·	·	·	·	·	·	·	·	·	·	·	·	·	·	·	·	·	·	·	·	·	·	·	·	·	·	·	·	A
Economic Commission for Europe *	33	·	·	·	·	·	·	·	·	·	·	·	·	·	·	·	·	·	·	·	·	·	·	·	·	·	·	·			·	·	·	·	·	·

* USSR, Byelorussia, Ukraine have separate seats

Source: Adapted from Jane Sharp. Deadline. vo. V, nos 5–6.

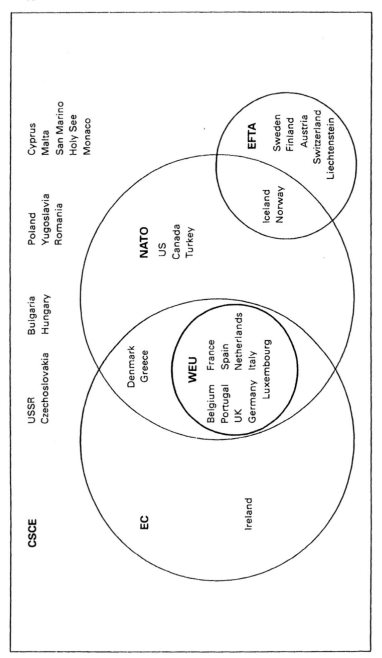

Source: Taken from *New Threats, New Responses*, Oxford Research Group, Autumn 1990.

FIGURE 2.3 *Membership of European institutions 1991*

(i) The Two Blocs: NATO and the Warsaw Pact

For Atlanticists in the West NATO remains the only reliable defence organisation, providing stability in a volatile situation, tying in the US guarantee and anchoring Germany in the Integrated Military Command. In addition it is suggested that NATO might take on a more extensive 'out of area' role including the creation of Rapid Reaction Forces. This is quintessentially a 'view from within'. The claim is that NATO can adapt appropriately to become a more political and less military institution, although what this means has yet to be explained. It may be that to the extent that the military dimension becomes less significant, so does NATO – particularly if European and American interests diverge. On the other hand some supporters of NATO see the alliance expanding to take in increasing numbers of countries to the East as democracy and the rule of law spread.[22]

Critics, of course, argue that the end of the Soviet threat and the demise of the Warsaw Pact have removed NATO's main raison d'être. It now stands in the way of the process of normalisation and integration. One suggestion was that the Integrated Military Structure should be merged with that of the Warsaw Pact – or else dissolved leaving the Atlantic Alliance in its original form. Or NATO's unified command and control structure and intelligence capabilities could be put en bloc under the United Nations. Or else, if the Alliance does survive and the Warsaw Treaty Organisation does not, then why should the Soviet Union not become a member of it?[23]

To the Soviet General Staff the Warsaw Pact represents a painfully depleted security buffer, now declared officially defunct as a military organisation. Nevertheless, it has been vital for coherent arms control and disarmament talks. It is through meetings of the 'twenty-two' in Vienna that the great reductions in conventional forces (CFE) have been negotiated. Whether follow-on negotiations (CFE 2) will be possible remains to be seen. Without them it will be much harder to coordinate a build-down, as crisscrossing individual national ceilings replace simpler bloc-to-bloc calculations.[24]

(ii) A strengthened European pillar: the Western European Union (WEU) and the Independent European Programme Group (IEPG)

Here the emphasis moves to the concept of an enhanced Western European defence coordination more or less firmly under the aegis of

NATO. In recent years the key institution has been seen to be the WEU, originating with the Brussels Treaty in 1948 but transferring its defence functions to NATO in 1950. France and Britain have been energetic in its recent revival. Its role, as defined in the 1987 Hague Platform, is 'to develop a more cohesive European defence identity'. But, whereas some see WEU as part of a stronger and more assertive Europe (i.e. France, Italy, Germany, Spain), others are keen that it should not weaken the role of NATO (i.e. Britain, Netherlands, Portugal). This ambiguity is perhaps the main strength of this option at a time of rapid change and conflicting priorities. On the other hand it is widely regarded for that reason as devoid of substantial content.[25]

Another organisation worth noting is the IEPG, created in 1976 to include all European members of NATO (except Iceland). This allows France to participate in a European effort to coordinate military R&D, standardise defence equipment, and maintain an effective European defence industrial base.[26]

(iii) A European Defence Community: the European Community (EC) and the European Free Trade Association (EFTA)

From this perspective what is wanted is a distinct European defence community to go with growing economic and political integration. Growing divergence between European and American security interests is said to reinforce this. Starting in 1971, and strengthened through the 1986 Single European Act, the European Community has entered the foreign policy field through the European Political Cooperation (EPC) process, which aims 'jointly to formulate and implement a European foreign policy'. It is thought inevitable that as part of an emerging 'United States of Europe' or 'European Confederation' (however defined) the European Community must also control its own security, including joint procurement, role specialisation and steps towards what might eventually become an integrated European army. One proposal is that the Western European Union be absorbed into the European Community as its security arm when the Brussels Treaty expires in 1998. French and British nuclear weapons are seen by some to constitute an embryonic European deterrent, and it has been suggested that their permanent seats on the UN Security Council might be transferred to a new united Europe.[27]

The ambition is for the EC to expand in stages to include, first, the seven EFTA countries (via the creation of a 'European Economic Space'), then the newly democratic states of Central Eastern Europe

(Poland, Czechoslovakia, Hungary), and eventually the other countries (but not the Soviet Union) as well, although there is fear in some quarters that expansion might mean dilution.[28]

This option seemed to have growing support through to the end of 1990 with a majority of EC members favouring progressive steps to integrate foreign policy, security and defence. Since then the Gulf crisis is seen by opponents to have shown up the enterprise as illusory if not hypocritical. The concept is criticised strongly both from the 'right' and from the 'left'. The former criticise it because it moves too far beyond the tradition of separate national defences, the latter because it does not move far enough in superseding it. Both agree in arguing that a defence capability for the European Community would cause problems for Eire and for other neutral countries wanting to join, and that it would appear threatening to the Soviet Union. Counter-arguments are that neutrality is ceasing to be a problem as bloc confrontation disappears, and that a new European defence community could establish a formal peace treaty with the Soviet Union in a way that NATO cannot.[29]

(iv) A Common European Security Space: the Conference On Security And Cooperation In Europe (CSCE) and the Council of Europe

Here we reach the only institution fully to satisfy those who espouse a 'view from above' in Europe, for the obvious reason that it includes all thirty-four nations and in particular the Soviet Union. The work of the CSCE has so far covered three areas or 'baskets' – human rights, economic and technological cooperation, and security. In the security field the Helsinki Final Act and all the follow-up agreements, including the principles and guidelines, the confidence and security building measures and the first permanent institutions agreed in Paris in November 1990, are seen as the first bricks of a Common European House. The Helsinki review meeting due in 1992 will be a further stage in the creation of a pan-European security order.[30]

Supporters of CSCE as the main security structure in Europe want to see it develop to the point where it supercedes both NATO and the former Warsaw Pact. Sceptics see CSCE as no more than an umbrella organisation to coordinate questions such as verification and the monitoring of human rights, and perhaps play a role in mediation and conflict resolution. Rather as with the UN, they see anything more as impossible in such an unwieldy forum. Many CSCE supporters, on on the other hand, envisage (in various combinations) a formal treaty, six-monthly foreign ministers' meetings, regular summits of heads of state, a committee of permanent representatives, a permanent secretariat, a rotating security council and joint peacekeeping forces, some of which have already been achieved.[31]

It is worth also mentioning the Council of Europe here. Although, or perhaps because, it does not have a defence dimension, this is the one Western organisation which might be expanded swiftly to include the East. Hungary joined in 1990, Poland, Czechoslovakia and Yugoslavia have applied to join, and Bulgaria and even the Soviet Union may follow (in which case the Soviet Union would for the first time be a member of a pan-European forum which excluded the USA and Canada). Founded in 1949, the aim of its members is to 'achieve a greater unity among the nations of Europe for the purpose of safeguarding and realising the ideals and principles which are their common heritage and facilitating their social and economic progress'. For Vaclav Havel, speaking in May 1990, 'the spiritual and moral values on which the Council of Europe is based and which are the common heritage of all European nations are the best of all possible foundations for a future integrated Europe'.[32]

Another important idea is that of various regional security subgroupings under the aegis of CSCE, such as a Baltic region, or a Danubian-Adriatic community – or even a Southern Mediterranean grouping which might include North African Maghreb countries.

Finally, it should not be forgotten that many of those who favour CSCE as the main security structure for Europe are equally insistent that it should form only one part of an overarching global system under the aegis of the United Nations. They do not want European security to be assured at the expense of the rest of the world. Here the United Nations' Economic Commission for Europe is significant, as is the UN Conference on Disarmament. International economic bodies like the World Bank (IBRD) and the International Monetary Fund (IMF), the new European Bank for Reconstruction and Development (EBRD) – an offshoot of the Organization for Economic Cooperation and Development (OECD) – also play an important, if controversial role.

For those who emphasise the role of the CSCE the 1990–1 Gulf crisis demonstrated how unsatisfactory the other alternatives are. Unilateral action by ex-colonial powers like Britain or France is considered regressive and dangerous. Intervention by NATO 'out-of-area' forces is condemned as inappropriate, as is the idea of action by

WEU or some future European Defence Community. The only acceptable response is seen to be through joint action by forces from any or all of the CSCE countries, including the Soviet Union, coordinated through the United Nations Military Staff Committee. This is regarded as the only appropriate way in which a new European security order should relate to continuing turmoil in other parts of the world.

4 WHAT SHOULD THE ROLE OF NUCLEAR WEAPONS BE?

In the late 1970s and early 1980s, first over the question of the neutron bomb, then over the deployment of American cruise and Pershing missiles, the nuclear weapon question became a dominant political issue in Western Europe. At the height of the agitation some five million people were demonstrating against the nuclear arms race in European cities. It was the catalyst which precipitated the peace movement and fired interest in the philosophies of non-offensive defence, common security and asymmetrical disarmament initiatives subsequently played back with such remarkable effect by reformist Soviet leaders. Since then the ending of the Cold War and the removal of all American and Soviet land-based missiles in the 500 to 5000 kilometre range as a result of the 1987 INF Treaty have defused the issue. Yet it remains a question of fundamental importance. What role should the most powerful weapons in the world play in the new Europe? As a result of historical accident four out of the five declared nuclear weapon states deploy nuclear weapons in Europe. All of them are maintaining their nuclear weapon establishments and evolving new generations of weapons for deployment later in the decade to last on twenty years or more into the next century. To determine the future of nuclear weapons in Europe is to come to terms with some of the deepest questions in international power politics. Nuclear weapons represent both the apotheosis and the *reductio ad absurdum* of traditional great power competition at maximum force levels.

Conclusions about the future role of nuclear weapons in Europe are derived from answers given to earlier questions. For example, in answer to questions about the nature of the threat that Western nuclear weapons were there to meet, the best counter-strategy, and the most appropriate institutional structure, the official Atlanticist reply throughout the 1980s was, the Soviet Union, flexible response, and NATO, respectively. NATO's whole deterrent posture depended

---

BOX 2.2 NATO NUCLEAR WEAPONS IN EUROPE, 1991

After the withdrawal of Pershing II and ground-launched cruise
missiles and warheads from Europe under the terms of the
Intermediate Range Nuclear Forces (INF) Treaty by the
summer of 1991 (which also includes German Pershing IA
missiles), there will be approximately 3700 American nuclear
warheads left. These comprise 155 millimetre and 8 inch artillery
shells, short range Lance missile warheads, gravity bombs and
antisubmarine depth bombs.

   In addition there are 400 American submarine-launched
ballistic missile (SLBM) warheads and about 100 Tomahawk
sea-launched cruise missile (SLCM) warheads allocated to the
European theatre, and two aircraft carriers carrying some 100
nuclear bombs and depth charges each.

   Finally there are the nuclear warheads deployed with the
British Polaris SLBM force (and the sub-strategic WE-177
bomb/depth charge) formally integrated into US and NATO
war plans, and French nuclear warheads (sea-, air- and ground-
launched) not formally integrated but known to be unofficially
available in case of war.

---

upon maintaining the link in Soviet perceptions between American
ground troops forward deployed along the Inner German Border and
the ultimate sanction of the American strategic deterrent. The former
would convince the Soviets that any incursion across the border would
involve war with the United States. The latter would convince them
that such a war could never be won. The main function of American
theatre nuclear weapons in Europe (and British nuclear weapons) was
said to be, via flexible response, to restore credibility to the deterrent in
the face of Soviet strategic counter-deployment. NATO's nuclear
weapons were not there just to deter Soviet nuclear weapons. Their
prime role was to deter a Soviet conventional attack, which, it was
believed, could not be reliably deterred in any other way. That was
why an option of first use had to be kept open. British nuclear
weapons were said to reinforce this by providing a second centre of
decision-making which would complicate Soviet planning. In addition,
NATO's nuclear weapons fulfilled political functions, like tying in

American commitment to defend Europe and European readiness to share the risks as well as the benefits of collective security. As well as this, British and French nuclear weapons were seen in some quarters as an embryonic European deterrent in case of American withdrawal. They were also popular with each of those nations individually as symbols of national status and guarantors of national independence.[33]

Each of these components is now under attack. How appropriate is the whole paraphernalia of a Western deterrent specially designed to meet a particular Soviet threat, if that threat no longer exists in that form? What use are nuclear weapons against ethnic unrest in Eastern Europe, or Iraqi conventional attack on Kuwait? Have they now any other credible function than that of deterring other powers from using or threatening to use their own nuclear weapons? Is a threat of first use viable any more? What does it mean to refer to nuclear weapons as a 'minimum deterrent' or an 'insurance policy'? And how does all this relate to the new communiqué language of 'last resort'? What about the tensions noted in Chapter 1 between declaratory military defence functions, semi-military intra-war deterrent functions, so-called political signalling functions, and non-deterrent stabilising and reassuring functions? How are these conflicting rationales to be reconciled? Or the divergent views of American and European planners? Or the contrasting perceptions of the disparate elements within the wider defence communities? Or the varied perspectives of different countries and political parties?[34]

As for particular systems, it seems that American ground-launched theatre nuclear weapons are on the way out. Can and should sea-launched systems fulfil the residual role of extended deterrence? Or is a new air-launched Tactical Air To Surface missile (TASM) (planned for the mid-1990s (US) and late 1990s (UK)) essential? Will NATO countries like Germany accept TASM? Or can and should a Franco-British TASM form part of a future European deterrent?[35]

BOX 2.3   THE TACTICAL AIR-TO-SURFACE MISSILE

At the moment most of the problems listed in the text are focused for NATO on one prospective system: the Tactical Air-to-Surface Missile (TASM). During the 1980s this was only one element in an extensive 'modernisation' programme for American nuclear weapons which included *ground-launched* intermediate range (Pershing and Cruise) missiles, short range (Follow-on-to-Lance) missiles and new artillery shells, as well as *sea-launched* strategic (Trident) ballistic missiles and intermediate range (Tomahawk land attack) cruise missiles. Since then, however, the INF Treaty and subsequent German reunification have ruled out the ground-delivered systems, and most strategists argue that sea-launched systems cannot sustain extended deterrence on their own. So everything is seen to depend upon a deployment of new *air-launched* systems, that is to say TASM. Without it, the argument goes, nuclear weapons will no longer be able to fulfil their primary role which is to deter aggression in Europe. The continent will be made safe again for conventional war.[36]

Yet it appears to be politically questionable whether such a NATO capability can be deployed. Every opposition party in Britain rejects it, even the Free Democrats in the ruling coalition in Germany resist the idea that it might be stationed there, while it seems unlikely that American nuclear weapons will be allowed in France. On the other hand, in view of longer warning-times of Soviet attack, it may be possible to make provision for dual-capable delivery systems in various European countries while the nuclear warheads are stored elsewhere (as happened with the enhanced radiation 'neutron bomb').[37]

There is the additional possibility that a joint British/French TASM could constitute the sub-strategic component of a future distinct European Nuclear Force, with British Trident and French M5 strategic submarine-launched ballistic missiles as the ultimate resort. But this faces equally formidable problems, including the delicate question of German participation. Without an equivalent of NATO's Nuclear Planning Group, or the dual-key arrangement whereby control of nuclear delivery systems and warheads is shared between non-nuclear and nuclear powers, it is hard to see how this could be achieved.[38]

Finally, there is the impetus for Britain and France to develop the capability for separate national reasons. This is what makes 'independent' nuclear forces popular in the two countries, but its operational relevance is doubtful.[39]

So it seems that it will be the question of the air-to-surface missile in its various mutually conflicting forms which will be the catalyst in forcing the evolution of nuclear deterrent thinking in Europe in the 1990s, as it was Pershing and ground-launched cruise missiles during the early 1980s and the replacement for Lance missiles during the late 1980s.

All of this also applies to Soviet nuclear weapon programmes. The Soviet withdrawal from Eastern Europe includes Soviet nuclear forces. Since the Reykjavik summit of 1986 there have been specific Soviet proposals to eliminate whole classes of US and Soviet theatre and strategic nuclear systems. Indeed, the declared aim has been to rid the whole world of nuclear weapons by the end of the century. Yet recent Soviet thinking seems to favour negotiation towards some mutual understanding of a shared concept of 'minimum deterrence' which will embrace naval tactical arsenals as well as land- and ground-based systems, and will include French and British as well as American capabilities. Meanwhile Soviet nuclear weapon programmes continue. What is their function in the changed environment of superpower cooperation within a new 'common European house'?[40]

In general, therefore, how do shifting strategic priorities and public rationales relate to the actual processes that are producing the next generation of nuclear weapons? What role is planned for them if further progress is made in Europe away from military postures mainly dedicated to deterrence and towards an increasingly political environment dedicated to pan-European security? What are the new criteria that should guide laboratory research? What is the brief for strategists? In sum, how are nuclear weapons to transcend their own antecedents?

Turning, finally, to the question of the global threat posed by nuclear weapon proliferation, this is where the tension between a 'view from within' and a 'view from above' is most acute. At one pole, for example, is the view from within the defence establishments of existing nuclear weapon powers that decisions about nuclear weapons are the sole business of national authorities in the countries concerned, that the indefinite retention of nuclear weapons by those powers is essential for world peace, but that other countries like Iraq should at all costs be prevented from developing them, if necessary by force. At the other pole is a view powerfully expressed in the United Nations General Assembly to the effect that, given the likely consequences of use, no nation has the right to untrammelled control of these weapons, so they must be brought under the aegis of international law with the preferred aim of eliminating them entirely in the near future. Leaving aside preferences, is it in fact possible to believe that a handful of countries will keep a monopoly indefinitely? Are the signs not now all the other way? Why is it thought possible and desirable to achieve a global ban on chemical weapons but not nuclear weapons? Is the policy of countries like the US and the UK of opposing a Comprehensive Test Ban Treaty (because they want to go on developing their own nuclear weapons) while urging universal subscription to the Non-Proliferation Treaty (because they don't want anyone else to do the same) viable? Or, if nuclear weapons have indeed kept the peace in Europe, why should they not go on to play a similar role in other parts of the world?[41]

5 HOW SHOULD RESOURCES BE SPENT?

'To cope with the full range of challenges we may confront we must focus on readiness and rapid response. And to prepare to meet the challenges we may face in the future, we must focus on research – an active and inventive program of defense R&D. Let me begin with the component with great long-term consequences – research. Time and again we have seen technology revolutionize the battlefield. The United States has always relied upon its technological edge to offset the need to match potential adversaries' strength in numbers. Cruise missiles, Stealth fighters and bombers, today's "smart" weapons with state-of-the-art guidance systems and tomorrow's "brilliant" ones: the men and women in our Armed Forces deserve the best technology America has to offer. And we must realise the heavy price we will pay if we look for false economies in defense R&D. Most modern weapons systems take a minimum of ten years to move from the drawing board to the battlefield. The nature of national defense demands that we plan now for threats on the distant horizon. The decisions we make today – the programs we push forward, or push aside – will dictate the kind of military forces we have at our disposal in the year 2000 – and beyond.'

This extract from President Bush's Aspen Institute address of 2 August 1990 (the day Saddam Hussein invaded Kuwait) expresses the essence of the 'view from within'. Military research and development must be protected at all costs. It represents the ultimate guarantee of national independence and security in an uncertain future. Whatever happens in terms of quantitative arms reductions, the absolute priority is to stay ahead in the qualitative arms race. The same sentiments are expressed with even greater fervour in the most critical area of all – nuclear weapon research. A former Director of the Livermore laboratory said:

'It is my perception that the three American nuclear weapons laboratories are not leaning into opportunities for developing new generations of penetrating or directional warheads as aggressively as they can or should. If we do not pursue them aggressively, the laboratories of other nations are likely to do so, perhaps without our knowledge. These nations could then take advantage of new capabilities and put them in the field, at which time we would be at a considerable disadvantage. So I would urge the three laboratories to get together and find ways to pursue these known opportunities more aggressively and competitively, as well as to assign teams of talented, creative individuals to explore new opportunities.'[42]

Moving out from the inner sanctum of defence R&D, concentric circles of critical defence capabilities are seen to spread out towards the peripheral areas where reductions are eventually made.

European governments share similar attitudes, both individually and collectively, in terms of creating a Europe wide defence industrial base. Up to now the main institutional expression for this has been the Independent European Programme Group, but some argue that future development of a single European Armaments Market and joint R&D programme should be coordinated through the European Commission. The crucial question is seen to be the extent to which individual nations should take on role specialisation and sacrifice unaffordable autonomy for the sake of overall European defence potential. In general the idea that there might be a large 'peace dividend' is thought to be illusory. The dramatic cost inflation of modern weaponry will take up most of the slack, as will the expense of making good existing shortfalls in equipment, evolving more mobile and technologically effective forces and providing support for those personnel who are demobilised. There are varied opinions about how best to cope with inevitable cutbacks in those defence industries geared to massive armoured confrontation between the blocs.[43]

From the perspective of the 'view from above', however, this whole approach is seen to be deeply misguided. It seems self-evident that the attitude expressed by President Bush in the Aspen speech is in itself myopic, and, when generalised, mutually disastrous. If every nation is acting on that philosophy there is no hope of ever limiting the endless proliferation of potential weapon systems. The president's conclusion from the fact of long lead-times is that all technological opportunities must therefore be vigorously explored on a basis of worst-case predictions about possible distant future threats. Yet, as he himself admits, force structures in ten years' time will be dictated by precisely those decisions. So, if this is being done by every nation, the outcome must be a further intensification of the qualitative arms race and a perpetuation of potential confrontation and insecurity. The alternative is to work towards a cooperative European and global security system in which massive reductions in military spending are linked to investment in those areas most likely to resolve underlying causes of tension and conflict. This can only be done by a fundamental shift away from thinking about international affairs in terms of conflicting state interests ultimately determined by military confrontation and towards a realisation that interdependence now demands cooperation in resolving common political, economic and environmental problems. Zero-sum thinking must be replaced by the understanding that we are now in a win-win or lose-lose situation. This 'idealistic' challenge to traditional 'realism' is further strengthened by the claim that heavy military expenditure is in any case self defeating, as can be seen if the experience of the Soviet Union and the United States since the Second World War is compared to that of Germany and Japan.[44]

It is finally worth stressing the central significance of the disagreement about the international arms trade here.

The 'view from within' is that arms imports and exports are essential to ensure that countries which do not manufacture their own capabilities can be properly defended (they are accordingly usually called 'defence exports'). To this end government agencies like the British Defence Export Services Organisation (DESO) coordinate support, analyse markets and stage arms exhibitions. It is often argued that, if such services were wound down in particular countries, it would just mean that others, perhaps less scrupulous, would step in with incalculable political consequences. Arms exports are also said to be necessary to make critical domestic programmes viable. Protestations that the whole system is carefully regulated so that weapons do not fall into the wrong hands accompany most official accounts.[45]

Criticism of this whole approach is trenchant:

'Nearly all the 170 odd wars fought since the Second World War have originated and been fought in the Third World and their length and ferocity have been largely dependent upon arms transfers from the industrialised world.'[46]

The most dramatic recent example was the import of over \$16 billion of military equipment (1985 prices) by Iraq between 1984 and 1988, from, among others, Czechoslovakia, France, Germany, Italy, Switzerland, the United Kingdom, the United States and the USSR. A large proportion of Third World debt (in some cases more than a third) is the result of arms purchases. In general, military aid dwarfs aid for development. The system is seen to be pernicious and immoral, driven by short-sighted self interest and greed and contributing significantly to increased instability and further impoverishment in the less developed parts of the world. There are urgent recommendations that mutually contradictory 'views from within' of this kind should now be replaced by an all-embracing 'view from above' under the aegis of the United Nations. An international arms register could provide a basis for coordinating subsequent cooperative security steps so that continuing heavy arms build-ups are no longer seen to be necessary. Since, as has already been pointed out, nine of the twelve top arms exporters are CSCE countries, this must be a top priority for the emerging new European security order.[47]

6 HOW SHOULD THE DECISIONS BE MADE?

'I am concerned because we in the Soviet Union have built up a tremendous military-industrial complex, which, so long as it was given all the food and money it needed, was obedient and did not create any problems. But now, when it feels the crunch, because the country simply cannot sustain such a big military establishment, it begins to raise its voice. And, if the foreign policy does not suit it, it finds reasons why the policy is wrong. Here, by the way, it is not so different from your American military-industrial complex. So one of the worst prospects as far as I'm concerned is a scenario I foresee in which there is, as it were, an international alliance of military-industrial complexes which have a tremendous need of each other in order to survive. For example, when our militarists take this line, what do they rely on? Things like Mrs Thatcher's speeches in which she stresses the importance of maintaining military force in the West.'

This assessment by former Soviet politburo member Georgi Arbatov given in an interview on 5 July 1990 echoes what many in the West also feel.[48] For example, Professor John Mack, addressing the American Psychiatric Association on 'The Psychodynamics of Big Defense Spending' on 2 May 1990, agrees:[49]

'What is clear is that we are confronted at the present time with an extensive network of organisations and bureaucracies with a strong investment, whether conscious or not, in their own self perpetuation, however much the actualities of the international political situation may have changed. It is this investment, or set of vested interests, which is the primary obstacle to shifting our economy away from the huge defense expenditures to which we have become accustomed. The resistance to change presented by this enormous structure needs to be better understood.'

From this perspective defence establishments in both East and West, inherited from a war-fighting past, cooperate in justifying each others' existence and in trying to preserve the decision-making monopoly that protects them by jointly invoking the elaborate paraphernalia of official secrecy. The 'view from within' is entrenched behind the bastions of state control, and those who believe that this view must now be transcended face the awe-inspiring task of overcoming, not only outmoded ways of thinking, but also outmoded structures of power. At the heart of the matter lies nothing less than the nature and status of the sovereign national state itself. This is seen to connect with the question of the 'democratic deficit'. NATO's North Atlantic Assembly, the Parliamentary Assemblies of the Council of Europe and the WEU, the Committee of Members of Parliament of EFTA and the European Parliament of the EC are all parliamentary bodies associated with the relevant institutions. But only the European Parliament is directly elected as such or has any sort of control over the executive arm, and even that is severely limited. The fiction is that national governments account to national parliaments for decisions taken within international bodies. But to critics of the current system the refusal of governments like the British government to account for, say, NATO decisions to the British parliament shows that this is indeed a fiction. Bodies like the WEU and IEPG are seen to represent international coordination between defence establishments to perpetuate the arms industry. What critics want are international bodies whose brief is, on the contrary, arms control and disarmament, and who are directly accountable to elected parliaments for it.[50]

Having based the whole of Chapter 1 on a 'view from above', and so far in this chapter having given the last word in each case to the 'view from above' as well, it is fitting to end the chapter with a 'view from within'. In this instance it is a view from within the defence communities of the West.

From this vantage-point what has just been written is entirely perverse. The fact of the matter is simple. Until the collapse of the Soviet Union in the late 1980s the West was faced with a monolithic tyranny bolstered by colossal military forces deployed in manifestly offensive posture. The subject peoples of Eastern Europe were held down by force. It was only the strength and resolve of the Western alliance, sustained for four decades, that finally convinced Soviet leaders that their military forces could not be used, and allowed time for the whole system to break down internally. The bankruptcy of Marxism-Leninism became manifest. The values defended by the alliance – fundamental human rights, parliamentary democracy, the market economy, in short freedom itself – demonstrated their natural superiority. The result has been to emancipate the world from the evil of Bolshevism and open the prospect of a new era of peace, freedom and prosperity in the world. Just as the Germans and Japanese today are thankful that their pre-war tyrannies were overthrown, so the demise of communism is as much to the long-term benefit of the peoples living in the Soviet Union as it is to everyone else. In view of all this it is absurd to equate the Western alliance with the Soviet despotism of the past (still not fully overcome), or to exaggerate the significance of shrinking defence budgets which average significantly less than 5 per cent of GDP. Armed forces in the West are controlled by freely elected governments, themselves answerable to national parliaments. Continued alliance solidarity and reasonable defences will help to ensure that remaining dangers and problems are safely resolved. Security, including the tackling of the urgent economic and environmental problems that now confront the world community, is enhanced, not eroded, by these policies. Nothing could be gained by abandoning them before the remaining items on the global agenda have been successfully negotiated. Recklessness and instability at great power level is certainly not in the interest of the Third World.

SUMMARY

Question 1   Where does the threat to security lie?

The view from within the Western defence establishments

The main security threats come from remaining Soviet military forces at the service of unpredictable future political masters, from instability in former communist East and South-East European countries, and from possible nuclear-armed dictators in places like the Middle East.

The view from above

The main security threats come from mutually reinforcing military strategies and weapons programmes, particularly nuclear, from gross imbalances in material living standards in Europe and the Soviet Union, and from the converging global developmental and environmental crises which threaten the future of humankind as a whole.

Question 2   What is the appropriate response?

The view from within the Western defence establishments:

The response must be to maintain collective alliance solidarity by continuing to anchor Germany and bind in the United States guarantee, to retain an adequate mix of up-to-date, flexible and responsive nuclear and non-nuclear forces, and to adapt integrated strategies in the direction of greater mobility without jeopardising the stability of credible deterrence.

The view from above

The response must be to restructure armed forces from the Atlantic to the Urals according to principles of non-offensive defence and common security, to overcome the structural economic discontinuities and imbalances in Europe, and to concentrate attention on a combined assault on global threats to a sustainable world future.

Question 3   What should the future security structure be?

The view from within the Western defence establishments

NATO must be retained as the immediate defence organisation, with an enhanced European pillar, possibly developing into a more coherent future European defence identity. The CSCE framework will allow wider collaboration in certain important fields, but cannot replace NATO as the main defence and security forum.

The view from above

NATO must eventually be merged into the wider CSCE process, which should therefore be progressively developed to take over an increasing number of security functions in an evolving pan-European security system. The European Community should not assume defence functions. CSCE itself must be viewed as one component in a future global security order under the aegis of the United Nations.

Question 4   What should the role of nuclear weapons be?

The view from within the Western defence establishments

Strategic and sub-strategic nuclear weapons must be maintained and modernised, American nuclear weapons must continue to be stationed in Europe, and British and French nuclear cooperation should be encouraged, whether or not as a possible future European nuclear force. The central feature of flexible response – the keeping open of the option of a first use of nuclear weapons – must be retained as a deterrent to war.

The view from above

All land-based sub-strategic nuclear weapons should be removed from Europe (including air-to-surface missiles), as should sea-based cruise missiles. During an interim period, however specified, the function of remaining nuclear weapons can only be as a minimum deterrent against a possible use of other nuclear weapons. A first use option must be forsworn, and a comprehensive test ban sought.

Question 5   How should resources be spent?

The view from within the Western defence establishments

Although defence budgets are likely to be reduced, this will not result in large 'peace dividends' in view of rising expenses and continuing defence needs. It is essential that energetic military R&D should be pursued and an adequate defence industrial base retained. Arms exports may be more stringently controlled, but will remain necessary. The equation often made between the size of military budgets and other social and economic budget requirements is a false one.

The view from above

The transfer of massive resources from military spending to urgent priorities elsewhere must be achieved as soon as possible. As much money, expertise and effort should be devoted in future to R&D and development programmes which will contribute to achieving sustainable progress for all, as has in the past been expended on military projects. Weapons research must be drastically cut, concerted efforts made to speed diversification and conversion programmes, and the international arms trade halted.

Question 6   How should the decisions be made?

The view from within the Western defence establishments

Defence decision-making should be left as it is. The realities of possible future threat can only be properly assessed by the official intelligence communities. Adequate defence remains one of the supreme responsibilities of government. Other social goods are only attainable when it is secure.

The view from above

The transformation in the nature of international affairs in the nuclear age means that not only inherited ways of thinking, but also inherited structures of power must be changed. Confrontation and militarism are built in to the nature of traditional defence establishments created during the age of great power war. Their control of information, monopoly of decision-making and habitual secrecy must be replaced by political processes more open to democratic debate and accountability.

NOTES

1. *The London Declaration on a Transformed Atlantic Alliance,* NATO press communiqué, Brussels 6 July 1990. On 19 November 1990 the 22 NATO and Warsaw Pact countries signed a joint declaration: 'In the new era of European relations which is beginning, they are no longer adversaries, will build new partnerships and extend to each other the hand of friendship.'
2. This is not to suggest that CSCE countries have not been and are not themselves involved, directly and indirectly, in such wars.
3. These phrases are from Secretary of State Baker's testimony to Congress, 5 September 1990, and Foreign Secretary Hurd's address to the United Nations, 26 September 1990.
4. For example, Edward Warner, 'New Thinking and Old Realities in Soviet Defence Policy', *Survival,* Jan/Feb 1989, and Christopher Donnelly, 'The Development of Soviet Military Policy in the 1990s', *RUSI Journal,* Spring 1990:

   'The model of adopting a strategic defensive posture, backed up by a limited counter-offensive capability and with a reliance on mobilisation may sound alright, but it flies in the face of Soviet military tradition and would take, under normal circumstances, several years of theoretical work to establish how it should best be done. There is no evidence that the Soviet General Staff has yet decided how to implement this policy despite Gorbachev needing results quickly. The result is tension between him and his military . . . The Soviet Armed Forces have been engaging in intense experimentation to establish improved force structures throughout the 1980s. These are designed to take account of the functions of new weapons currently coming into service. Attempts by Soviet Generals to explain this as "defensive" restructuring is little more than deception.'

5. The Pentagon's January 1990 *Defense Guidance* long-range planning document was still based on 14 days warning. The two-year estimate was quoted in *The Times,* 3 August 1990. 'Warning times do have significant implications, for example in the level you could have of front line forces, in the scope that you can depend more on reserves for reinforcement and therefore on what the original deployments are', Tom King, evidence to House of Commons Defence Select Committee, July 1990.

6. 'Demographers and government officials estimate that as many as five million refugees could soon be in European Community states', Jonathan Eyal, *Guardian*, 30 November 1990. Austria has reinforced its border guards. Finnish icebreakers are making sure there is no ice bridge from the Baltic states.

7. 'In the eighteenth century we [the British] made extensive use of mercenary troops in Europe – notably Saxons. Are we to become the mercenaries at the behest of those richer Saxons now?', R. W. Johnson in an article in the *New Statesman*, July 1990, in which he argues for an Anglo-French alliance to meet the German threat.

8. Admiral Khvatov, C.-in-C. Soviet Pacific fleet, and General Ivan Mikulin, speaking at the 28th Congress of the CPSU, 5 July 1990, *Soviet News*, no. 6534.

9. Alexandr Prokhanov, 'The Tragedy of Centralism', *Literaturnaya Rossiya*, 5 January 1990, quoted in Christopher Donnelly, *The Development of Soviet Military Policy*.

10. The idea of East–West relations during the Cold War as a baleful collaboration of this kind was elaborated during the 1980s by, among others, E. P. Thompson, *Exterminism and the Cold War*, New Left Books, 1982, and George Konrad, *Antipolitics*, Quartet 1984.

11. This view has been powerfully argued by Johan Galtung, for example at the IPPNW symposium at Coventry in September 1990, 'Health and Security 2000: New Thinking in Europe'.

12. An example of this Western 'view from within' is provided here:

> 'The deeper lesson for the West is that, far from being an era of global tranquillity and enormous peace dividends, the post-communist world is likely to be one in which we face formidable and unfamiliar dangers. Foremost among these is the threat of militant Islam, which will not disappear even if Saddam Hussein and his regime are destroyed. Whatever happens in the Gulf, the West would do well to look to its defences and prepare for the long haul' (John Gray, *Independent*, 4 September 1990).

As for refugees, a European Commission study estimated that, whereas the EC population would increase by 2.4 million over the next decade (0.7 per cent), in North Africa it would be 49.6 million (20 per cent). Ninety-five per cent of all population growth in Europe and the Mediterranean would be concentrated in North Africa with the bulk of the population under the age of 20. Reported in *The Times*, 1 December 1990.

13. Ronald Higgins, *The Seventh Enemy: The Human Factor in the Global Crisis*, Hodder and Stoughton, 1978.

14. This thinking has been central to 'dependency theory' for many years. A useful critical survey can be found in J. Caporosa (ed.) 'Dependence and Dependency in the Global System', *International Organization*, vol 32, no. 1, 1978.

15. The complex process of reformulating NATO force structure and strategy, coordinated through the High Level Task Force, is likely to

be announced in outline during 1991. Political considerations urge a single stage reformulation, but practical uncertainties may make this difficult. Of the three likely vertical tiers in the Central Region, the multinational covering force to the East would perhaps concentrate on surveillance and long-range firepower, the quick reaction forces in the centre be also organised for possible rapid deployment elsewhere (including out of area), and the armoured manoeuvre forces retained to the West constitute a powerful reinforcement potential.

16. One of the main problems here is that former Warsaw Pact territory is not in the NATO area, so, in the absence of a direct assault on NATO territory, it is not clear whether or how the Alliance could intervene at all in this region, even in a 'peace-keeping' mode.

17. There is an enormous literature on 'non-provocative defence', a recent example being Philip Webber, *New Defence Strategies for the 1990s: From Confrontation to Coexistence*, Macmillan, 1990. The concept of 'mutual defensive superiority' is explored in Robert Neild, *An Essay on Strategy*, Macmillan, 1990. On role specialisation, applying principles developed by Andreas von Bülow and others in Germany, Sir Hugh Beach has suggested non-offensive 'shield' forces to the East provided by Germany (and perhaps Belgium, the Netherlands and Denmark), while the United States, Britain and France concentrate on enhanced manoeuvre 'sword' forces to the West, *Restructuring of Military Forces and Doctrines*, 40th Pugwash Conference, September 1990, background paper.

As to the relationship between unilateral modernisation and multilateral arms control, the idea that continued modernisation is compatible with arms control is embodied in NATO's Harmel doctrine and post-1979 dual track policy. This approach was criticised from one side by those who advocated unilateral modernisation and discounted arms control. The classic exposition of the contrary view is in Charles Osgood, *Neither War Nor Surrender*, University of Illinois Press, 1962. The aim here is to break the spiral of mutually reinforcing unilateral armament measures (collectively known as 'the arms race') by reversing it. Tension would be released in carefully calculated unilateral disarmament steps and then the ratchet would be held to see if the other would reciprocate. The process is called 'graduated reciprocation in tension reduction' (GRIT). Once the process is under way it can be formalised by multilateral agreement. Supporters of this approach claim that this is precisely what Mikhail Gorbachev has done since 1985. From this perspective the opposite idea of mutual 'negotiation from strength' is logically self-defeating.

18. There is considerable terminological ambiguity here. The term 'common security' was popularised in the Palme Commission report *Common Security: A Programme for Disarmament*, published at the height of the 'second Cold War' in 1982. At that time common security, which embraced the idea of both alliances taken together, was contrasted with the collective security embodied in the idea of NATO on its own. The term 'collective security' is also used, however, for the security provided within a single all-embracing organisation like the League of Nations or

the United Nations, and here, of course, there is no clash with the concept of common security.

19. For Sir Hugh Beach, speaking on BBC 2's 'Fifth Column' programme, 11 July 1990, the whole point of achieving a pan-European security system is to 'confront with some prospect of success the real security issues of the 21st century: famine, disease, pollution, global warming, drugs, terrorism, fundamentalism. These are the things which threaten us all and only if we act together can we get on top of them', Media Transcription Service, ref. no. 831.

20. There are those who welcome this confusion and express impatience with the idea that there might be a neat 'bureaucratic' solution. The language of architecture is seen to be inappropriate in conditions where ad hoc adjustment will be both most likely and most sensible. Nothing in this section is intended to contradict this. There has been a bewildering mass of suggestions about future security frameworks since the autumn of 1989. Particularly useful in sorting this out have been Adrian Hyde-Price, *European Security Beyond the Cold War*, IISS, February 1990 (used in draft form), and Jane Sharp, 'Europe's New Architecture', SIPRI, in *Deadline*, vol. V, nos 5–6 (bulletin of the Center for War, Peace and the News Media), Fall 1990.

21. The 'nation state' model of a 'Europe des Patries' finds favour with political groupings to the right, but, insofar as it is associated with resurgent nationalism, is regarded as reactionary and dangerous by those towards the centre and left.

22. For NATO's Secretary General, Manfred Wörner, 'we must preserve NATO's integrated military structure. It is a unique achievement and ensures that no one will be tempted to renationalise security', NATO press release 18, October 1990. For British Foreign Secretary Douglas Hurd 'NATO is the rock of our defence, the guarantee of collective security', whereas the European Community is 'on the economic and political side', Radio 4, 19 November 1990, Media Transcription Service, ref. no. 1074. An out of area role for NATO was demanded by British Defence Secretary Tom King at the North Atlantic Assembly session, 28 November 1990, *Daily Telegraph*, 29 November 1990. For Roseanne Ridgeway, president of the Atlantic Council, the point of NATO is 'to express as an institution the fact that there are interests that the United States and Europe share in politics, in defence, in economics and in the world order', Radio 4, 20 September 1990, Media Transcription Service ref. no. 987. In Berlin in December 1989 US Secretary of State James Baker described the role of NATO as crucial in the 'new Atlanticism' sketched out by President Bush: 'as we construct a new security architecture that maintains common defence, the nonmilitary component of European security will grow. NATO will become the forum where Western nations cooperate to negotiate, to implement, to verify and to extend agreements between East and West.'

23. 'We don't want the European continent to be divided into military alliances. We want an all-European system of security. NATO stands for Navies, Aircraft, Tanks, Obsolete', Gennady Gerasimov, 6 July 1990. It is suggested that some Soviet planners favour the survival of NATO

because it justifies their own dispositions although they strongly resist the desire of some former Warsaw Pact countries to join the Alliance. It is not only Soviet commentators and the peace movement who do not see a continuing role for NATO: 'The Atlantic Alliance was established in the face of the Soviet threat. Then came the integrated military structure in response to the Warsaw Pact. With the disintegration of the Warsaw Pact what is the reason for the continued existence of the Atlantic Alliance and the integrated command?' Jean-Pierre Chevènement, French Defence Minister, at the NATO ministerial meeting at Turnberry, 7 June 1990 (France left NATO's integrated military structure in 1966). The idea of merging the Alliances has been implicit in German Foreign Minister Hans-Dietrich Genscher's suggestion of developing cooperative security structures (speech to Western European Union 23 March 1990), while the notion of widening NATO to embrace all CSCE countries has been suggested by Walther Stützle, director of SIPRI (*Die Zeit*, May 1990).

24. Jonathan Dean, former US ambassador to the MBFR talks, has suggested that the cooperative verification procedures set up between the two alliances to monitor the CFE agreement could be developed within pan-European institutions (i.e. inspection teams could become prototypes for future peacekeeping forces). Cited in Jane Sharp, *Europe's New Architecture*.

25. Former Dutch defence minister, Willem van Eekelen, secretary general of the WEU, is understandably enthusiastic about the prospects for his institution. So are others, such as Edward Mortimer: 'what is needed is a specifically *West* European body with an explicit mandate for collective defence . . . The WEU *is* the European pillar in outline. Its members should start building it as a military organisation, before the American pillar begins to crack under the strain', *Financial Times*, 1 July 1990. The British Foreign Secretary suggested an expanded role for the WEU including a rapid reaction force which could intervene in conflicts outside Europe, speech in Berlin 10 December 1990, reported in *The Times*, 17 December 1990.

26. *Towards a Stronger Europe*, vol. 1 EDIG Report, 1987.

27. Single European Act, 1986, Title III, Article 30.2. Some predict that present moves to create a European Defence Community will meet a fate similar to those which failed in the 1950s. But the Inter-Governmental Conferences in December 1990 suggested otherwise. Under Italian presidency it was proposed that the WEU should be absorbed into the EC as its security arm. France and Germany supported the principle of moves to integrate security and defence concerns. Although the British government remains sceptical, influential individuals like Lord Carrington and Leon Brittan argue that the process is inevitable.

28. Margaret Thatcher's speech at Aspen, Colorado, on 6 August 1990 suggested that the widening of the European Community would be preferable to deepening it. Others do not see these as alternatives. Jacques Delors envisages concentric circles leading to eventual integration of the whole of Europe. François Mitterrand speaks of an 'All-European Confederation', Helmut Kohl of a 'United States of Europe'.

29. A European Defence Community is opposed on the right by National Conservatives and on the left by radical Social Democrats and Greens. Neither of the two main British political parties yet supports the idea.

30. The idea of an enhanced role for the CSCE has been pressed for some time by German Foreign Minister Hans-Dietrich Genscher, and some of this thinking has since been incorporated, first in the 6 July 1990 NATO London Declaration, then in the 20 November 1990 Paris agreements. Ambitious plans have been sketched out in Soviet foreign minister Eduard Shevardnadze's conception of a 'greater Europe' (*Izvestia*, 30 May 1990) and elaborated by thinkers like Frank Blackaby, former director of the Stockholm International Research Institute (British American Security Information Council report).

31. The November 1990 Paris CSCE summit agreed a number of confidence and security building measures, affirmed basic pan-European principles and guidelines for future meetings, laid plans for an 'Assembly of Europe' and established the first permanent CSCE institutions: regular summits and ministerial meetings, a secretariat, a conflict prevention centre and an election observation office.

32. Vaclav Havel, address to the Parliamentary Assembly of The Council of Europe, *Ceteka Daily News and Press Survey*, 10 May 1990.

33. An outline of NATO nuclear weapon policy in the 1980s can be found in Oliver Ramsbotham, *Modernizing NATO's Nuclear Weapons*, Macmillan 1989, Ch. 2. A critique can be found in Ch. 3.

34. The idea of a 'minimum deterrent' has been elaborated at strategic level, particularly with reference to US-Soviet relations. It is often taken to refer to a nuclear deterrent whose sole function is the direct deterrence of enemy nuclear blackmail or attack. As such it does not include the functions of extended deterrence and flexible response (i.e. keeping open a first use option). This is how it is understood, for example, in Stephen Shenfield, *Minimum Nuclear Deterrence: The Debate Among Soviet Civilian Analysts*, Center for Foreign Policy Development, Brown University, November 1989. Unfortunately nearly all deterrent forces are officially described as 'minimum', so the term has no generally accepted meaning.

35. France retains land-launched intermediate range S3 missiles and has not yet renounced the possibility of fielding new short-range Hadès missiles. Both France and the Soviet Union both already deploy nuclear air-to-surface missiles in Europe.

36. In the 6 July 1990 London Declaration, NATO heads of state and government affirmed that NATO's nuclear weapons 'will continue to fulfil an essential role in the overall strategy of the Alliance to prevent war by ensuring that there are no circumstances in which nuclear retaliation in response to military action might be discounted. However, in the transformed Europe, they will be able to adopt a new NATO strategy making nuclear forces truly weapons of last resort'. The first sentence affirms the central principle of flexible response. The second seems difficult to reconcile with it. This wording is widely understood to have represented a compromise between British and German views.

37. The precise British Labour Party position is to reject a British TASM and conclude that 'no other European member of NATO is prepared to accept those weapons' (Martin O'Neill, House of Commons debate on the Defence Estimates, 18 July 1990, Hansard col. 699). However, if NATO allies do want an American TASM, then 'we would accept our responsibilities as an Alliance member'.

38. Anglo-French collaboration on an extended range version of the current French Air-Sol à Moyenne Portée (ASMP), the Air-Sol Longue Portée (ASLP) has been discussed since the 1986 Reykjavik summit. A joint statement by the British and French defence ministers on 21 April 1990 read 'the UK is considering a missile derived from ASMP . . . with a UK nuclear warhead to replace the WE177 gravity bomb'.

39. The rationale for a new British sub-strategic capability in addition to Trident has not been fully set out, beyond the judgement in the 1989 *Statement on the Defence Estimates* that 'strategic weapons alone, for all their awesome power, could not be morally tolerable, practically feasible or politically credible for every scenario'.

40. Sergei Kortunov, 'Negotiating on Nuclear Weapons in Europe', *Survival*, Jan/Feb 1991. The 800 km range AS13 (Kingbolt) is sometimes described as the Soviet equivalent of TASM, although there is some confusion over the roles, functions and in some cases existence of a number of Soviet air-to-surface missiles, *Jane's Missiles 1989/90*.

41. The British government, according to the UK delegation to the United Nations, considers that 'the most important of the existing arms control treaties, and incontestably the one with the widest adherence, is the Nuclear Non-Proliferation Treaty', but 'an immediate move to a Comprehensive Test Ban Treaty would be premature and even destabilising. For the foreseeable future the United Kingdom's security will depend on deterrence based, in part, on the possession of nuclear weapons. This will mean a continuing requirement to conduct underground nuclear tests to ensure that our nuclear weapons remain effective and up to date', *Arms Control and Disarmament Quarterly Review*, October 1989. The unstated belief is that Britain is a mature, stable and reliable power, whereas a number of others are not.

42. John S. Foster, former Director of Lawrence Livermore National Laboratory, *Los Alamos Science*, no. 17, 1989.

43. 'The swords into ploughshares arguments are, of course, as implausible now as they ever have been. It is as absurd to think that it is possible to abandon defence and switch the money and resources immediately into "green" products as it was some years ago to try to spend it on cancer research. It would take years to convert the research and development and output of defence-orientated companies to equipment that could help preserve the environment, just as it did for the mighty tobacco empires to change their businesses and for the government to find replacement resources. It is in any case much too early to consider that defence is a thing of the past. The world is far from being out of that wood' (*Jane's All the World's Aircraft 1990–1*, foreword).

44. 'During my entire adult life my thinking has been a function of the Cold War. It is time to break out of that, although it's difficult to do so . . . We

are in an increasingly interdependent world: interdependent economically, independent politically, interdependent environmentally and interdependent militarily. No nation and no single group of nations can stand alone in isolation in this increasingly globally interdependent world . . . If we go down this road that Gorbachev has pointed us in the direction of then I believe that within six to eight years we, in the US, could cut our defence budget about half in relation to GNP, from 6 per cent GNP to 3 per cent GNP. That would free up in 1989 dollars a hundred and fifty billion dollars a year. If I were Defense Secretary today, I would be considering how that could be done six to eight years from now without endangering the security of the West' (Robert McNamara, BBC Radio 4, 6 October 1989, Media Transcription Service ref. no. 567).

45. 'Our competitive approach towards buying equipment for our own Services is helping British industry towards many export successes . . . This makes a large contribution both to employment and to the balance of payments . . . Export success depends primarily on the efforts of industry, but the Defence Export Services Organisation plays an important role in support . . . This success does not imply any relaxation of the strict controls needed to prevent weapons or other sensitive equipment falling into the wrong hands. The DESO cooperates closely with other Government Departments to ensure that an informed view is taken of the balance between the legitimate pursuit of commercial interests and the necessary application of government controls' (*Statement on the Defence Estimates*, 1989).

46. *The Arms Trade*, British Council of Churches, March 1990.

47. 'No doubt trade in weapons is becoming a global problem calling for an early solution. In this context serious consideration should be given to the proposals listed in Soviet Foreign Minister Shevardnadze's letter to the UN Secretary General. Its main point is to work out new approaches to the issue of international sales and deliveries of weapons. The letter views the phenomenon as, on the one hand, a dangerous source of the proliferation of the arms race to different parts of the world. On the other hand every state has an inalienable right, recognised by the UN Charter, to collective and individual self-defence. Aware of these two factors, the Soviet minister proposes the following. In the first place, one should consider the principle of transition from excessive military build-ups to a reasonable sufficiency . . . Then legality and openness should be ensured in weapons trading . . . If the principle of openness is implemented, data on arms budgets, arms production, export and re-export, could be published, say, in the UN standard annual reports, which would, in turn, lessen suspicions and increase mutual confidence . . . Finally, the task of drafting a UN convention limiting international sales and supplies of arms is on the agenda' (V. Pogrbenkov, Soviet News, 29 August 1990, no. 6541).

48. BBC Radio 4, 'The World At One', Media Transcription Service, ref. no. 822.

49. *The Risk of Malignant Professionalism in Our Time*, Harvard Medical School.

50. On secrecy and lack of accountability, see Scilla McLean (ed.) *How Nuclear Weapons Decisions Are Made*, Macmillan, 1986, and Hugh Miall, *Nuclear Weapons: Who's In Charge?*, Macmillan 1987, both from the Oxford Research Group.

3 The Two Poles of the Debate

It is time to look more closely at the 'view from within' and the 'view from above'. So far this distinction has been assumed rather than justified. Is it true that there are two main poles to the new European security debate? And, if so, is this an appropriate description of them?

Let us set the two approaches out again in general terms so that it is clear what is in contention.

The first approach assumes as its starting point the existence of the nation state as it has evolved since the sixteenth century and of the system of international power politics built upon it. International affairs are interpreted in terms of conflicting cultures, ideologies and interests, themselves expressions of human nature itself. It is the prime duty of political leaders entrusted with responsibility for defence to recognise these realities. Not to do so is regarded as inexcusable. In practical terms, therefore, things are seen from the point of view of particular governments, countries or alliances. Security means the protection of 'our' interests or values from what is outside. In the autumn of 1989, for example, from a Western viewpoint, it was the political upheavals in Eastern Europe and the Soviet Union that were dangerous (though welcome), and the maintenance of NATO's military infrastructure that was seen to underpin stability. The stress was on strong national defence, deterrence and collective alliance solidarity. This is an approach habitual to military planners and defence intellectuals, and widespread among a broad swathe of 'tough-minded' politicians, journalists and members of the public.

Margaret Thatcher's response to the fall of the Berlin Wall illustrates the first approach:

'We must remember that times of great change are times of great uncertainty, even danger. The librarian of the United States

68

Congress put it very well when he said: "there is no more insecure time in the life of an empire than when it is facing the devolution of its power, no more dangerous time in the life of a religion (communism being after all a secular religion) than when it has lost its inner faith but retains its outer power". Very wise words. Now is the time for us in the West to stay true to the policies and principles that have brought us safely through the years of confrontation and Cold War since 1945. I don't believe that the great changes now happening would have come about had it not been for NATO and the strength and resolve it has shown. And it must be through NATO that we continue to keep the peace by tried and tested means, while welcoming every step that allows us to do so safely at lower levels of forces and weapons.'

13 November 1989[1]

The second approach assumes at the outset that the world is now faced with global problems which threaten the very survival of mankind. Prominent among these are the arms race and the nuclear menace. They entirely eclipse sectional interests and can only be overcome if inherited traditions of state sovereignty and militarism, which have largely created them, are transcended. The same applies to the concentrations of capital and economic exploitation protected by this system. The real problems are common problems and the solutions can therefore only be common solutions. This means that political leaders must learn to see things independently of particular nations or alliances. From this perspective it was the military confrontation in Europe that was seen to be the danger in the autumn of 1989, and the political changes as providing a unique opportunity to end it. Mutual deterrence and collective bloc confrontation was seen to constitute the problem; progressive mutual disarmament and common security to offer the solution. This approach is central to the thinking of many Social Democrats, Liberal Democrats, Greens, and, increasingly, Liberal Conservatives.

One of Mikhail Gorbachev's speeches, delivered a few days before the fall of the Berlin Wall, illustrates the second approach:

'Peace envisages a general agreement between states that no problems, past or present, can be solved with the help of weapons. If this is so, armaments should be reduced to the level of sensible defensive sufficiency, while power politics, hegemony and interference in the internal affairs of other states should be renounced.

Phenomena like the presence of troops on foreign territories, military alliances and vast areas kept off limits, which are so habitual but are incompatible with the peaceful period, should be phased out. Peace means creating a generally recognised legal basis for relations between states. Peace means taking care to form a truly international, genuinely global economy, which would promote the stable development of each country. Peace means broadly based and open cooperation in tackling global problems. Finally, peace means the interaction of countries and peoples in ensuring and protecting human rights in all their diversity on a world-wide scale. These constitute the pivotal and humanising contents and the main meaning of peace. Can mankind effect this breakthrough towards a fundamentally new quality of mutual relations?'

26 October 1989[2]

From the perspective of the 'view from above', the 'view from within' seems hopelessly locked into a past mind-set structurally conditioned by defence establishments originally created in the age of war. From the perspective of the 'view from within', however, the 'view from above' is in fact a view from nowhere. Its dream of an age of mutually assured security does not correspond to current political reality.

But is this neat dichotomy adequate? Are these not caricatures of a more complex reality? Are there not different national perspectives and traditions? Within nations are there not varied viewpoints? Are 'defence establishments' the monoliths projected by critics? Are there not wide divergencies of opinion within and between treasury departments, offices of heads of state, foreign ministries, defence ministries, not to mention intelligence communities, different branches of the armed services, research laboratories, defence manufacturers? Can the confusion of party political opinion in Europe be reduced to these simple alternatives? And what about the luxuriant profusion of academic theory loosely designated 'international relations'? How do 'the view from above' and the 'view from within' relate to all of this?

It is exactly because the situation is so complicated that a simple dichotomy turns out to provide most insight. Holding on to these two poles and seeing how the tension between them plays across the international debate shows up the fundamental issues in a way that more complicated models could not. Perception is not obscured by intervening theory. That these are real poles to the debate is demonstrated in Chapters 4 to 8 with reference to German and British politics. Looking below the level of so-called 'national' perspectives and concentrating on the spectrum of opinion articulated both within and between political parties reveals these underlying centres of gravity. Why parties of the 'right' should gravitate one way and parties of the 'left' the other is a deep question in the philosophy of politics beyond the scope of this book. The claim is that, for whatever reason, they do. Chapter 9 adds the further ambitious claim that this dialogue is of historic significance and can be directly linked to the extraordinary changes now transforming international affairs.

So far the two poles have been described as 'the view from within' and the 'view from above', but these terms will now be temporarily discarded. They are accurate insofar as belief is related to power and those with responsibility for decision-making within discrete power structures are seen to view the situation accordingly (which is no doubt why parties of the left tend towards a 'view from within' as they approach office, whereas former decision-makers often gravitate towards a 'view from above' on retirement). But, if power is abstracted, in terms of pure relations of belief the description fails. Those who hold what has here been called the 'view from within', for example, do not see it as a view from within. They see it as a perception of reality. In other words 'realism' of this kind claims to be a view from above. Conversely, from the same perspective, what has here been called the 'view from above' is seen as a view from within – for example a view from within the narrow confines of left-wing ideology or the peace movement. These difficulties also complicate other descriptions. For example, the terms 'realism' and 'idealism' seem to beg the question of what is real in favour of the first pole. On the other hand, descriptions like 'old thinking' and 'new thinking' seem to beg the question of what is relevant in favour of the second pole.

What, then, are we to call the two poles to the debate? Up to now they have been presented as if they were alternative philosophies. But strictly speaking they are not as distinct as that. They are not alternative paradigms in general international relations theory (like realism, structuralism and pluralism), nor broad philosophical approaches (like realism in another sense and idealism), nor politico-historical interpretations of international affairs (like orthodoxy, revisionism, post-revisionism and radicalism) – although all of these will be related to them in what follows. They do not lie on the surface of the debate at all, but beneath it. They are focal points around which a number of such paradigms, approaches, philosophies and interpretations cluster.[3]

Nevertheless, despite all this, distinct labels will be assigned to the two poles for ease of reference. The first will, after all, be called 'realist', because the wider connotations of this term are appropriate and it is already suitably ambiguous. The second will be called 'transformationist' in an attempt to introduce a comparable rough appropriateness and ambiguity. Each is associated with a cluster of traditions, attitudes and beliefs.

1   THE REALIST POLE

Here nations, states and blocs are seen as the main actors on the international stage, relations between them being characterised by conflict of interest and regulated by manipulation of power. Three strands can be distinguished, which link loosely with approaches and interpretations already mentioned and are relevant to what follows.[4]

There is the strong tradition which places its main emphasis on the idea of the nation. Here, however much of a fiction it may appear from some points of view, the identity of nation and state is seen to be paramount. Since existing state boundaries do not coincide with concepts of nationhood in many cases (and could not, since such concepts often mutually conflict), there is tension between this powerful historical instinct and other aspects of realist thinking about the state. This tension is found throughout Europe as putative nations aspire to statehood (particularly in the East) and existing nations hesitate to merge sovereignty in supra-national organisations (particularly in the West).[5]

Then there is the more purely realist tradition which prides itself on a hard-headed appreciation of the fact that in the real world autonomous states regulate affairs between themselves without sentiment, to their own advantage and according to perceived relations of power. Diplomacy oils the wheels of power politics. So far as Western Europe goes, this tradition militates strongly towards the creation of a federal Europe which will be able to protect its interests and compete on equal terms with the United States and the rising power of Japan into the next century.[6]

Finally there is the more romantic Atlanticist tradition in which realist perceptions that there will always be conflict in international affairs is joined to Anglo-Saxon moralism to produce the idea that the Western alliance is engaged in a crusade to spread economic and political freedom through the world. The triumph of parliamentary democracy over totalitarianism and free-market capitalism over socialism are seen to be two sides of the same coin. In Europe this tends to be associated with emphasis on the fundamental importance of the Atlantic Alliance as the guarantor of a particular value system and vehicle for its further dissemination.[7]

These three strands (nationalist, statist and Atlanticist) intertwine in many policy positions to produce overlapping but at times also contradictory prescriptions.

2 THE TRANSFORMATIONIST POLE

The transformationist approach also combines disparate but complementary elements. Here the main actors on the international stage are still seen by some to be states, but others emphasise peoples, classes, identity groups or world society as a whole. Attention tends to shift from interests to needs, and from power politics to conflict resolution. In general there is less concern with managing power and more with transforming society. Once again different strands can be discerned.[8]

First there is the broad liberal tradition, drawing on the natural law idea of a world community and the rationalist idea that competing national interests can be reconciled through reason. Influential between the wars when realist ideas were discredited after the horror of the First World War, this approach was itself discredited by being associated with a failure to prevent the Second World War. Now it is once again powerfully reinforced through a growing appreciation of mutual vulnerability and interdependence in the international arena. The emphasis is on transforming relations between countries through international cooperation, international institutions and international law.[9]

Then there is the international socialist tradition, at times more combative, which emphasises the reproduction of economic structures as the dynamic of history, and in particular the relationship between exploiter and exploited. From this perspective, for example, the Atlanticist variant of realism is seen, not as a moral crusade for freedom, but as a vehicle for the preservation of economic power. The ambition, therefore, is to transform economic relations worldwide in the direction of a new international economic order so that gross disparities between rich and poor can be eventually overcome. Unregulated 'free market capitalism' is seen to be, not only inadequate to cope with mounting global problems, but itself the cause of many of them.[10]

Finally there is the radical approach which shares the ambition of transforming the nature of world society with the other two approaches, but is impatient with the formal structures of power still acknowledged in the liberal tradition and the economic determinism still found in some versions of international socialism. Perhaps the central inspiration here is the idea of the civil society, defined as the whole set of interrelated autonomous groups that people naturally identify with at local as well as national, regional and global levels. The emphasis is on respect for individual and group preferences, cultural variety and international solidarity. As in the revolutions in Central and Eastern Europe in autumn 1989, social change should come spontaneously from below rather than being imposed by élite groups from above.[11]

These variants of the transformationist approach (liberal, socialist, radical) overlap and at times contradict each other, just as the variants of the realist approach do. It must also be acknowledged that elements associated in the main with one of the two poles can in some lights be seen to share qualities with the other. Atlanticism, for example, in its triumphalist crusading guise can be more 'transformationist' than the more cautious manifestations of the liberal and socialist traditions. Conversely, liberal and socialist thinking, when addressing power-problems like political disputes, confrontational military strategies or massive concentrations of capital, can often appear more 'realist' than, say, the more emotional response of romantic nationalists. Nevertheless, enough has been said to convey the essence of the idea that there are now two main poles around which the new European security debate revolves.

3 THE NATURE OF THE DEBATE

It remains to point out some further general features of the debate as a whole before coming on to offer particular examples of it by comparing what is being said in Germany and Britain.

It has become fashionable to contrast various 'national' approaches to the new security agenda in Europe, and to analyse the debate accordingly. France, for example, is said to embody the pure statist position, having first adopted the Gaullist idea of a 'Europe des patries', then during the 1980s unemotionally concluded that French national interests now demanded that this be adapted in the direction of creating a powerful confederated European state. Britain, on the other hand, is said to embody the Atlanticist tradition, clinging to the idea of inherited sovereignty and identifying a world mission in partnership with the United States. The Soviet Union is seen to embody the socialist approach, reflected in the idea of a Common European Home. Whereas Germany, more complexly, has been seen to respond to its unique position by accommodating both the French and the Soviet positions, but perhaps coming to be particularly identified with the broad liberal approach as exemplified in its espousal of the reconciliatory CSCE ideal.[12]

There may be truth in such generalisations. But in this book the focus of attention is not the nation, but party political opinion within the nation. The idea is that, as Cold War antagonisms fade, security interests as a whole in Europe are converging (even though, as the disarray during the Gulf crisis showed, there are still pronounced local divergencies). A single European political space is opening up as pluralist politics begin to multiply in what was the former Eastern bloc. It remains to be seen whether countries like Yugoslavia, Romania and Albania will be drawn into it, or even the Western republics of the Soviet Union. In this context, more developed in the West than the East at the moment, political parties in different European countries often share more with each other than they do with other parties in their own country. For example, the British Labour Party shares much the same platform in the security field as the German SPD and is in this sense closer to the 'German' than the 'British' position. As later chapters show, the same applies to the various strands of opinion *within* the political parties in the two countries. Similar patterns are found in other West European (and increasingly East European) countries. All of this is manifested in embryonic institutional form in the international political groupings within the European parliament. In addition there is the wider international academic debate, the trans-national cooperation among non-governmental organisations and the multiplying television and radio communications which are slowly helping to develop a European consciousness. In short, the 'dialogue' between realist and

transformationist approaches, which now lies at the heart of the
European security debate, is not so much a dialogue between nations
as a dialogue between the two poles of an emerging pan-European
political continuum.[13]

This is not to suggest that the wider public debate directly affects
decision making. Decision making is confined to small élites in most
countries (and even more so in international organisations like NATO
or the EC). Particularly in the security field national parliaments tend
to be weak, and international parliaments dramatically so. Accountability is on the whole easily managed through control of information,
and policy formulation is decided in private and justified in public
afterwards. If anything, as the significance of multinational bodies
increases this becomes more accentuated. The long-standing Atlanticist élite associated with NATO is now matched by the growing
importance of the Western European élite associated with the
European Community, and both are notoriously impervious to outside control. Elected ministers (or ministers appointed by elected heads
of state), who are part of the élite, are themselves often effectively
sidelined as policy 'choices' are drastically narrowed in advance by
unelected permanent officials. It is hard to generalise about the quality
and range of debate that goes on within decision-making bodies
(although the claim always is that it is thorough and vigorous), or to
assess how it affects and is affected by the wider public debate of which
it is formally part. The public debate is often led (or manipulated) by
those in positions of power, and decision-making élites tend to be
scornful of outside opinion if it strays beyond well-recognised para-
meters. The converse process whereby broad shifts of public opinion
(however defined) filter through various policy-forming structures to
appear in the programmes of political parties and pressure groups is
obscure, as is the further process whereby official policy itself changes.
Party political decision making is often as élitist as national and
international decision making.

Despite all this, the contention here is that the dialogue between the
realist and transformationist poles of the new European security
debate is of fundamental significance, however it manifests itself,
whether within or outside official or semi-official decision making
bodies. The chapters which follow trace the evolution of the debate in
Germany and Britain, suggesting that, despite wide differences in
geographical position, historical experience and political culture, its
contours are now similar in the two countries.

NOTES

1. Speech in Guildhall, London, *Arms Control and Disarmament Quarterly Review*, Foreign and Commonwealth Office, no. 16, January 1990.
2. Speech in the Finlandia Palace, Helsinki, *Soviet News*, 2 November 1989. The sentiments expressed here are a condensed version of the celebrated United Nations speech of 7 December 1988, seen by many as an epoch-making moment in great power relations and international affairs.
3. These concepts and terms are confusing – particularly the term 'realism'. The realist paradigm deals with inter-state relations, in contrast to the structuralist preoccupation with economic relations and the pluralist concern with a multiplicity of interdependent social relations. But the quarrel between realism and idealism in international studies is a dispute within the realist paradigm. Here realism means a particular interpretation of the nature of interstate relations. This must be distinguished again from the long and varied tradition of philosophical realism which asserts the independent 'reality' of whatever the entities are that are being called in question. Finally, there is the everyday sense in which realism means facing up to the way things are rather than the way we wish they were. In this latter sense each of these paradigms, philosophies and approaches claims to be realist.
4. There is no claim here that the three strands are mutually exclusive or exhaustive. It is nevertheless useful to distinguish them.
5. The term 'nation state' is not strictly applicable when nations are not states (like the German nation in the middle ages, or the Jewish nation in the centuries when the state of Israel did not exist, or England, Scotland and Wales today), and states are not nations (like dynastic empires in the past, and the Soviet Union and in some eyes Britain today). The nationalist strand is not reflected in much explicit theoretical writing, nor is there any satisfactory definition of what a nation is, but the cultural instinct to identify with a nation is perhaps all the more powerful for that.
6. There is the classic realism of Thucydides, Machiavelli, Hobbes, Clausewitz, and the twentieth-century extension of it by writers like E. H. Carr, *The Twenty Years Crisis 1919–1939*, Macmillan, 1940 and H.J. Morgenthau, *Politics Among Nations: The Struggle For Power And Peace*, Knopf, 1985, and by 'neo-realists' like K. N. Waltz, *Theory Of International Politics*, Addison-Wesley, 1979. Of the politico-historical interpretations of the Cold War period it is post-revisionism which is the most strictly statist, reading the conflict as a classical struggle of interest and power. The 1990–1 Gulf crisis is interpreted in a similar way.
7. The Atlanticist strand has been grafted onto the broad realist tradition, and is powerful within the élites, particularly in Washington and London, but also in other NATO countries. The Atlanticist interpretation of the Cold War as a defence of freedom against the expansionist threat of totalitarianism is the orthodox view. There is a comparable response to the 1990–1 crisis in the Gulf: it is seen as a struggle of principle against a dangerous tyrant.

8. Once again there is no claim that this is the only taxonomy. Once again, though, it has proved useful to adopt this analysis.
9. The liberal strand draws on stoic ideas of universal law, developed by Grotius in the seventeenth century, and the rationalist tradition of Erasmus and Kant. Kant, in particular, has stimulated recent interest, both by his 'federalism' (the idea of a federation of republican states leagued together for the sole purpose of abolishing war) and his 'universalism' (the rather different idea of a global world government). This extract from his *The Idea For A Universal History With A Cosmopolitan Purpose*, Hans Reiss (ed.) *Kant's Political Writings*, Cambridge, 1970, seems perfectly attuned to the mood of the 1990s:

    > 'Although this political body exists for the present only in the roughest of outlines, it nevertheless seems as if a feeling is beginning to stir in all its members, each of which has an interest in maintaining the whole. And this encourages the hope that, after many revolutions, with all their transforming effects, the highest purpose of nature, a universal cosmopolitan existence, will at last be realised as the matrix within which all the original capacities of the human race may develop.'

    This tradition has been developed in a number of ways, many mentioned earlier in this book. Note also the application of game theory, as in R. Axelrod, *The Evolution Of Cooperation*, Basic Books,, 1984, and the explosion of interest in conflict resolution, for example J. W. Burton (ed.) *Conflict: Human Needs Theory*, Macmillan, 1990. See also R. A. Falk, *A Study Of Future Worlds*, Free Press, New York, and Collier-Macmillan, London, 1975.
10. The socialist strand, closely associated with structuralism, is widely reflected in political literature. At theoretical level it has been developed most thoroughly within the neo-Marxist tradition of Gramsci and Althusser, but also in general interpretations such as I. Wallerstein, *The Capitalist World Economy*, Cambridge University Press, 1979. The revisionist interpretation of the Cold War as a struggle to contain the spreading tentacles of capitalism is in this tradition. In the 1990–1 Gulf crisis it is identified with the view that the conflict was mainly about energy: the Western motive was to maintain political puppets in control of the oilfields.
11. Here we find a multiplicity of approaches which should properly be separated. For example there is the Buddhist universalist tradition, the Hindu tradition of non-violence associated with Gandhi, the Christian pacifist tradition such as that of the Quakers. Then there are all the grassroots movements represented in the Helsinki Citizens' Assembly for Peace and Democracy in Europe established in Prague on 19 October 1990:

    > 'The Assembly is composed of individual citizens and representatives of social and political movements, civic institutions, non-governmental organisations, clubs, circles, citizens' initiatives, groups and associations from all over Europe as well as North America and the Asian part of the Soviet Union . . . The biggest challenge that Europe will

face in the coming years is the integration of Europe. We will have to overcome all kinds of social problems that can cause divisions in Europe. These problems include poverty and unemployment; environmental degradation; social, national, ethnic, linguistic and religious conflicts; cultural deprivation; the situation of women; racism and xenophobia; consumerism and so on. They can only be solved by governments and citizens working together . . . Our aim is to integrate Europe from below, to construct a pan-European democratic civil society' (Jaroslav Sbata and Mient Jan Faber, co-chairmen, open letter to the Heads of State and Governments at the CSCE summit in Paris, 19–21 November 1990).

In *The Imaginary War: Understanding the East–West Conflict*, Blackwell, 1990, Mary Kaldor identifies this approach with a radical interpretation of the Cold War conflict as a collusion between Stalinism and Atlanticism to manage internal conflicts within their own systems, and contrasts this with the orthodox, revisionist and post-revisionist interpretations. In the 1990–1 Gulf crisis the radical response was reflected in the citizen's action peace camps.

12. See, for example, Ole Waeve, 'Three Competing Europes: German, French, Russian', *International Affairs*, vol. 66, no. 3, 1990.
13. This continuum can now be said to extend to the Soviet Union, where hard-line 'realist' views are in violent tension with the 'transformationist' foreign policy views so dramatically developed from January 1986 by Mikhail Gorbachev and Eduard Shevardnadze.

Part II
The German Debate

4 German Politics and the Question of Security 1949–1989

The tremendous events of 1990 – the East German elections on 18 March, the German-Soviet accord of 12 September, unification itself on 3 October, the first federal elections for a united Germany since 1933 on 2 December – drew a line under forty-five years of German history. No longer singularised at the centre of a divided Europe or directly threatened as the prospective battleground between the great blocs, a fully sovereign Germany could now look forward to a far greater freedom of action in future than in the immediate past. The prospect of Soviet withdrawal and relative American decline left Germany as the pivotal power in Europe, geographically placed between West and East and with ample scope to translate growing economic strength into political influence. The shackles had been removed. What would the nature of the new Germany be (see Figure 4.1)?

This question was asked with growing urgency both inside and outside Germany as it became plain that nothing could prevent the landslide towards unification. Fears and memories were revived. Fears for the future and memories of the past. Would a united Germany keep to the path followed thus far by the Western Federal Republic (FRG)? Or would it revert to the Germany of the past? The trouble with the second question was that there were several pasts.

1 THE SHADOW OF THE PAST

The boundaries of the post-war Federal Republic had in fact been closest to those of Lewis the German's original ninth-century kingdom

Germany 1937

Germany 1949

Germany today

Source: The Economist, 30 June 1990.

FIGURE 4.1   *German borders 1937–90*

– the old duchies of Saxony, Franconia, Thuringia, Swabia and Bavaria. But German colonisation during the centuries that followed spread German influence hundreds of kilometres to the East through predominantly Slav lands. Although battles were fought and states were carved out (for example, the lands of the Teutonic Knights in East Prussia), this 'Drang nach Osten' (push to the East) was on the whole peaceful. German became the lingua franca of commerce and learning throughout the region, the language of Hanseatic merchants and Reformation scholars. The First Reich (which lasted from 961 to 1806 when it was abolished by Napoleon) became little more than a geographical expression. It hardly seems that this could be the model for a united Germany in the 1990s.[1]

In the nineteenth century the urge to create a unitary German state in emulation of Britain and France intensified. In 1848, the 'year of revolutions', it looked briefly as if this might be achieved by the cluster of smaller states in the old lands mainly to the West of the river Elbe. But the failure of this impulse eventually left the field clear for Prussia. The core of Prussia lay in the territories to the East of the Elbe (Ostelbia) which had been ex-colonial border fiefdoms in the middle ages. Less populous and less socially varied than the older lands to the West, they were dominated by great landed estates owned by a 'Junker' aristocracy. It was this aristocracy, in alliance with the ruling Hohenzollern dynasty, which, from the seventeenth century, had built the militarised and authoritarian traditions of the Prussian state. The Prussian king became emperor (Kaiser) of the new Germany in 1871, and, despite the efforts of chancellor Bismarck up to the time of his dismissal in 1890, his creation eventually proved unstable as Kaiser Wilhelm II challenged Britain and France for European hegemony. The Second Reich foundered in the débâcle of the First World War. This seems no more likely to serve as a model for a new post-bloc Germany whose centre of gravity lies in the West and whose self-interest dictates close cooperation with Common Market partners.[2]

Finally there is the searing experience of Hitler's Third Reich, built on the ruins of the 1919 Weimar Republic. Could this be the model? Again it seems impossible. In 1933 the Third Reich was created in the middle of a prolonged economic depression which virtually wiped out middle-class savings. Parties of the extreme left and right flourished and a breakdown of public order was threatened. There was widespread resentment at the way other European countries had treated Germany and seized her territories after the First World War. In the 1990s, on the other hand, unification has been driven by the astonishing economic success of West Germany. Political extremism on the left and on the right seem if anything less significant than they were a few years ago. Despite traces of resentment in some quarters about former German lands across the Oder, there is no sense that Germany has been done down in the post Second World War settlement. On the contrary, there is near unanimity that it is only through acceptance of existing boundaries and integration into the wider European community that stability and prosperity has come. Plans for economic expansion (which are, of course, in themselves alarming to some) depend upon avoiding the political upheavals of the past.

None of these pre-1945 models seem relevant to the German situation today. The main reason for this lies in what has happened since then – the experience of West Germany in the forty years of its existence.

2   THE FOUNDING OF THE FEDERAL REPUBLIC

The Federal Republic of Germany was born in catastrophe and ruin. In the spring of 1945 the great Eastern and Western pincer movement which crushed the Third Reich met along what became the inner German border. For the people living in the zones occupied by the three Western powers this was the 'Stunde Null' (zero hour). Unlike 1918 they were allowed no say in their own future. Denazification, decentralisation and demilitarisation were imposed by the Allied Control Commission. But, within a remarkably short space of time, in May 1949, the new Federal Republic was established as a semi-independent democratic state. Under its first Chancellor, Konrad Adenauer, it dedicated itself to federalism, democracy, rapprochement with France, integration into the Western alliance and economic rehabilitation.

West German democracy was founded on the Grundgesetz (the Basic Law), agreed by the 65 representatives of the 10 (with West Berlin 11) Länder (regional states) of the Western zones of occupation, who met in the former natural history museum in Bonn in 1948. Two features of the Basic Law are worth emphasising.

One feature is federalism. Considerable powers were retained by the Länder so that a centralised totalitarian state could never again be created. The Länder help shape national policy through the Bundesrat, the second chamber of the federal parliament in Bonn, which plays a critical role in determining constitutional questions and enjoys considerable delaying powers. They were also given membership on the central council of the Bundesbank, itself formally independent of central government control. A Land government retains a number of reserve powers and can develop programmes which are significantly at variance with national government policy and in defiance of official party platforms. This has led to marked regional differences.

The second feature is proportional representation, guaranteed through the 'additional member' voting system. Half the seats in the Bundestag are filled as in Britain by constituency MPs elected on a 'first-past-the-post' system. But electors also have a second vote. This is cast, not for candidates, but for parties. The basic law stipulates that the proportion of second votes won by each party must be mirrored by the proportion of MPs that each party has. So the remaining half of the seats in the Bundestag are apportioned to make sure that this is so. These seats are filled by MPs chosen from party lists at Länder level in order to balance the various groups and interests within the party in proportion to numerical strength. To qualify for representation in parliament a party must win either three constituency seats or 5 per cent of the second vote. Below this there is no representation, in order to exclude a multiplicity of splinter parties (as a result the eleven parliamentary parties of 1949 were by 1989 reduced to four).[3]

3 THE CHRISTIAN DEMOCRATS AND THE WESTPOLITIK 1949-66

The new West German state was committed from the beginning to European integration to an extent that few in Britain can appreciate. In its founding call to action on 26 June 1945, Konrad Adenauer's party, the Christian Democratic Union (CDU), dedicated itself to 'a new democratic order founded on the ethical and spiritual powers of Christianity'. Its commitment was to political and economic integration in Western Europe as the only reliable antidote to the unbridled nationalism which had been tearing the continent apart since the time of the French Revolution. In this it met a sympathetic response from Italian Christian Democrats led by Alcide de Gaspari and French Popular Republicans (MRP) led by Robert Schuman. In Britain, on the contrary, with inexcusable short-sightedness, neither Attlee's Labour administration from 1945 to 1951, nor the Conservative governments that followed, showed any sympathy for the idea at all.

Adenauer's Westpolitik was based on a revolutionary Frankreich-politik – a determination to put Franco–German relations on an entirely new footing. The way a century of bitter enmity was overcome so soon after the end of the war teaches a fundamental lesson about how similar enmities between East and West can be overcome today. The quid pro quo mentality which had ruined similar attempts in the 1920s (particularly during the Locarno years from 1925 to 1929) was transcended. The idea of economic integration was the key to the new policy, accompanied by cultural interchanges of all kinds. On the French side, in marked contrast to the ferocity of France's anti-German policy after 1919, the remarkable vision of Jean Monnet, the architect of French post-war economic planning, more than reciprocated. Monnet's proposal of 16 April 1950 for a European Coal and Steel Community was the germ from which the mighty structure of the European Community has grown. Fired by the idea that 'a totally new situation must be created: the Franco–German problem must become a European problem', he suggested that France would place her own coal and steel industries under the control of an international authority if West Germany would do the same. Coal and steel were 'the key to economic power and the raw materials for forging weapons of war', so 'to pool them across frontiers would reduce their malign presence and turn them instead into a guarantee of peace'.[4]

Adenauer's response was immediate. He was 75 years old. For years he had schooled himself in the grim discipline of hard negotiation and wounded pride. He could hardly believe that France was all at once offering cooperation and full equality. During the one and a half hour interview in which Jean Monnet outlined what was now called the 'Schuman plan', he reacted with astonishment and growing emotion. Setting aside his original reserve, he described the plan as 'a matter of morality' and said

'I have waited twenty-five years for a move like this. In accepting it, my government and my country have no secret hankerings after hegemony. History since 1933 has taught us the folly of such ideas. Germany knows that its fate is bound up with that of Western Europe as a whole.'[5]

In this way the principle that international security could only be assured by a readiness to cede a measure of national sovereignty became the cornerstone both of federal policy and of the new Europe that West Germany was helping to build.

Despite stubborn opposition from the parties of the left, including passionate controversy about West German rearmament after 1950, the Westpolitik came to be accepted as the framework for German recovery. By the mid-1950s the 'German economic miracle' was generating a growth rate of 15 per cent a year. In 1955 West Germany was admitted as a full member of NATO. In 1957 the Common Market was established and in 1963 the Franco-German (Elysée) Treaty of Friendship and Cooperation was signed. In the 1957 federal elections Adenauer's CDU, together with its sister-party the Bavarian Christian Social Union (CSU), won more than 50 per cent of the votes, the only time a West German party achieved such a feat.

4   THE SOCIAL DEMOCRATS AND THE OSTPOLITIK 1969–82

The Social Democratic Party (SPD), meanwhile, had remained stuck at around 30 per cent of the vote in the 1949, 1953 and 1957 Bundestag elections. Its leader until 1952, Kurt Schumacher, waged a grim and hopeless rearguard action against Adenauer's policies of free market expansion and Western integration, branding him the 'allied chancellor'. But by the late 1950s it became plain that such old-fashioned class-based and nationalistic socialism was a recipe for eternal opposition. So in 1959–60 the party remodelled itself as an up-to-date social-democratic party by adopting the Godesberg Programme. Both the free market and the Westpolitik, including military conscription and membership of NATO, were accepted. The transformation was successful. In 1966 the SPD joined a Grand Coalition government with the CDU/CSU and the small Free Democratic Party (FDP). In 1969, when the Grand Coalition collapsed, the SPD emerged as the dominant partner in a coalition with the FDP and Willy Brandt became chancellor.

Willy Brandt was mayor of West Berlin, when, on 13 August 1961, the East German authorities had begun to build the Berlin Wall. 'The barbed wire will not last for ever', he had proclaimed on that day, and dedicated himself to the task of overcoming it. The policy for achieving this was an 'Ostpolitik' of détente with the Soviet Union and her East European allies combined with a 'Deutschlandpolitik' of fostering all possible links and connections with East Germany. The programme was proposed in 1963 and developed, formulated and explained to the party and to society at large during the following seven years. It was then put into practice, first by Willy Brandt and his Free Democrat (FDP) foreign minister Walter Scheel, then from 1974 by his successor Helmut Schmidt in partnership with another Free Democrat, Hans-Dietrich Genscher.

The Ostpolitik was a bold policy. It meant rapprochement with Russia just after the 1968 invasion of Czechoslovakia, and above all renunciation of all claims to pre-Second World War German territory East of the Oder-Neisse line. Both components were unpopular with the right wing of the CDU and particularly the CDU's Bavarian sister party the Christian Social Union (CSU). But the achievements of the Ostpolitik came to silence its critics. For Willy Brandt, if France was the former enemy which had to be embraced in the West, in the East it was Poland:

'Reconciliation with Poland had the same historical significance as Franco-German rapprochement. It was a moral and political duty because no land had suffered more from Hitler's war and the extermination policies of his state, party and military machine.'[6]

Bilateral treaties with the Soviet Union and Poland (1970–1), East Germany (1972) and Czechoslovakia (1973) set the scene for the broader Conference on Security and Cooperation in Europe (CSCE) process initiated in 1972. In the CSCE Final Act signed in Helsinki on 1 August 1975 by every state on the continent (except Albania) together with the United States and Canada, existing frontiers were guaranteed against violation by armed force. It was the German language version of the Helsinki Final Act, prepared jointly by East and West Germany, Austria, Switzerland and Liechtenstein, that was generally considered to be the most authoritative.

As for the Deutschlandpolitik, in addition to government–government accommodation, the idea was to break down the division between the two Germanies by a multiplying network of links and exchanges of all kinds – political, economic, cultural. The result would be a complex tissue of interconnections, a 'capillarisation', that would undermine the military–political frontier. This was to be 'Wandel durch Annäherung' (change through communication) in the phrase coined by Egon Bahr, Willy Brandt's deputy mayor in West Berlin. How crucial this process has been in bringing about the eventual reunification of Germany remains controversial. But, however achieved, by the late 1980s the 17 million East Germans, hermetically sealed off by force behind the Iron Curtain for more than three decades, were already culturally integrated into the West.

TABLE 4.1　*Bundestag elections 1949–87*[7]

	1949	1953	1957	1961	1965	1969	1972	1976	1980	1983	1987
Distribution of seats (excluding Berlin)											
CDU	115	191	215	192	196	193	117	190	185	191	174
CSU	24	52	55	50	49	49	48	53	52	53	49
SPD	131	151	169	190	202	224	230	214	228	193	186
FDP	52	48	41	67	49	30	41	39	54	34	46
Grünen	–	–	–	–	–	–	–	–	–	27	42
Others	80	45	17	–	–	–	–	–	–	–	–
Percentage of second vote											
CDU/CSU	31.0	45.2	50.2	45.3	47.6	46.1	44.9	48.6	44.5	48.8	44.3
SPD	29.2	28.8	31.8	36.2	39.3	42.7	45.8	42.6	42.9	38.2	37.0
FDP	11.9	9.5	7.7	12.8	9.5	5.8	8.4	7.9	10.6	7.0	9.1
Grünen	–	–	–	–	–	–	–	–	1.5	5.6	8.3
Others	27.9	16.5	10.3	5.7	3.6	5.4	0.9	0.9	0.5	0.4	1.3

5　THE EMERGENCE OF A NEW AGENDA 1982–90

In 1982, largely for domestic reasons, the SDP/FDP government of Helmut Schmidt fell as the FDP switched to coalition with the CDU/CSU. From a peak of 45.8 per cent of the national vote in the 1972 election the SPD slumped to 38.2 in 1983 against a background of budget deficits and unemployment, and a growing challenge from the new Green party (Die Grünen) (see Table 4.1). The transition from being a class party to being a 'Volkspartei', symbolised in the figure of Willy Brandt, had widened the appeal of the party but weakened its traditional hold on the big cities. After more than fifteen years in government its leadership had come to be associated with traditional industrial and defence policies now rejected by a growing number of radicals.

By the late 1970s both the CDU's Westpolitik and the SPD's Ostpolitik had been assimilated into a broad national consensus in the Bundestag. The party-political controversies of the 1950s over rearmament and membership of NATO, and of the late 1960s and 1970s over détente and the Ostpolitik, had largely died away. For example, whichever parties were in power, the difficult business of reassuring France that rapprochement with the East did not mean a drift to neutrality, and the Soviet Union that NATO's 1979 dual track

policy (stronger defence and continued negotiation) did not mean the
end of détente, had become a common task.

Yet beneath the surface deep shifts of attitude were taking place.
Growing economic strength and the rise to prominence of younger
post-war generations began to change the conditioning climate at
home. The intensification in the Cold War during the early part of the
decade, and the abrupt thaw during the latter part changed the climate
abroad. Triggered by the 1977 controversy over the 'neutron bomb'
and the 1979 decision to deploy American intermediate range Pershing
II and ground-launched cruise missiles in West Germany, the nuclear
weapon question, largely dormant since the 1950s, became a catalyst
for the reappraisal of the status of Germany, East and West, in
relation to the Soviet Union on the one hand, and trans-Atlantic
and European allies in NATO on the other. The feeling against
German 'singularisation' grew. Behind the reaction to the INF Treaty
lay resentment at high-handed American action and British pressure.
Behind mounting resistance to the deployment of new short-range
nuclear forces lay a new sense of German national interest and
readiness to assert it. Behind hostility to NATO military exercises
lay the belief that it was now time for the special role of the Second
World War victors in Germany to end. All of this found expression in
the rapturous welcome for the Soviet President on his visit to West
Germany in June 1989.[8]

In general, as in Britain, a resurgence of conservatism coincided with
a radicalisation of left-wing politics – although in the case of West
Germany the effect on security policy was different. The polarisation
during the first half of the decade between the Atlanticist tradition
accepted up to that point by the leaders of both the main parties and
the rising tide of the peace movement gave way by the end of the
decade to a new broad consensus. The protest movement was largely
absorbed into the fabric of federal politics, and government policy was
at the same time substantially modified. Tidal movements of public
opinion, charted in opinion polls and manifested in local, Land and
federal elections, accompanied a decisive shift of emphasis at national
level away from Atlanticist orthodoxy and towards the opening up of a
new agenda committed to the prospect of fundamental change. The
advent of Mikhail Gorbachev in March 1985 provided both the
occasion and the opportunity for the transformation. The revisionism
inherent in West German foreign policy conditioned the response. But
a vital further contributory factor was the flexibility of the West
German political system.

It is worth looking at each of, the four main parties in turn and noting how characteristic features of the German political system contributed to the way alternative security policies developed.

(a) The Greens (Die Grünen)

Alarm at the intensification in the Cold War, frustration at what was felt to be the stifling establishment consensus between both main parties, and the advent of a younger generation impatient with the consumerist and Atlanticist assumptions of the post-war era led to the creation of the Green alliance in 1979. It was made up of a kaleidoscope of extra-parliamentary environmentalist, socialist and special interest group movements rallying around the 'four pillars' defined at the party conference in Offenbach in October 1979 as 'ecology, social responsibility, grassroots democracy and non-violence'. Unlike new British parties, once the West German Green Party crossed the 5 per cent electoral barrier it secured a proportionate representation at local and national level. For example in 1987 it won no 'first-past-the-post' constituency seats but its 8.6 per cent share of the second vote earned it 44 MPs in the Bundestag, more than half of whom were women. At regional level the federal system meant that in Hesse a 'Red–Green' coalition with the SPD could run the Land government in defiance of central SPD policy. This strengthened the 'realist' wing of the Greens which accepted that nationally it was more realistic to aim for a radicalisation of SPD policy through Green partnership in a coalition government than insistence on an undiluted alternative agenda. In Hamburg and West Berlin, on the other hand, the more radical 'eco-socialists' predominated. These strands were carried through to national level as Green representation in the Bundestag was made up from regional party slates.[9]

Also crucial to the success of the Greens in building themselves up into a national party was the party funding system. Since 1967 each party polling more than 0.5 per cent of the national vote had been entitled to a state subsidy which by 1984 was nearly £2 for every vote cast (averaged up as if every eligible voter in fact voted). This could be used for research as well as political campaigning. In addition, another £200 million, proportional to votes, was given to party organisations, and further federal and regional state sums provided to support party research and educational foundations of all kinds. When they were founded as a national party for the European elections in 1979, for example, the Greens qualified straight away for a £1.5 million initial grant.[10] Finally, each MP was paid a salary of some £3000 a month and a further £2000 a month expense allowance together with another £3000 for personal assistants, researchers and office staff (1988 figures). Since Green MPs only accepted a salary of £1000 a month (the average wage of a skilled worker) and £700 a month for allowances (plus £200 a month for every dependent relative), the rest went to the party's 'ecology fund'. Somewhat to the embarrassment of some of the Greens themselves the lavish resources of the party's 'Ökofund' came to support a network of dependent groups and projects.[11]

(b) The Social Democrats (SPD)

In parallel with what was happening in the British Labour Party, the 'Wende' (turn) away from the moderate tradition of the 1970s in security policy in the SPD was clearly in evidence by the 1983 Cologne party conference. But the development of SPD policy was more complex than Labour's lurch to unilateralism. Challenged by Greens to the left, rather than SDP-Liberals to the right as in Britain, most of the SPD moderates stayed in the party. Above all the federal constitution, the nature of coalition government and the committee system in the Bundestag meant that opposition parties were not completely excluded from power, regionally or nationally, while party affiliated research institutes and advisers directed a constant stream of information, comment and suggested policy alternatives to party policy makers. It will be useful to take these features one at a time.[12]

At Land level, for example, SPD majorities could pioneer what amounted to an alternative agenda for the party. This happened in the Saarland, one of the smallest of the Länder, where Oskar Lafontaine used his independent power base to advocate radical security ideas, including a questioning of continued German membership of NATO. In defiance of central party policy he outflanked the local Greens by offering an electoral pact, and then incorporated much of their programme into his own 'work, peace and environment' campaign. The result was to reduce the Green vote in the Saarland to 2.5 per cent and increase the SPD to 49.2 per cent in the 1985 Land election. In this way he also outflanked the more moderate national party leadership and became SPD candidate for Chancellor in the December 1990 federal elections. During the 1980s various Länder developed their own links in Eastern Europe, and the SPD as a whole continued to

conduct what the CDU disparagingly called its own 'Nebenaussen-
politik' in this area.[13]

At federal level many SPD MPs preferred to influence national
decision-making through work on parliamentary committees, inter-
governmental consultative bodies, the Bundestag/Bundesrat mediating
committee, and so on, than devote their energies to permanent
adversarial criticism. It is true that the Bundestag was often formally
ignored, as in the run-up to German unification, when Chancellor
Kohl's ten-point plan of November 1989 was almost the only major
change announced there. This tendency for decisions to be made 'in
back rooms' and then rubber-stamped in public is deplored by
campaigners like Hildegard Hamm-Brücher (FDP). But the significant work in the Bundestag never has been set-piece plenary debates.
It is in committee that the intra- and inter-party bargaining goes on.
Between 1949 and 1980 there were 1810 plenary floor debates in the
Bundestag and 22000 committee meetings. Some twenty permanent
departmental committees parallel government departments, themselves
shadowed by party committees. In addition there are ad hoc
committees, investigative committees and enquiry committees. Sixty
per cent of government bills are modified at committee stage, which
largely explains the marked absence of friction when they finally
appear in the full chamber. It is hard to draw up a final balance on
the question of how important inter-party bargaining is, and how
much scope there is for the Chancellor to ride roughshod over
opposition within and outside his party. But during the 1980s one
important factor was that the policy of FDP foreign minister Genscher
was in general closer to the SPD than to his own coalition partners in
the CDU/CSU. When foreign minister and chancellor disagreed,
therefore, prominent SPD spokespersons would be tipped the wink
and would be found making speeches endorsing the foreign ministry
line. An informal SPD/FDP understanding in foreign affairs commanded a shadowy majority in the Bundestag. The chancellor as often
as not gave way.[14]

Of equal significance was the fact that one or two officials from each
of the various government ministries were seconded to the relevant
offices of the different parliamentary parties as policy advisers. In the
security field this meant that the SPD, even though in opposition,
would have, say, two senior personnel from the foreign office and two
from the ministry of defence, paid out of state funds, permanently
advising party spokespersons and policy-makers. Although in this
capacity ex-ministry advisers no longer had access to state papers, they

were able to communicate with former colleagues who did. They were free to return to the ministries when they wanted.[15]

As for alternative policy formulation, the 1980s was a period of intense activity within the research institutes associated with the SPD. The patronage lavished by the Friedrich Ebert Stiftung based in Bonn is the envy of British parties of opposition. Funded to the tune of some £50 million a year, the foundation employs 130 researchers in other countries in addition to those in Germany. This provides international outreach in the United States and Europe which ensures broad debate based on up-to-date information from Washington, London and Paris. A network of peace research institutes sprang up during the 1970s funded by public foundations and supportive Länder governments (subsequently on occasion decommissioned by unsupportive ones). University reform meant that a number of university professors sympathetic to the SPD could also contribute to the formulation of party policy. Part of the funding for the Hamburg Institute for Peace Research and Security Policy (IFSH) comes from the university there. In this way great tracts of analysis into non-offensive defence, common security, stage-by-stage denuclearisation, and so on, were developed and knit together into the evolving fabric of the party's traditional Ostpolitik.[16]

(c) The Free Democrats (FDP)

There was no equivalent in Britain to the role played by the West German Free Democrats during the 1980s. Since it was only in 1957 that any one party has won more than 50 per cent of the second vote, there has nearly always been a coalition government in West Germany. Many voters deliberately foster this by choosing a constituency MP from, say, the CDU with their first vote, but then voting for, say, the FDP with their second vote to ensure a coalition which will temper CDU policy in the desired direction. During the forty-year existence of West Germany the FDP oscillated between 30 and 67 Bundestag seats (out of 496 in the 1987 election), coming perilously close to elimination in 1983. Yet it has enjoyed a share in government for most of this period. For the past twenty years it has been continually in office, first in coalition with the SPD, then, since 1982, in coalition with the CDU/ CSU. Walter Scheel and Hans-Dietrich Genscher have maintained a remarkable FDP monopoly of the foreign affairs portfolio throughout this period. It is extraordinary that Hans-Dietrich Genscher has been foreign minister since 1974 as a member of SPD- and CDU/CSU-led governments. This embodied the national consensus on the basic issues and goals of both the Westpolitik and the Ostpolitik that had developed by the 1980s. Despite challenge from right and left, the consensus survived, providing an underlying stability to West German policy.[17]

Nevertheless, as already mentioned, within this broad framework of consensus, there was often tension between Genscher's foreign office and mainstream opinion within the CDU/CSU in security policy. The two wings of the FDP (inherited from the nineteenth-century Progressive and National Liberals) tended to shed and acquire support as the party shifted in coalition between the larger parties of left and right. But the tendency throughout was for the party to be closer to the CDU/CSU on economic and to the SPD on foreign policy and security matters. As one of the architects of the Ostpolitik, Genscher maintained the impetus of the original SPD/FDP initiative at the heart of government. In the early part of the decade in the nuclear weapon field this manifested itself in an emphasis within NATO on the multilateral 'arms control' track of the 1979 'dual track' policy rather than the unilateral 'modernisation' track. In the later part of the decade it developed into a strong advocacy of creative response to the initiatives of Mikhail Gorbachev.

A number of those on the political right in West Germany resented what they saw as the undue influence of a small party and regarded FDP MPs as careerists. In the same way the foreign policy flexibility of 'Genscherism' was castigated as weak opportunism by Margaret Thatcher and Ronald Reagan, and attacked as a sell-out to communism by the outspoken CSU leader Franz-Josef Strauss. But by the end of the decade, as the Gorbachev phenomenon gathered momentum, this approach began to acquire substance, and to represent, if anything, the centre ground in West German politics. The declared aim was 'not to win against the East, but with the East', to build a strong integrated European Union within a wider pan-European Peace Order from the Atlantic to the Urals, to de-militarise and de-ideologise East–West relations and to eliminate hostility from international relations.[18]

A large measure of Hans-Dietrich Genscher's success was due to the fact that he brought non-conventional thinkers into the foreign office and set up task forces to re-evaluate the world situation and come up with long-term perspectives or possible scenarios. In general, responding to the steady relative decline in US influence, he expanded the framework of West German foreign policy thinking from a West European to a pan-European (if not yet fully global) scale.[19]

(d) The Christian Democrats (CDU)/Christian Social Union (CSU)

Through much of the 1980s Helmut Kohl struggled to assert his authority, not only over his coalition, but also over his party. The inter-party bargaining characteristic of coalition government operated at every level: 'the informal practices of coalition management secure a permanent involvement of the leading members of the parliamentary majority parties in the decision-making process'. This included not only balancing the transformationist FDP thinking in the foreign office with Atlanticist (Manfred Wörner) and nationalist (Rupert Scholz) realism at the defence ministry, but also, particularly before the death of Franz Josef Strauss in 1987, assimilating similar pressure from the CSU from an opposite quarter. Much of the chancellor's apparent (and real) vacillation was the result of his having to bridge different positions in this way and address policy statements to different domestic audiences. This was compounded by the fact that in the federal tradition political power is derived from independent power-bases in the provinces, like the CSU stronghold in Bavaria. The same applied to his own party. Minister-presidents from the CDU enjoyed a semi-independent status and could build a local reputation to the point where they became a serious challenge to the leadership.[20]

In theory devolution went even further than that, as this semi-official description shows:

'Within each party's parliamentary grouping (Bundestagsfraktion) majority decisions have to be taken in those cases in which it is not possible to reduce the various views to a common denominator. Sometimes such debates among members of a parliamentary group are marked by greater controversy than the oratorical battles between government and opposition parties in the plenary sessions of the Bundestag. This can afford individual members a major opportunity. The more open the process of arriving at a common policy within the individual parliamentary group, the greater the chance through commitment and persuasion of bringing his or her influence to bear.'[21]

Certainly British visitors are surprised to find radical alternative policy papers, clearly at odds with official party policy, pressed upon them by West German politicians from all parties to an extent that is not practised in Britain, and it does seem to be the case that the highly differentiated organisation and working of parliamentary parties prevents complete domination of intra-party decision-making within the ruling coalition by the cabinet. But the question of the balance that is and should be struck between dispersion of power and 'Kanzlerdemokratie' remains an open and controversial one.[22]

NOTES

1. This brief paragraph of course elides most of the main themes of a thousand years of German history, including the failed Ottonian/ Hohenstaufen attempt at unification in the tenth to thirteenth centuries, and the Habsburg attempt in the fifteenth to seventeenth centuries.
2. The post-war political and economic division of Europe has been seen to correspond to the much older division described in this paragraph.
3. The 5 per cent clause was introduced and progressively tightened in 1949, 1953 and 1956. The second vote was introduced in 1953.
4. Jean Monnet, *Memoirs*, Doubleday, 1978, p. 293.
5. Monnet, op. cit., pp. 309–10.
6. Willy Brandt, *Begegnungen und Einsichten*, Hoffman u. Campe Verlag, 1976, p. 242, quoted in Edwina S Campbell, *Germany's Past & Europe's Future*, Pergamon-Brassey, 1989.
7. Compiled from West German statistical yearbooks, Eckhard Jesse, *Elections: The Federal Republic Of Germany In Comparison*, Berg, 1990.
8. There was considerable alarm at the deal nearly struck at Reykjavik between Ronald Reagan and Mikhail Gorbachev in 1986, and resentment at the pressure put on West Germany by the United States and Britain to include the German Pershing 1A missiles informally in the INF deal (the so-called 'second zero'). The issue of low flying aroused extraordinary anger.
9. A useful account can be found in Sara Parkin, *Green Parties, An International Guide*, Heretic Books, 1989, Ch. 7. See also Werner Hülsberg, *The German Greens*, Verso, 1988.
10. Hülsberg, *The German Greens*, pp. 121–2 (1984 figures).
11. Figures taken from Carl-Christian Kaiser, *The German Bundestag*, Bundestag Public Relations Division, 1988, pp. 57–8.
12. The SPD was founded in 1875 and is still in many ways encumbered by an archaic organisation. Some of the features indicated here which preserve variety were seen to have been shown up as weaknesses in the 1990 federal elections. For example the fact that the leader of the party need not be the candidate for chancellor can confuse the electorate if there is a difference in style. These weaknesses have been exposed as the solid class basis of the party has been weakened and the muddle in ex-GDR Länder has added to the disarray.

13. The term 'Nebeneussenpolitik' referred to the private negotiations conducted by the West German opposition parties with the official parties in Eastern Europe.

14. See N. Johnson, 'Committees In The West German Bundestag', in J. D. Lees and M. Shaw (eds) *Committees in Legislatures*, Martin Robertson, 1979.

15. Information communicated by Dr Gerd Wagner, seconded as adviser to Horst Ehmke, SPD foreign affairs spokesman, from the foreign office.

16. Similar foundations exist for the other parties represented in the Bundestag, such as the CDU's Konrad Adenauer Stiftung, as do networks of research institutes such as that at Ebenhausen for the CDU.

17. The importance of the second vote 'ticket-splitting' for the FDP is stressed in E. Kirchner and D. Broughton, 'The FDP in the Federal Republic of Germany', in E. Kirchner (ed.) *Liberal Parties in Western Europe*, Cambridge University Press, 1988. A poll in 1987 showed that 70 per cent of the electorate wanted the FDP to survive.

18. E. Kirchner, 'Genscher and What Lies Behind "Genscherism"', *West European Politics*, vol. 13, April 1990, no. 2, pp. 159–77.

19. Whether Germany should take on a world role, and exactly what that role should be, remains controversial. Without a strong ex-colonial tradition to match that of Britain and France, and conditioned by post-war anti-militarism, there is a reluctance to play the kind of role that still comes naturally to those two countries. The SPD and FDP insist that any enhanced German military contribution must be firmly under the aegis of the United Nations. There may be less inhibition to take on a more active economic role.

20. For example Lothar Späth in Baden-Wurttemberg. A long-standing CDU rival to Helmut Kohl, Kurt Biedenkopf, is impregnable as premier of Saxony in former East Germany. On coalition government see K. von Beyme, 'Coalition Government in Western Germany', in V. Bogdanov (ed.) *Coalition Government in Western Europe*, Heinemann, 1983.

21. Kaiser, *The German Bundestag*, p. 37. It is in fact not surprising if debate within parliamentary groups is livelier than in plenary sessions, since the latter are no more than staged set pieces.

22. Compare Thomas Saalfeld, 'The West German Bundestag After Forty Years: The Role of Parliament in a "Party Democracy"', *West European Politics*, vol. 13, July 1990, no. 3, and R. Mayntz, 'Executive Leadership in Germany: Dispersion of Power or "Kanzlerdemokratie"?', in R. Rose and E. Suleiman (eds) *Presidents and Prime Ministers*, American Institute for Public Policy Research, 1980.

5 The New German Security Debate

The federal elections in December 1990 underlined the fact that in the security field there was now a new agenda in German politics. From 1949 to 1989 the question of security had been conditioned by the underlying long-term project of overcoming the division of Germany. Now that this had been achieved, the whole context of security thinking changed. The national consensus which had emerged in the second half of the 1980s was a broad one, accommodating wide divergencies. Traditional 'realist' instincts were still powerful, but were now challenged by an increasingly articulate and convincing 'transformationist' programme. It was within this continuum that the new agenda was defined and argued out. The hope seemed to be that the new Germany could now play a key role in the further development of (West) European integration and East–West normalisation, and thereby begin to take on a world role under the aegis of the United Nations.

Since then the shock of the conservative backlash in the Soviet Union and the Gulf War have dispelled the euphoria. The foreign policy consensus still evident up to December 1990 may now be threatened as the political right blames foreign minister Genscher for failing to take a lead in supporting the anti-Iraq alliance, thus opening a rift between Germany and the former Second World War allies, Britain, France and the United States. He is accused of humiliating failure in the first crucial test of post-unification Germany's political maturity. It remains to be seen how serious and far-reaching this disagreement is and how it affects the complex balances of German domestic politics.

There have been attempts to discern a unitary 'German vision' for the new Europe in which settled borders and political integration clear the way for uninhibited economic expansion from a dominant position

BOX 5.1 ALL-GERMAN ELECTIONS, 1990

	Seats	Percentage overall	Percentage in West		Percentage in East	
CDU	268	36.7	35.3	(34.5)	43.5	(42.7)
CSU (DSU in East)	51	7.1	9.1	(9.8)	1.0	(6.6)
FDP	79	11.0	10.6	(9.1)	13.4	(5.6)
SPD	239	33.5	35.9	(37.0)	23.6	(20.8)
PDS/Linke Liste	17	2.4	0.3	–	9.9	(15.2)
Bündnis 90/Grünen(E)	8	1.2	–	–	5.9	–
Grünen (W)	–	3.9	4.7	(8.3)	–	–
Republikaner	–	2.1	2.3	–	1.3	–
Others (16 parties)	–	2.1	–	–	–	–

Notes: Figures in brackets are for percentage of second votes in the 1987 elections (West) and March 1990 elections (East).

Helmut Kohl, written off in 1989 as a bungler who lacked a long-term view, emerged triumphant as the architect of reunion. But his victory was not as emphatic as had at one time been supposed. The combined CDU/CSU percentage of the vote fell. In contrast the increase in the FDP vote was seen as a personal triumph for Hans-Dietrich Genscher, in whose birthplace in former East Germany, Halle, the FDP candidate won a direct mandate, the first time the party had achieved this. The FDP won enough seats to make it possible to bring the SPD back to power if it decided to change partners as in 1982.

The result was a disaster for the SPD, which in the immediate aftermath of November 1989 had looked likely to be dominant in the East German Länder. But SPD strategists comforted themselves by their share of the younger vote and the expectation that the unification lustre would soon wear off revealing the social and economic problems of which Oskar Lafontaine warned.

The real losers were the West German Greens, discredited by internal squabbles between realists (*realos*) and fundamentalists (*fundis*), weakened by the policy of rotating MPs so that well-known figures were continually being replaced by unknowns, and identified with opposition to unification. Disarmament was no longer the vote-winner that it had been, and ecological clothes had been stolen by the other parties, particularly the SPD. The East German Greens formed an electoral pact with the Bündnis 90 alliance of citizens' groups. The old East German Communist Party (SED), renamed the Partei des Demokratischen Sozialismus (PDS), formed a pact with West German affiliates in the Linke Liste (left list). After the election the West German Greens and the East German Greens combined. According to the Federal Executive Committee of the Greens, had this been done before the elections there would now be around 35 Green MPs.

in Mitteleuropa, and to contrast this with a 'French vision', a 'Soviet vision', etc. But the emphasis in this chapter, as in the last, is rather on the variety of party political perspectives to be found within Germany. There is not just one 'German vision', but many. Indeed, it is not only differences of opinion between parties that are significant here, but also differences of opinion inside them. National political parties are themselves vast coalitions of interest and belief. If the unexpected upheaval of autumn 1989 and the avalanche of dramatic events th.1t followed intensified existing debate in Germany rather than silenced .t as in Britain, this was because the basic issues were already articulate.1 across the spectrum of party politics. In what follows the spread ·)f opinion will be related to the six main questions isolated in Chapter 2.[1]

1 THE THREAT TO SECURITY

By December 1990 a broad consensus had emerged on this question. There were a handful on the political right who still saw the Soviet Union as the enemy and advocated an advance of the Western frontier to the borders of Russia. But even in the CSU the orthodoxy now was to view the residual strength of Soviet armed forces as a limited and probably temporary threat 'that we must be planning to look beyond'.[2] Former hard-headed 'Gaullists' in the CDU acknowledged that the size and geographical proximity of the Soviet Union (800 kilometres as against 5000 for the United States) were a factor so long as the Soviet Union holds together, but stressed that other threats, like instability in the Middle East and multiplying Islamic populations to

FIGURE 5.1   *The sixteen German Länder*

the South of Europe's soft Mediterranean underbelly, might make the Soviet Union an ally rather than an enemy.[3] Towards the liberal wing of the CDU the Vienna negotiations between NATO and Warsaw Pact countries which resulted in the CFE agreement of November 1990 were seen as the beginning of a fundamental shift from working 'gegeneinander' (against one another) to working 'miteinander' (with one another).[4] Nevertheless, the strong possibility of a reversal of Soviet foreign policy is envisaged within the élites, and there was a powerful demand for the retention of effective defences as an insurance policy.

FDP spokespersons saw the Soviet threat as having effectively vanished. A temporary residual danger was acknowledged while withdrawal from Eastern Europe was taking place, but, to give an idea of relative scale, this was described as being if anything less of an immediate threat to security than the danger to young people's lives from drug pushing in public lavatories.[5] The abandonment of the Soviet 'Feindbild' (enemy image) had been advocated for many years by the foreign minister. Once again, the upheavals in the Soviet Union in 1991 have instilled caution, but not a change in fundamental long-standing priorities.

Within the SPD the stress was on the global and environmental problems facing not only Germany, but all other countries as well. The danger of instability in Europe to the East and South was recognised but seen to be more of a political and economic than a military problem. The attempt by certain Bundeswehr officers to justify a large army establishment by appealing to a continuing Soviet threat was described by one foreign policy adviser as 'pitiful'.[6] A prominent spokesperson on the right of the party, formerly in the Luftwaffe, saw the enemy as 'within ourselves, it is our own perceptions that must be overcome'.[7] Another, this time on the left, described deprivation as the greatest threat: 'it is unbearable that we in the richer part of the world should go on living at the expense of the Third World – this can only store up trouble for ourselves'.[8] 'The North–South divide and environmental degradation are now by far and away the most important threats to security and must be our top priority', according to a spokesperson for the Young Socialists.[9] The chair of the SPD parliamentary security working party did not even mention the Soviet threat.[10] It was not thought that a reversal of Soviet domestic policy in the face of political break-up and economic collapse could revive the Soviet position in Eastern Europe. Nor would there be an incentive for a new hard-line regime to compound domestic problems by reviving Cold War hostility.

For the Greens in general 'there are no "enemies" against which "we" have to defend ourselves'.[11] But Green fundamentalists saw militarism itself as the enemy, embodied in the two alliances and particularly in Western capitalist society. 'The most important thing is to work on the base, to change things at the base'[12] – it was the deep structural and attitudinal roots of militarism that must be eradicated. After the electoral débâcle for the West German Greens in December 1990 it was no longer clear how the alternative agenda would be represented in the Bundestag. The belated merger with the East German Greens might mingle West German radicalism with the outlook of former East Germans as expressed in the defence policy of the DDR between March and December 1990.[13]

2 THE RESPONSE

With such a diffuse and in many cases indistinct sense of where the threats to security are coming from, there is a matching variety of recommended responses. Nevertheless, confining attention to the military-political dimension, there is general agreement that what is now needed is a comprehensive analysis of the nature of residual risk and a concomitant assessment of appropriate future dispositions. A fundamental reorientation will be required over the next few years at national, alliance and wider European levels. Short-, medium- and long-term aims need to be defined which take prudent account of possible interim contingencies while at the same time keeping a clear sight of preferred final goals. It is taken for granted, first, that narrow 'defence' decisions must be determined by broader 'foreign policy' judgements, and, second, that this is a legitimate matter for full participation across the party political spectrum. The cross-party Bundeswehr-Kommission, for example, is due to report in autumn 1991 on the 'Sinnfrage der Bundeswehr' (the question of the purpose of the federal armed forces) in tandem with the NATO review.[14] Only those right-wing nationalists who see no need to adapt proven practices and those left-wing fundamentalists who reject even temporary compromise with existing dispositions fall outside this continuum.

Within the CDU a characteristic view towards the right of the party is the idea that defences must be credible and this necessitates change. This should be achieved in stages. Allied troops should remain in Germany in reduced numbers and sensitivity must be shown to Soviet concerns. 'Forward defence' needs to be redefined with defences now forward at the Polish border but with supporting offensive forces held back. 'Flexible response' must also be revised. Old thinking which envisages relatively weak conventional forces and early recourse to battlefield nuclear weapons is now unnecessary and politically unsustainable. So there should be swift movement to conventional defence sufficiency together with a background minimum nuclear deterrent threat.[15] Liberals on the left of the party want foreign troops in Germany to have a different status now, more the guarantors of stability than a defence aimed against the Soviet Union.[16] The idea of multinational forces is favoured, as is the concept of mobility so that (to borrow a Gaullist phrase) they face 'à tous azimuts' (in all directions) not just East. Indeed, the further question is sometimes asked, why, if there are French and British troops in Germany, should there not also be German troops in France and Britain?[17] CDU thinking in general seems to favour the idea that the 1949 constitution should be amended to allow a deployment of German troops 'out of area', but that this should be under United Nations auspices, and in the form, not of national contingents, but multinational forces within, say, the framework of the Western European Union.

Centrist SPD views now overlap over the short-term not only with the fluidity of 'Genscherism' but also with some of the thinking towards the left of the CDU. The understanding reached between Chancellor Kohl and President Gorbachev that the size of the Bundeswehr of a united Germany should not exceed 370 000 has ended earlier disputes about numbers, although radical recommendations have been made that a future Gesamteuropäische Armee (army of a united Europe) would only need to be some 500 000 strong.[18] There are plans to cancel larger numbers of frigates, main battle tanks and combat planes, including the European Fighter Aircraft.[19] But it is thought important in the shorter term to retain the multinational integrated military structure in NATO as a hedge against the danger of German Gaullism. It is generally agreed that 'NATO strategy is already dead', and strenuous work is being done to adapt the 1980s concepts of Strukturelle Nichtangriffsfähigkeit (structural inability to attack) and Gemeinsame Sicherheit (common security) to the new circumstances.[20] Since these ideas were worked out in detail against the background of bloc-to-bloc confrontation across the inner German border, they now have to be rethought. 'Common security', for example, is being superseded by more complex models which embrace numbers of separate countries and sub-alliances within a single overall security system. Confusingly for the British this is known as SKS – System Kollektiver Sicherheit (system of collective security). Central to this thinking is the significance of the broad band of neutral or semi-neutral states that now separates the NATO area from the Soviet Union.[21] As for 'out-of-area' operations, FDP thinking seems to stress the need to speed up West European political integration so that German troops can participate in multinational contingents while an SPD report on 'the future shape of armed forces in a united Germany' insists that these must be 'peace troops' trained to work in international groups within a CSCE context under UN auspices.[22]

Beyond the military-political dimension there is a multitude of suggested economic and political responses to the European and global threats to security which lie beyond the scope of this book.

3 THE FUTURE SECURITY ARCHITECTURE IN EUROPE

The 15 perspectives listed in the Table 5.1 may give some idea of the variety of inter-party opinion in Germany on the question of a future security architecture. Despite the apparent complexity, a clear pattern can be discerned. Movement across the broad central party political consensus from right to left (perspectives 3 to 11) highlights in turn the roles of the four main focal points described in Chapter 2 – NATO, the Western European Union, the European Community and the Conference on Security and Cooperation in Europe. It is as if a searchlight beam is moved from Washington to Moscow, panning back to take in more and more of the landscape as it does so. This fact is of great significance. The important questions in the European security debate are indeed party political questions. Within the consensus it is not so much a question of 'either/or' as of priority, emphasis and timing, so the descriptions of the 15 positions outlined below should be understood to indicate points of focal concern rather than watertight recommendations which exclude other elements.[23]

Neither the virulently right-wing Republican Party (perspective 1),[24] nor the radical alternative agenda of the 'New Social Movements' (perspective 14)[25] are represented in the Bundestag. Nor, even though they are (or in the case of West German Greens were) represented in the Bundestag, can the National Conservatives (nicknamed 'Stahlhelmer' – steel helmets: perspective 2)[26] on one side, and the Green Fundamentalists (perspective 13)[27] on the other be said to belong within the broad national consensus.

TABLE 5.1   *Fifteen perspectives on a future European security structure*

1.   Die Republikaner – a revived greater German nationalism
2.   CDU/CSU National Conservatives – a Europe of Fatherlands
3.   CDU/CSU Atlanticists – emphasis on NATO
4.   CDU Centrists – emphasis on a strengthened WEU
5.   CDU Liberals – emphasis on a European Defence Community
6.   CDU Euromilitarists – emphasis on a European superstate
7.   FDP Rightists – emphasis on multiplicity and cautious change
8.   FDP Leftists – emphasis on multiplicity and rapid change
9.   SPD NATO Revisionists – adapt existing practices
10. SPD Gradualists – CSCE eventually absorbs NATO/WTO
11. SPD Radicals – CSCE swiftly absorbs NATO/WTO
12. Green Realists – ensure SPD radical programme succeeds
13. Green Fundamentalists – emphasis on a Europe of regions
14. New Social Movements – reconstruction based on new values
15. Ex-GDR Approach – Germany as bridge between East and West

Elsewhere there is a continuum. In the CDU/CSU the formerly dominant Atlanticist position (perspective 3)[28] is now rarely argued openly, although it remains a strong instinct within the defence élite. The Centrist position (perspective 4),[29] which emphasises the role of the WEU as the 'European pillar' of NATO, was originally staked out by outspoken 'Gaullists' in the mid-1980s who were critical of American high-handedness. This subsequently became central ground for the party. The centre of gravity is now, perhaps, shifting again towards the idea of some kind of independent European Defence Community linked by formal treaty (a 'new Atlanticism') to the United States, but also eventually achieving a formal relationship with the Soviet Union (perspective 5).[30] The handful of Euromilitarists (perspective 6)[31] welcome the idea of a new European superstate with its own (Anglo-French) nuclear deterrent.

The two wings of the FDP share the instincts of a small party manoeuvring between larger parties in a country that has itself been manoeuvring between the superpowers. Continuous influence in the foreign office means that long-serving rightist personnel merge into defence establishment orthodoxy (perspective 7),[32] but the leftist tradition in security thinking is nevertheless the stronger within the party (perspective 8).[33]

Experienced SPD advisers from the ministries, sceptical about 'quaker concepts' like 'defensive defence', would be likely to gain in prominence if there were an SPD government (perspective 9).[34] But the party as a whole has shifted dramatically since 1982. There is now agreement that the aim is to absorb the two former blocs into a Gesamteuropäisches Sicherheitssystem (pan-European security system) developed from the CSCE (KSZE) 'Helsinki process', which is looked on with pride as an SPD achievement. But, whereas SPD Gradualists (perspective 10)[35] are happy in the meantime to accept German membership of NATO's integrated military structure as a hedge against revived nationalism and Euro-Gaullism, SPD Radicals (perspective 11)[36] are not. They want an immediate transformation of NATO comparable in effect, if not in nature, to that going on in the East, followed by the swift supercession of both.

Finally, although the GDR has now been swallowed up, its former strongly non-nuclear anti-alliance attitudes together with its antipathy to foreign troops will now find expression in the special arrangements being made for it, and may surface in the policy preferences of constituency and party slate MPs from the five ex-GDR Länder. This, together with similar attitudes found among neighbouring ex-Warsaw Pact allies, may exert a stronger influence in Germany over the next few years than a number of Western commentators seem to think.[37]

4 THE ROLE OF NUCLEAR WEAPONS

When we come to the nuclear weapon question, we find that, in contrast to the debate in Britain as presented through the British media, it is firmly embedded in the broader strategic and foreign policy debate that has just been reviewed. Conclusions about nuclear weapons follow from prior judgements about the nature of threat, the character of appropriate response and the political framework within which security issues should be determined. During the 1980s, particularly after the advent of Mikhail Gorbachev, the German nuclear weapon debate came to focus on the relationship between the two tracks of NATO's 1979 'dual track' policy, unilateral modernisation (the first track) and multilateral negotiated arms control (the second track). At the beginning of the decade advocates of unilateral modernisation were still in the ascendancy, but by the end arms controllers urging multilateral zero options to eliminate further classes of nuclear weapons on both sides had seized the initiative.

In 1991 there is a consensus that short-range ground-launched systems (missiles and artillery) must go. Plans for likely early use of theatre nuclear weapons must be abandoned and they must at most constitute a background threat of possible last resort. Proper conventional defence sufficiency can now be achieved and this will make all these changes operationally feasible. There is also a near consensus which falls short of the radical wing of the SPD that in the middle term, while the Soviet Union still has nuclear weapons, the American extended deterrent will have to be retained. But there is controversy about what this entails.

The official CDU position is for the maintenance of a 'minimum nuclear deterrent on German soil'. It is thought important to retain a German say in NATO nuclear policy – and a German influence in any evolving Anglo-French 'European' deterrent. The German establishment wants to retain the options of 'nuclear participation' (maintaining carrier systems) and 'co-dispersal of nuclear weapons' (shared possession of nuclear weapons within a European framework). Within the German defence establishment it is therefore considered essential not only to accommodate the proposed new Tactical Air-To-Surface Missile (TASM), but to provide German carriers for it. But the public defence rationale for such a capability has shifted almost entirely away from military use to political signalling. Indeed, the defence minister no longer describes it in terms of 'deterring an expressly designated political opponent', but in terms of 'assuring and stabilising a system of reciprocal security in Europe cemented by treaty'.[38]

For the FDP Hans-Dietrich Genscher called for a nuclear-free Europe at a party conference in Hanover in August 1990, saying that there was no longer a place for 'short-range nuclear missiles and other nuclear missiles' in the new Europe.[39]

The official SPD position is that 'all nuclear and chemical weapons have to be withdrawn from Germany'. They should be confined to the countries that produce them. In particular the SPD 'would not allow stationing of aircraft carrying TASM in the Federal Republic of Germany'. Renunciation of its own nuclear weapons by a unified Germany should be incorporated in the Grundgesetz (basic law).[40] Those who feel that there is a continuing interim role for the American strategic deterrent are satisfied that sea-based systems are adequate. It is recognised that denuclearisation is a stage-by-stage process and programmes such as Sicherheit 2000 sketch out progressive steps towards European elimination by the year 2000 in coordination with a multiplicity of broader strategic and political changes.

As for the question of French and British nuclear weapons, some in the CDU/CSU envisage the possibility of Franco-British capabilities constituting a future European deterrent. But in general the opinion seems to be that if France and Britain want to keep them for psychological reasons, let them. Beyond that, there is not too much interest.

5 THE ALLOCATION OF RESOURCES

With this question we reach an area where a great deal of research is concentrated.

Until recently on the right of the political spectrum the idea of a 'peace dividend' was regarded as illusory. In the CDU/CSU it was pointed out that West Germany spends less than 3% GDP on defence compared to Britain's nearly 4%. West German companies are in any case less dependent on defence contracts and arms exports to the Third World than British companies, and most of them sensibly began to diversify rapidly from the mid-1980s.[41] Since then, however, the need for defence cuts to help pay for restructuring the former GDR has changed the complexion of the debate. The defence minister's call for an increased budget was greeted with incredulity and influential spokespersons in the CDU began recommending reductions from the current 54.5 billion DM to below 50 billion.[42]

For the SPD this is a major question and is widely regarded as in the deepest sense a moral one. Research modelling has indicated that if a 50% reduction in real terms were attempted by the end of the century, there would be no significant dividend until about 1993, but that thereafter it would grow exponentially. The conclusion is that serious planning in this direction must start straight away.[43] It is pointed out that, although West Germany spends less than Britain as a percentage of GDP, the overall figure is comparable because German GDP is higher. There is general agreement that arms exports to the Third World should be stringently prohibited.[44]

The Greens have been carrying out extensive research in this area for a number of years and have put forward detailed amendments to draft budget bills for state funding of industrial conversion. For example in November 1988 a £1 billion conversion fund was proposed, drawn from sums saved in military procurement cuts, 'to subsidise the conversion and retraining of production plants and personnel previously involved in the manufacture of weapons or civilian aircraft for the manufacture of other products'. Detailed costings were drawn up in liaison with employees of defence companies who had formed 'working groups on alternative manufacturing' and specific suggestions for alternative 'environment-friendly' products to be made by the shipbuilding, tank- and aircraft-manufacturing sectors were made.[45]

It seems to be generally agreed that the whole enterprise of conversion and diversification must be ordered at local and Länder level, where the specific needs and capabilities of particular areas can be most accurately assessed and most effectively handled.[46]

6　DECISION MAKING

As has perhaps already become evident, despite having the largest army in Europe outside the Soviet Union, defence decision making in Germany is a more open process than it is in Britain. Just as British national pride at sending troops to the Gulf is not understood, nor is the secrecy with which all aspects of military planning in Britain is allowed to be jealously guarded by Whitehall. The Bundeswehr-Kommission mentioned above, for example, is not something likely to be set up in Britain. This is largely the result of the post-1945 revulsion against authoritarianism and militarism, which led to extensive parliamentary control and the democratisation programme in the armed forces. It is a tradition which has continued to this day. Nevertheless, there is strenuous criticism of covert military planning, particularly from the left-wing of the SPD and the Greens, in areas like NATO nuclear weapon policy and arms exports. Through to the end of 1990 the offices of Green MPs in the Bundestag were lined with ongoing files on specific issues of this kind.[47]

7　PARTY POLITICAL PROGRAMMES FOR THE DECEMBER 1990 ALL-GERMAN FEDERAL ELECTIONS

The Christian Social Union[48]

The CSU's parliamentary election programme stressed that there was now an historic challenge facing Germany. Communism and socialism have conspicuously failed, freedom has won over unfreedom, and Soviet disarmament has come about thanks to the resolute Western twin-track policy of strong defence and negotiation. SPD demands for unilateral Western disarmament have fortunately been resisted. As a result the military threat from the East has diminished and NATO can become a more political organisation, taking on new responsiblities for further disarmament and peaceful resolution of conflict. The great goal is to continue to preserve peace at lower levels of armament, through balanced reductions and strict verification regimes.

But the price of freedom is vigilance. The Soviet Union remains a military superpower possessing a powerful nuclear arsenal. Only the United States is an appropriate counterweight so the Atlantic Alliance remains the basis of German security. Germany must remain firmly in NATO. The Bundeswehr deserves gratitude for its stalwart defence of freedom. There is now scope for savings, particularly in cost-intensive weapon programmes, the number of military manoeuvres must be reduced and low-flying stringently curtailed. The new Bundeswehr must not be deprived of any of its peace-keeping power, however. A well-functioning army of this kind will not be directed against anyone. It will not be threatening. But strong armed forces are an essential attribute of a sovereign state.

The Christian Democratic Union[49]

'Ja zu Deutschland, ja zur Zukunft' ('Yes to Germany, yes to the future'). Under this slogan the CDU set out its election policies, claiming unification as a personal triumph for Chancellor Kohl. The security promise was for 'peace and freedom' within a strong Europe – 'Germany is our fatherland, Europe is our future'.

Germany must maintain a small but modern Bundeswehr. A national service reduced to twelve months must be retained to ensure that it really is an 'army of the people'. Conscientious objectors will be able, as in the past, to do valuable civilian service for the old and handicapped.

But the main emphasis is on the building of a European Union as a basis for the growing-together of the whole of Europe. German-French friendship remains the engine of this process of integration. Economic and political union (including strengthened rights for the European parliament) is central. But only if this includes a common foreign and security policy can Europe effectively represent its common interest in the world and contribute effectively to overcoming the shared problems of humanity. NATO also remains essential, having secured four decades of peace and freedom. A stable security structure in Europe requires the Transatlantic link. So the CDU plan is for a 'new

European security structure' in which the European Community, the Western European Union, NATO and the CSCE complement each other.

Turning to the wider European agenda, the expanding borders of an evolving European Union must be given a new character, no longer excluding those outside but allowing free movement. Central, Eastern and South-Eastern Europe must be progressively included as the economic division of Europe is broken down. International recognition in law must be accorded to the rights of ethnic groups throughout the region to their own cultural identity within their own homeland. German-Soviet relations are crucial for the development of the new 'peace order' based on the building-blocks of arms control and disarmament. Since 1982 the CDU has succeeded in securing the INF Treaty, the withdrawal of US chemical weapons from Germany and the CFE Treaty. This work must continue. German mediation with the Soviet Union is essential, and help must be given to the Soviet Union where needed.

Finally, a united and sovereign Germany must now take on larger responsibilities for peace in the world once a clear-cut basis for this has been defined in German law, including scope for out-of-area contributions. A partnership must be built with the countries of the Third World, so that the overcoming of the division of Europe leads on to the overcoming of the discrepancy in levels of development in the world. In general, apart from immediate relief help, aid should be directed where most progress has been made in the direction of democracy, a free social order and human rights.

The Free Democratic Party[50]

For twenty years the FDP has pursued the goal of peace in Europe by overcoming East–West antagonism and the division of Germany. Foreign ministers Scheel and Genscher have succeeded in achieving this through a sensible and consistent foreign policy against opposition both from left and right. Without this there could have been no INF Treaty, troop cuts or reduction in the length of national service.

The FDP is the party of Europe. The European Community must now develop further into a federal European Union with a common policy in relation to the outside world commensurate with its economic strength. A single foreign policy must also extend to cover all aspects of security. Nor is there a contradiction between deepening and widening the community. It is open to other states to join as and when they are ready and have reached an appropriate stage of development. As a future European government the European commission should be elected by the European parliament which must have comprehensive legislative powers and budget rights.

The FDP supports the idea of the Bundeswehr being integrated into a multinational European force. But its role should be seen to extend further, to peace-keeping in a pan-European context, and, strictly under the aegis of the United Nations, a world context. The former GDR territory is now in a special category agreed in the two-plus-four talks. This represents the first step in what should become a new pan-European structure. The essential task is to work out the principles of a proper 'defensive defence capability', for which a special commission has been set up. The European Fighter Aircraft should be cancelled and a substantial peace dividend sought. Short range nuclear weapons should be negotiated down to zero and further modernisation halted. It remains essential for Germany to stay in NATO, but the alliance needs a new definition of its aim, strategy and relations to non-NATO states. Antagonism and violent means must be set aside and the transition from confrontation to cooperation achieved. Its political character must be strengthened to preserve the security link with the USA and contribute to coordinated progress in arms control and disarmament. Germany must renounce chemical, biological and nuclear weapons as a part of its constitution, and support a global ban on nuclear weapon testing.

The overarching context for all this must be the creation of a new European 'peace order' from the Atlantic to the Urals, a common space of democratic, legal, political, economic, environmental and military security. The driving force (Träger) and forum here is the CSCE process. It must play the decisive role and develop into the basis for a cooperative European system. The goal must be transparency so that information is exchanged about planned as well as actual weapons systems and arms control can become preventative and not just regulatory. One of the main common tasks is to speed the replacement of military with civilian production. This should be done cooperatively with the West helping the Soviet Union. It is also vital that disarmament in Europe should not lead to second-hand weapons being exported to the third world. Specific clauses to guard against this should be included in disarmament agreements. Restrictions against arms exports should be tightened in general. In order to achieve all this CSCE must be institutionalised to assure routine exchanges between ministers and military staffs, develop confidence-building mechanisms (i.e. for verification), and acquire capacities for effective conflict resolution. A parliamentary assembly is an essential ingredient here.

The Social Democratic Party[51]

The SPD claimed to draw the real consequences from the end to the East–West conflict. The military blocs have lost their function and the aim should be to broaden the CSCE process to replace them. A pan-European security system should be created by treaty. One aspect of this must be follow-on talks after the first CFE agreement to achieve drastic further reductions and a cooperative restructuring of forces so that they are generally seen to be defensive. This should be accompanied by step-by-step nuclear disarmament, including a rejection of flexible response with its reliance on a first-use option. These changes are not to be cosmetic. Beginning with the former East German Länder, the whole of Germany should become nuclear free. Germany should commit itself under international law not to produce its own nuclear, chemical or biological weapons, or allow stationing of these weapons on her soil. In the meantime Germany must be treated like any other member of NATO. Foreign troops should not have a different status in Germany than they have elsewhere. The European Fighter Aircraft should be abandoned, military manoeuvres (especially those involving low-flying) drastically reduced and the number of military bases in Germany cut down. Neither NATO nor the WEU should be given an out-of-area role. If German forces do operate out of area, then it must be as peace-keeping forces under the aegis of the United Nations.

This fundamental reshaping of the European security space must be accompanied by an emphatic transfer of resources from military to civilian projects. For Germany the necessary direct investment in the former GDR Länder, which will be much heavier than the CDU is claiming, must be funded above all from defence savings. An immediate 9 billion DM should be slashed from the German defence budget, with a 50% reduction achieved in the middle term. This money should also be devoted to easing the painful transition of defence conversion, and at least one billion DM a year should be given straight away in aid to the Third World. On no account should disarmament in Europe lead to increased arms exports elsewhere. The immorality of the arms trade is now plainly evident in the Gulf crisis. There must be an effective ban on arms exports to developing countries which cannot afford them, to areas of tension, to dictatorial regimes and to governments known to be abusing human rights.

The SPD goal is 'a United States of Europe' built on a stronger EC expanded to include the EFTA countries and the new Central and East European democracies. The role of the European parliament must be enhanced. And regions must be strengthened so that the new United States of Europe becomes a truly federal body. The centralised nation state is too small to deal with many of the big problems and too large properly to manage many of the local ones. One of the great tasks of this new international entity is to achieve the ecological modernisation of the Eastern European countries and decisively to overcome the great East–West economic divide.

The West German Greens,[52] East German Greens/Bündnis 90,[53] Party of Democratic Socialism (PDS)/Linke Liste[54]

Although the West and East German Greens have now amalgamated, they fought the December 1990 election as distinct parties, the East German Greens in an electoral pact with the East German Bündnis 90 citizens groups. There was also the communist East German PDS (the renamed SED) and its West German affiliates in the Linke Liste (left list).

The programme of the West German Greens opened by emphasising the opportunity that now existed for total disarmament and the demilitarisation of Germany. Both the Bundeswehr and the NVA should be disbanded and conscription ended. The dissolution of the blocs should lead to the swift creation of a pan-European peace order under the aegis of the CSCE. Sovereign nation states and military alliances should be transcended (and the transformation of the European Community into a super-state avoided) both by a merging into wider pan-European and global organisations, and by decentralisation into a Europe of regions. All nuclear, chemical and biological weapons must be eliminated. Foreign troops must withdraw from Germany. The defence budget must be drastically slashed. Arms exports must be strenuously prohibited.

In contrast, the East German Greens and Bündnis 90, reflecting the experience of the peaceful revolution of autumn 1990, emphasised above all their philosophical commitment to active non-violence – active resistance against injustice as the essential complement of the commitment to non-violence.

The manifesto of the East German Partei des Demokratischen Sozialismus (PDS) and its associated Linke Liste was equally radical. It called for German demilitarisation by the year 2000, withdrawal of foreign troops, an end to all military manoeuvres, an end to all military production, and a total conversion programme with emphasis on environmental projects including redeployment of personnel from armed forces into a European environment programme. 'Demilitarisation and democratisation are two sides of the same coin.' Germany must leave NATO, which should be replaced by a security system which includes the Soviet Union. Disquiet was expressed at the thought of Germany taking on a world role, including intervention overseas. Instead of seeing the Third World as a threat, the aim should be to end exploitation of the Third World, for example by cancelling debt.

NOTES

1. The analysis in this chapter is based on texts of speeches from the bulletin of the Presse- und Informationsamt der Bundesregierung; the thematic selection of newspaper articles provided by the IFIAS Pressespiegel; policy statements from each of the parties represented in the Bundestag, and interviews with party spokespersons carried out in February 1990 and updated since. In addition, Lothar Gutjahr's analysis of CDU foreign and defence policy 1986–90, *Konservative Reaktion auf das Ende von Jalta*, Hamburger Beiträge, IFSH, 1990, has been used as the basis for the analysis of CDU/CSU attitudes.
2. Dr Wolfgang Bötsch, chairman, CSU parliamentary party.
3. Markus Berger, personal adviser to Alfred Dregger, chairman, CDU parliamentary party.
4. Karl Lamers, disarmament spokesperson, CDU/CSU parliamentary party.
5. Dr Klaus Citron, Head of Policy Planning, Foreign Office.
6. Dr Gerd Wagner, personal adviser to Horst Ehmke, SPD foreign affairs spokesperson.
7. Manfred Opel, SPD MP.
8. Katrin Fuchs, SPD spokesperson on disarmament and arms control issues.
9. Ingo Arendt.
10. Erwin Horn.
11. Final Declaration, joint party BRD/DDR congress Magdeburg, 14 March 1990.
12. Petra Kelly.

13. Of the East German MPs from the East German Greens/Bündnis 90 alliance, only two are from the East German Green Party, the rest are from the citizens' groups.
14. *Frankfurter Rundschau*, 8 September 1990.
15. Alfred Dregger, chairman, CDU parliamentary party.
16. Karl Lamers, disarmament spokesperson, CDU/CSU parliamentary party.
17. *Die Welt*, 7 September 1990.
18. *Darmstädter Signal*, as reported *Frankfurter Rundschau*, 27 August 1990.
19. *Fortschritt 90*, SPD working group for the party manifesto, Frieden und Abrüstung, special issue, March 1990.
20. There is an enormous literature on both these concepts. A useful review of 'non-offensive defence' proposals made during the 1980s can be found in Jonathan Dean, 'Alternative Defence: Answer to NATO's Central Front Problems?', *International Affairs*, Winter 1987–8.
21. This work is being coordinated by Egon Bahr and Dieter Lutz at IFSH (Hamburg).
22. Joint BRD/DDR report, Erwin Horn and Peter Zumkley.
23. The analysis in this section is drawn from the resources referred to in n. 1. A sample of representatives of these fifteen perspectives, in many cases personally interviewed, is: 1 Franz Schönhuber; 2 Bernhard Friedmann; 3 Manfred Wörner; 4 Alfred Dregger; 5 Karl Lamers; 6 Hans-Gert Pöttering; 7 Klaus Citron; 8 Olaf Feldmann; 9 Gerd Wagner; 10 Karsten Voigt; 11 Katrin Fuchs; 12 Christa Vennegerts; 13 Angelika Bier; 14 Otfried Nassauer; 15 Frank Marcinek.
24. Despite local electoral gains this party has yet to win a seat in the Bundestag. Its views are a more extreme version of perspective 2, including hostility against Gastarbeiter (immigrant workers) and irre-dentist claims to lost lands East of the Oder-Neisse line.
25. These are activists, influential at regional and local level, who regard even fundamentalist MPS as tarred with the brush of compromise. Structures of all kinds are rejected here, so the premise on which question three is formulated is not recognised in the first place.
26. These are traditionalists within the CDU/CSU attracted to the Gaullist vision of a Europe of Fatherlands. For them the move back to Berlin represents a rejection of 'new' values associated with the Federal Republic and a revival of old German nationalism.
27. The Green fundamentalists (fundis) oppose the Green realist (realo) policy of gaining access to power through alliance with the SPD. Perhaps the most distinctive concept here is a rejection of the CSCE structure as envisaged in SPD/FDP thinking, because it is made up of nations. Instead what is favoured is a Europe of regions with power coming from below rather than imposed from above.
28. The dominant security element here is seen to be NATO, embodying the leading role of American frontline troops and the US extended deterrent based in Germany. Although there is talk of NATO as a more 'political' and less 'military' alliance, there is still a stress on capabilities rather than intentions and a reluctance to alter existing NATO structures and strategies more than is strictly necessary until new Soviet dispositions

have been implemented. The fact that NATO's integrated structures remain intact means that Atlanticist thinking is still powerfully represented within the defence élite. It is more an institutionalised attitude than a conscious programme.

29. Here the spotlight moves to play equally on Washington and Brussels. The emphasis is on the 'twin pillars' of the Western Alliance, with Western Europe playing as prominent a role as the United States. The 'Gaullists' of the late 1980s like Alfred Dregger were subsequently joined by 'arms controllers' like Heiner Geissler and 'moderate Atlanticists' like Volker Rühe.

30. Here the spotlight is focused on Brussels and begins to play equally either side on Washington and Moscow. The United States remains a guarantor of the new European order, but the Soviet Union must be included as well. It is thought inevitable that the significance of NATO will dwindle and that a security and defence dimension will be added to the growing economic, political and foreign policy integration of the European Community. These different aspects of sovereignty cannot be separated.

31. The few Euromilitarists hope for the creation of a European superpower on a par with the United States and Japan, able to defend its interests and shape the evolution of world politics.

32. This tradition within the FDP, reaching right back to the nineteenth-century 'national liberals', ensures that there is continuity with the predominant CDU/CSU element in the ruling coalition. Some liberal conservatives within the CDU are more radical than the more cautious FDP professionals.

33. There can be no doubt that the overall direction of FDP policy in the foreign policy and security field comes from here. But the instinct of successive FDP foreign ministers has been to manipulate the situation pragmatically. There is a suspicion of blue-prints and 'architectures' and a preference for ad hoc adjustment to existing institutional multiplicity in the overall direction of a new 'peace order' in Europe.

34. Although former SPD Atlanticists like Helmut Schmidt no longer describe themselves as such, there is still a distinct strain within the party which envisages piecemeal adaptation of inherited structures rather than a bold break with the past. They are prepared to envisage creative ambivalence in the medium term, for example reconciling traditions of extended deterrence with new impulses towards a non-nuclear Germany. This is not so much a developed position as an instinctive approach among those with experience in the ministries.

35. Here the spotlight plays evenly across the entire continent 'from the Atlantic to the Urals'. But the collapse of the Berlin Wall sharpened the distinction between 'gradualists' and 'radicals' in the SPD. The gradualists interpret the programme as one of building out from existing structures. They accept membership of NATO's integrated military structure in the middle term, together with a minimum deterrent.

36. For the radicals, however, the time to temporise is over. The Eastern bloc has already collapsed and there is a swathe of semi-neutral states stretching from Scandinavia to the Balkans. This means that we already have a de facto zone of common security and the days of integrated

commands and extended deterrents has passed. 'The real guarantees against war are not military strength, but drastic reductions and defensive restructuring of forces on both sides, and the development of new European institutions within the CSCE framework. These must be accompanied by policies of economic cooperation and integration', Katrin Fuchs, SPD spokesperson on disarmament and arms control.

37. Attitudes from within the former GDR have been underplayed in this book, but the political confusion there has been so great since November 1989 that any analysis would be likely to be outdated before it was complete. Assessment of the impact on the evolution of politics in the united Germany, therefore, will have to be made when the situation becomes clearer.

38. Gerhard Stoltenberg, West German defence minister, *Washington Post*, 1 May 1990.

39. Allgemeine Deutsche Nachtrichten, 11 August 1990.

40. Official SPD position adopted 25 April 1990 and sent by Horst Ehmke in a letter to Hans-Dietrich Genscher (BRD) and Marcus Meckel (DDR). Communicated by Wolfgang Biermann, SPD security adviser.

41. Ortwin Lowack, chairman CSU parliamentary party foreign policy and security working group.

42. Neue Ruhr Zeitung, 5 September 1990; Haribert Scharrenbrauch, chair CDU/CSU parliamentary group, *Neues Deutschland*, 9 August 1990.

43. Erwin Horn, chair SPD parliamentary party security working group.

44. *Fortschritt 90*.

45. German Bundestag 11th legislative term, amendment motion, Drucksache 11/3350, 11 November 1988.

46. Address by Walter Kroy of MBB to the Institute for Public Policy Research, 25 November 1990.

47. An example of parliamentary intervention was the insistence that control be kept of the 'selling on' rights of the joint German/French/Italian/Dutch NH90 helicopter, *Stuttgarter Zeitung*, 7 September 1990. The FDP parliamentary party was prominent here. FDP MP Hildegard Hamm-Brücher campaigned for many years for more parliamentary involvement, winning the support of more than 150 MPs on a number of occasions.

48. CSU Bundestagswahlprogramm, Heimat Bayern, Zukunft Deutschland, 10 November 1990.

49. CDU Wahlprogramm zur gesamtdeutschen Bundestagswahl am 2 Dezember 1990.

50. Das Liberale Deutschland: Programm der FDP zu den Bundestagswahlen am 2 Dezember 1990.

51. SPD Regierungsprogramm 1990–4, Der Neue Weg, 28 September 1990.

52. Wahlprogramm Die Grünen, October 1990.

53. Wahlplatform Die Grünen/Bündnis 90.

54. Wahlprogramm PDS/Linke Liste.

Part III
The British Debate

6 The British Defence Debate in the 1980s

The contrast between the West German security debate and the British defence debate is striking. The events of autumn 1989 quickened and intensified the debate in Germany, but did not seem to link up at all with what had been going on in Britain. Media commentators concluded that 'defence' was no longer a party political issue, and the British debate ended at exactly the moment when the critical phase of the European debate began. How had this come about?

1 AN INSULAR TRADITION

Although the Berlin Wall, the symbolic barrier between East and West, was removed in November 1989, another barrier further West was not – the English Channel. This stretch of water has had an effect on British identity out of all proportion to its twenty-two mile width. After painful and protracted hesitation, Britain's membership of the European Community was finally confirmed in the referendum of 5 June 1975, but most Britons do not yet seem to feel European. For the bulk of the population there is a greater cultural affinity with the United States or Australia than with France. Britons still refuse to learn the languages of their European neighbours, and in general know little about European affairs. With one or two notable exceptions, such as the Heath government between 1970 and 1974, neither of the two main British parties has yet embraced the European ideal with the enthusiasm of mainland counterparts.

This is an old tradition. Although for five hundred years after the Norman Conquest England played the role of a major European land power, from the sixteenth century her interests began to turn West. Through command of the sea and vigorous commercial and industrial enterprise, England/Britain became a colonial and then imperial world power. Her aspirations switched from Europe to the ever-expanding destiny of the 'English speaking peoples'. Her policy in Europe was reduced to the negative one of trying to ensure that no continental land power came to predominate, and in particular control the coastline just across the Channel.

2   THE ATLANTICIST CONSENSUS – 1945–79

In 1940, however, Britain came close to defeat. She was engaged in a desperate struggle for survival, facing the very situation her traditional policy had always sought to avoid. German airpower nearly succeeded where for centuries continental naval power had failed. Britain stood alone. It was a moment of supreme national peril, 'the finest hour', and, although it was not realised at the time, a turning point in British foreign policy.[1]

In hailing national salvation in his celebrated Battle of Britain address, Winston Churchill had still been able to suppose that the British Empire, more extensive in 1945 than ever before, might 'last for a thousand years'. In fact it lasted seven, effectively ending when India gained independence in 1947. The German threat was immediately succeeded by the Soviet threat, and it became plain that British security was from now on dependent on the continued presence of American troops in Europe. The signing of the North Atlantic Treaty in April 1949 formalised this logic. The defence of the West came to rest on forward deployed American ground troops supported by the American strategic nuclear deterrent. NATO became the vehicle through which the United States defended Western Europe.[2]

Humiliating though it was for an ex-imperial power to have to admit it, Britain was now only a 'bit-player' in this vast multinational enterprise. From 1949 to 1979 successive Labour and Conservative governments implemented the policy, disguising British decline under the fig-leaf of a 'special relationship' with the United States. At its heart was an ambivalent nuclear deterrent policy which stressed independence and interdependence at the same time. Unlike France, which found a post-imperial identity under De Gaulle by creating her own nuclear 'force de frappe' ostensibly independent of the United States and detaching herself from NATO's integrated command, Britain committed 95 per cent of her conventional forces and all her nuclear forces to the Western Alliance. Her strategic deterrent was tested in Nevada and targeted in Omaha. France concluded that her future greatness lay through leadership in Europe, whereas Britain cast around for a continuing off-shore role and hesitated on the brink.[3]

For forty years British policy was dominated by the long and reluctant process of accommodation to relative economic decline. Successive defence reviews became synonymous with defence cuts. The 1957 Sandys review, for example, reduced the British Army Of The Rhine by almost exactly the same amount as that proposed in the July 1990 interim statement on the 'options for change'. Budgetary constraints exacerbated the centuries long debate about maritime versus continental commitments. Despite criticism when in opposition, Labour and Conservative governments pursued the same course. Conservative governments sometimes made the most radical cuts. Labour governments sometimes initiated new nuclear weapon programmes. Neither party tried seriously to reverse the actions of the other. Labour did not attempt to undo the policy of deterrence. The Conservatives did not try to return East of Suez. Both remained loyal to the Atlanticist principles embodied in NATO.

And throughout this period governments from both parties maintained the Whitehall tradition of secrecy on defence matters. To a degree unmatched in other Western countries, the tight-knit defence establishment of ministers, senior civil servants and military chiefs excluded the rest of the body politic from active participation. The high level of secrecy surrounding nuclear matters in particular generated a 'nuclear priesthood' which understood the arcane 'theology' of nuclear strategy and communicated with each other in highly classified papers that even junior ministers were not permitted to read. It thus became possible for a small group of senior ministers and civil servants to control policy with little outside influence. Despite the fact that defence spending accounted for more than 10 per cent of government expenditure, Parliament was only allotted one two-day debate on the Defence Estimates, three individual service days and a short debate on the Consolidated Fund each year. No major debates were held on nuclear weapons from 1965 to 1979, apart from the debates on the Defence Estimates. Neither major party wanted a debate, and neither released full information about the policies it was pursuing. 'Defence' was treated in isolation from politics.[4]

3 LABOUR UNILATERALISM – THE ELECTORAL ALBATROSS

In 1981, however, the post-war British defence consensus collapsed. A policy of unilateral nuclear disarmament was adopted by the Labour party and in 1983 'defence' became a major electoral issue. In marked contrast to the evolving complex of the West German SPD's multi-faceted Ostpolitik, however, with its well-researched policy options of stage-by-stage denuclearisation, arms control, non-provocative defence and common security, the Labour Party was clear about what it did not want, but not about what it did. Not a single proper research study accompanied the change. It was a powerfully emotive single issue campaign, not a defence policy at all.[5]

It was also electorally unpopular. The intention to abandon the British deterrent went down badly at home. The plan to remove American nuclear weapons misfired abroad. Without a properly researched alternative defence policy which took full account of Labour's commitment to continued British participation in NATO's integrated command structure, party spokespersons left themselves open to equally parochial criticism. How would a Labour government respond to Soviet nuclear blackmail? What would Neil Kinnock do if Russian tanks massed at Calais? In the eyes of the public the British defence debate was reduced to a local tussle between insular ideas of an 'independent deterrent' and equally insular ideas about 'unilateral disarmament'.[6]

By 1987 attempts had been made to link Labour Party unilateralism to West German SPD policies for a revised NATO strategy, drawing on the increasingly sophisticated work being done by the peace movement in Britain with its full involvement in the European debate. But the British media remained preoccupied with the former and ignored the latter. Neither political commentators nor the general public had the knowledge or the interest to take part in the European debate. Instead of the extensive research back-up available to West German opposition parties, the Labour Party had to rely on the heroic work of a couple of defence researchers at Walworth Road, one or two assistants to shadow defence and foreign policy spokespersons and the dwindling resources of the Fabian Society.[7]

BOX 6.1 LABOUR PARTY POLICY AT THE TIME OF
THE 1987 GENERAL ELECTION[8]

By 1987 Labour Party policy had been coordinated with that of
other European socialist and social democratic parties, particularly in NATO countries. An attempt was made to derive
defence policy from broader security and foreign policy considerations. The question of Britain's nuclear weapons was seen
to be one aspect of the question of NATO's nuclear weapons,
which was itself assessed against the background of NATO and
Warsaw Pact conventional force strategies within a context of
dramatic detente with the Soviet Union.

Current NATO nuclear deterrent strategies were severely
criticised. The fact that mutually deployed nuclear forces were
unusable was pointed out and the concept of extended
deterrence consequently rejected. The United States could not
be expected to risk suicide in defence of Europe. The dangerous
likely effects of time-urgent first-strike weapons and nuclear
war-fighting strategies on crisis stability were stressed. The idea
that there was a Soviet military advantage which could not be
met at non-nuclear level was denied. NATO reliance on nuclear
weapons was seen to do no more than inhibit a proper
modernisation of conventional forces and defensive strategies
(described as 'defensive deterrence'), made more feasible by the
development of emerging technologies. Existing 'deep strike'
strategies were condemned as dangerous and destabilising. The
Reykjavik summit, with its proposal to eliminate strategic
ballistic missiles by 1996 and remove land-based nuclear
systems from Europe, was welcomed. It showed how confidence-building unilateral gestures could pave the way for far-
reaching multilateral agreement.

In all these areas the Conservative Party was seen to be
dragging its feet, clinging to the Trident option and determined
to obstruct changes which might jeopardise it. Motivated largely
by pressure from the military-economic-bureaucratic establishment whose interests it represented, and by outmoded delusions
of grandeur, the government was seen to have turned its back
on all the more progressive movements in the world. Britain had
become a client of the United States, tied to it by nuclear apron-
strings. Foreign aid had been effectively cut, commonwealth ties

weakened by refusal to act against apartheid, and the opportunity to achieve an historic rapprochement between East and
West jeopardised.

These criticisms were accompanied by an equal emphasis on
strong defences. The nationalistic notion peddled by the
Conservatives that an 'independent' deterrent had anything to
do with effective defence was dismissed as a dangerous delusion,
as was the idea that Britain and France might pool resources to
create a 'Eurobomb' for a new European superstate as
advocated, among others, by David Owen. The charge that
Labour policy would divide and weaken NATO was denied. A
majority of NATO members were said to reject existing strategy
anyway, and the United States would come to understand that
its true European interests would be not only safeguarded but
enhanced by Labour policy. A new agreement about the status
of remaining US bases and facilities in Britain would re-
establish the partnership as a relationship between equals. But
the main thrust of the argument was the accusation that it was
the Conservative government which was in fact undermining
defences as a result of unpublicised reductions in the defence
budget and heavily increased spending on nuclear weapons. The
resources being poured unnecessarily into the defence of the
Falkland Islands and other out-of-area operations should also
be reduced and procurement procedures tightened to get proper
value for money from defence contracts. The money thus saved
would enable a Labour government to arrest and reverse this
serious decline.

4 CONSERVATIVE UNILATERALISM – THE UNDETECTED POLICY

The irony of the situation was that within the context of the European
debate it was not the Labour Party but the Conservative government
that was unilateralist. All the main British parties agreed that Britain
should remain part of NATO's integrated military structure. That
meant that all Britain's nuclear weapons were committed to NATO
and targeted accordingly. Britain could try to persuade her allies to
join her in changing NATO strategy. She could leave the integrated

command. She could leave NATO. But the one thing she could not do was to stay in the integrated structure and 'unilaterally' repudiate its strategy. It was only the Alliance as a whole that could act 'unilaterally' or 'multilaterally' in the field of its own nuclear strategy. As was clearly understood across the Channel, NATO acted unilaterally when it did things without reference to the other side, and multilaterally when it did things through negotiation. In the case of NATO's nuclear policy, therefore, 'unilateralism' meant unilateral modernisation and 'multilateralism' meant multilateral arms control. These were the two tracks of NATO's 1979 'Dual Track' nuclear policy, and it was the relationship between the two that lay at the heart of this aspect of the European debate.[9]

Throughout the 1980s the British Conservative government was in this sense unwaveringly unilateralist, with the single exception of the INF Treaty. It insisted on unilateral rearmament for NATO not only with new nuclear Trident missiles, but with an assignment of new nuclear sea-launched cruise missiles, new nuclear air-to-surface missiles, new longer-range nuclear Lance missiles and new nuclear 8 inch and 155 mm artillery shells. The British government was adamant that none of these was negotiable, neither down to equal ceilings, nor down to zero.[10]

The Labour Party, on the other hand, together with the Liberal-SDP Alliance in Britain and socialist and social democratic parties abroad, favoured multilateral negotiation with the Soviet Union down to equal ceilings or zero. The remarkable 1986 Reykjavik Summit, which filled the Conservative government with alarm because Mikhail Gorbachev and Ronald Reagan seemed suddenly on the verge of eliminating all nuclear ballistic missiles on both sides, was greeted by the Labour Party and the Alliance with delight. Towards the end of the 1980s, in response to the change in Soviet policy, the multilateral arms controllers came increasingly to predominate over the unilateral rearmers in most NATO countries. By early 1990 the British government appeared increasingly isolated in its unyielding unilateralism.[11]

One of the scandals of British politics in the 1980s was the fact that this entire debate – the real nuclear weapon debate of the 1980s in Europe – passed unnoticed in Britain. Neither Labour Party and Alliance multilateralism nor Conservative unilateralism was recognised. Apart from Trident, not a single other component in the NATO nuclear modernisation programme was communicated by the Government to Parliament. None of it was mentioned in Foreign Office and

Ministry of Defence publicity papers. British political media commentators ignored it, just as they ignored almost every other component of the great European security debate going on just across the Channel.[12]

This was all part of the continuing British tradition in which defence and foreign policy was largely the preserve of the Prime Minister, the Foreign Secretary, the Secretary of State for Defence and a handful of others. Almost all the professionalism in this field was confined to the ministries and the closed world of Whitehall. The rest was strikingly amateur. Even the wider political community in Westminster was kept in the dark with Tory MPs knowing no more than anyone else. Select Committees tended to be lost in detail and debate on the floor of the House of Commons to divide predictably along party lines.[13]

BOX 6.2 CONSERVATIVE PARTY POLICY AT THE TIME OF THE 1987 GENERAL ELECTION[14]

The main Conservative Party claim was that it was its staunch insistence on strong NATO defences during the early years of the decade that had made possible the recent spectacular improvement in East–West relations by demonstrating conclusively to Soviet leaders that massive military expenditure was counter-productive. Only an adequate mix of conventional and nuclear weapons appropriately deployed could achieve this. Forward defence, deep strike strategies and flexible response were essential to convince Soviet planners that any aggression would expose the Soviet Union to damage out of proportion to any expected gain. Ideas of 'no first use' and 'defensive defence' meant little and would be entirely counterproductive. The whole of NATO's posture was manifestly defensive and the alliance had made the only meaningful declaration of no first use – a commitment never to be the first to use any weapons. Since these forces remained essential for effective deterrence they must be kept up to date. Obsolete weapons deter nobody.

The two main opposition party charges were rejected. Conservative Party policy, far from obstructing East–West détente, was the only way to ensure it. Unilateral disarmament of the kind advocated by the Labour Party would be a recipe for disaster. Without a replacement for Polaris Britain would be defenceless against a nuclear-armed adversary and would be exposed to blackmail or attack. Labour Party plans to pull out of NATO's integrated nuclear planning would severely weaken deterrence, while insistence on the removal of American nuclear facilities from Britain would destroy the Atlantic Alliance. All Britain's allies agreed about this. The net result would be to undo the forty-year achievement of the alliance and remove any incentive for Soviet leaders to negotiate multilateral asymmetrical reductions, like the imminent INF Treaty. It would play into the hands of the hardliners. It was absurd to accuse the Conservative government of obstructing moves towards East–West détente when the Prime Minister was one of the first to recognise the opportunities opened up by the advent of Mikhail Gorbachev. Strong defence and détente were not antithetical. They were complementary. The aim was to achieve substantial reductions in the vastly superior Soviet conventional forces and to enhance security at much reduced force levels.

Finally, the accusation made by both main opposition parties that Conservative policy was weakening British conventional defences was dismissed peremptorily. In the case of Labour it was seen as a transparent device to draw attention away from the implications of its own catastrophic plans.

5 THE FATE OF THE CENTRE PARTIES

In 1987 the West German FDP with 9 per cent of the national vote gained 48 seats in the Bundestag and a continued share in coalition government. Its contribution to the evolution of West German foreign policy during the 1980s was profound. In Britain in 1983 the Liberal-SDP Alliance won 25.4 per cent of the national vote, gained 23 seats in Parliament, and was ignored.

The Conservative Party, with 42 per cent of the vote, won nearly two-thirds of the seats. Protected by an overwhelming parliamentary majority, the Government could disregard the alternative policy formulations of other parties. Internal party discipline and the remarkable absence of independent thinking within the parliamentary Conservative Party meant that it could also ignore alternatives from within its own ranks. In the House of Commons Conservatives asked Ministers if they agreed with well-known aspects of Government policy. Ministers thanked them and said that they did. Deliberations in Whitehall were kept secret, both from Conservative and opposition MPs. The wider world was informed through nuanced communiqués. The British media accepted the system, grateful for briefings from those in power and unprepared to listen to those who were not. All of them together, MPs, the media and the public at large ran off after the illusory hare of Labour Party 'unilateralism' and failed entirely to subject government policy to the kind of scrutiny that would have been routine in other countries.[15]

The saddest fate was that endured by the Alliance parties. Political commentators, encouraged by the Government, presented the defence debate as one between Labour renunciation and Conservative retention of the British deterrent. Nothing else featured. The Alliance's thoughtful 1986 *Defence And Disarmament* report, together with the separate policy papers that preceded it, was passed over. The fact that it advocated both collective and common security was perhaps too complicated for a British public used to the stark simplicities of adversarial politics. Both Labour Party and Conservative Party policies were criticised, the former as inconsistent and irresponsible, the latter as a damaging perpetuation of the Cold War. Commentators were unable to make anything of this.

BOX 6.3   ALLIANCE PARTY POLICY AT THE TIME OF THE 1987 GENERAL ELECTION[16]

Alliance policy differed most radically from the Conservative Party on the global setting for British policy, and from the Labour Party on its specific recommendations for it.

Although the reality of Soviet nuclear and non-nuclear power was seen to rule out precipitate unconditional measures, the Alliance Parties accepted that NATO and WTO nuclear war-fighting strategies were irresponsible, and that NATO's dependence on the likely early use of nuclear weapons, in particular, was dangerously misguided. The removal of all land-based nuclear weapons from the European theatre must be a central aim of Western policy. The Conservative Party's perpetuation of Cold War paranoia and clinging to the myth that there was a 'delicate' theatre nuclear balance in Europe were seen to have seriously obstructed progress towards détente and a nuclear weapon build-down. It was disgraceful that the British government should so lamely endorse American adventurism and oppose every opportunity to secure an end to nuclear testing and the elimination of ballistic systems by the superpowers. The 'special relationship' as practised by Margaret Thatcher meant being tied to American apron-strings. Instead, the British government should be vigorously pressing for a whole range of arms-reduction and confidence-building measures in a search for common security between East and West.

But the search for common security through détente and restraint must go hand-in-hand with robust collective security within the Western Alliance. If Conservative Party policy jeopardised the former by failing to recognise that long-term security could only be achieved through cooperation, Labour Party policy jeopardised the latter by failing to understand that Britain could only take a lead in working towards this goal through her membership of a strong and united alliance.

On the question of British nuclear weapons, the Trident option was seen to lock Britain permanently into dependence on American technology. Instead, the possibility of cooperation with France within a European context should be explored. Trident would represent a huge leap in targeting potential over Polaris. The direction ahead lay in strengthening links with European partners in order to build a more equal balance between the European and American pillars of the Western Alliance.

6 EXCLUDED DISSENTERS

Finally there was the shaming story of the new Green Party. As Labour Party policy moved steadily towards the centre there was clearly room in British politics for a party to represent the radical alternative agenda of the 1980s. In West Germany the Greens entered the Bundestag and contributed significantly to the quality of West German debate. They played an energetic part in parliamentary committees, researched and suggested a whole series of amendments to federal legislation, much of it passed, and in general introduced a refreshing new dimension to evolving parliamentary pluralism. Even after the débâcle of the 1990 federal election the 8 Green/Bündnis 90 and 17 PDS MPs continue to play this role.

In 1989 the British Greens won 15 per cent of the vote in the European elections, more than Green parties in any other country. But, uniquely, because proportional representation for European elections had been rejected by Britain in 1977, not a single Green Euro-MP was returned. British Green voters were simply not represented in the European Parliament. Instead it was only as a result of a decision taken by Green Euro-MPs from other countries that British Greens were able to participate in the policy-making process at all.[17]

BOX 6.4   THE RADICAL AGENDA AT THE TIME OF THE 1987 GENERAL ELECTION

Although, unlike West Germany, Britain did not have a party represented in parliament which endorsed the radical agenda (perhaps in some respects the SNP came closest), it is worth noting that there was an articulate body of opinion which rejected at least three policy positions accepted by the main British parties.

First, unlike the Labour Party, the idea that savings on the nuclear weapon programme should be spent on conventional defences was rejected. Indeed, defence spending as a whole should be substantially cut, and the resources transferred to domestic industrial and welfare enterprises and to foreign aid.

Second, instead of the Labour Party/Alliance policy of staying in NATO and working for a change of strategy from inside, the recommendation was for Britain to withdraw from NATO immediately and join the other non-aligned countries which belonged to neither armed camp.

Third, in addition to refusing to man NATO nuclear weapon delivery systems and insisting on the withdrawal of American nuclear weapons from Britain, it was proposed to remove the entire American military presence from the country. Apart from anything else, facilities such as the ballistic missile early warning station at Fylingdales in Yorkshire, and the submarine tracking station at Brawdy in Pembrokeshire were seen to play a more important role in US nuclear deterrent strategy than F-111 airfields or Cruise Missile bases.

7 THE BRITISH MEDIA AND THE DAY THE DEFENCE DEBATE DIED

After the 1987 general election defence policy was one of the seven policy areas to be reviewed by the Labour Party. The deliberations of the defence group were considered the most delicate of all in view of the emotive symbolism that unilateralism had come to assume. The new policy was largely the creation of the shadow foreign affairs spokesman, Gerald Kaufman, the final version being typed out on budget day, 14 March 1989. With its abandonment of a commitment to eliminate Trident unilaterally and remove American nuclear weapons from Britain, it was steered through the review group meetings in April. Finally, on Monday and Tuesday 8 and 9 May, the NEC met to consider it. There was resistance, but Neil Kinnock surprised his colleagues with an impassioned endorsement, on the grounds, first, that after the Reykjavik summit multilateral disarmament was now clearly the right route, and, second, that policy-makers he had argued with in the White House, the Kremlin and the Elysée simply could not understand what the point of 'unilateralism' was. The review policy was carried by 17 votes to 8.[18]

The reaction of British television reporters and journalists was characteristic. The carefully formulated foreign policy context of the Labour Party review was brushed aside. Details of the defence policy itself were left to defence correspondents and confined to little-read inside pages. Political correspondents, who monopolised prime time viewing, front page articles and centre spreads, were really only interested in domestic political fall-out. So, when news of the vote was given, almost the only question asked again and again like an incantation was 'will Kinnock press the button?' The issue was important, but obsessive preoccupation with it obliterated everything else. The idea was that if he said 'no' the new policy would be shown to be empty, if 'yes' then he would be betraying his own deepest stated convictions. The entire British defence debate of the 1980s had been reduced to this Procrustean question. It was constantly reiterated in interviews and press conferences. It was shouted at members of the Shadow Cabinet whenever they appeared.

Neil Kinnock deliberated for two days. On Thursday he consulted his advisers late into the night. By Friday he had found the form of words which he hoped would bury the issue:

'We will negotiate with Trident and with the policy line that comes with all that operational weaponry, the policy line that never says "yes" or "no" to the question "will you press the nuclear button?" That is the combination of nuclear weaponry and the doctrine of uncertainty that is woven into it that we shall inherit. And it is that combination, the whole package, that we shall use in negotiations to secure nuclear disarmament by ourselves and by others. It is an inextricable combination, and the reason for that is that as long as the weapons exist, the assumption by others will be that there may be circumstances in which those weapons might be used.'

In October the Labour Party conference voted on the new defence paper. The 1988 majority in favour of unilateralism was easily overturned. Vigorous debate continued within the party but from now on the leadership line was assured. The last hurdle had been cleared. At the Conservative Party conference a week later Margaret Thatcher tried to rescuscitate the debate that had brought her so much electoral gain during the 1980s. She argued that the Labour Party was still unilateralist at heart and that the changes were only cosmetic. This is likely to continue to be a leitmotif of Conservative Party campaigning through to the next general election. But, so far as British political commentators were concerned, October 1989 was the month in which the stormy and idiosyncratic British defence debate of the 1980s finally expired.

NOTES

1. Revolutions in English/British foreign policy are rare. It is possible to argue that since the end of Roman Britain there have only been three: the Norman Conquest, when, through its ruling dynasty, England became a continental land power; the sixteenth century, when, with the loss of Calais and acquisition of transatlantic interests, England began to become a maritime/colonial power; the second half of the twentieth century, when Britain lost her empire, and, with some reluctance, began to accept a future in Europe. There are those who still dream that it might be possible to return, if not to post-Norman and post-Tudor land and sea empire, then at any rate to Anglo-Saxon off-shore independence. King Harold is the tragic symbol of this cause.
2. 'The Soviet threat is the starting point for everything we do in defence', George Younger, Secretary of State for Defence, in Oliver Ramsbotham, *Choices: Nuclear and Non-Nuclear Defence Options*, Brasseys, 1987, p. 458.

As a result 'the vast majority of our forces are committed to four main roles in NATO and make a major contribution to the Alliance strategies of flexible response and forward defence', *Statement on the Defence Estimates*, 1989, HMSO, vol. 1, p. 13.

The four main roles being:

    a. A contribution to extended deterrence through the Polaris submarine force at strategic level, and free-fall bombs, nuclear depth bombs, Lance surface-to-surface missiles and nuclear capable artillery at sub-strategic level. Polaris missiles are targeted for selective theatre use through NATO's Supreme Allied Commander's Supplementary Plan, and for general nuclear response through the American Single Integrated Operational Plan.

    b. A contribution to the task of protecting the Atlantic supply routes for US reinforcements and the UK itself as an 'unsinkable' offshore aircraft carrier in case of Soviet advance on the mainland.

    c. A contribution to the forward defence of the European mainland through the commitment of one army corps (BAOR) to the Northern Army Group in West Germany, and fifteen squadrons of aircraft (RAF Germany) to the Second Allied Tactical Air Force.

    d. A contribution of maritime forces to 'forward maritime defence' in the Eastern Atlantic and the Channel.

However psychologically understandable the obsession of the British defence debate of the 1980s with the question of 'independent' deterrence or defence may have been, it can be seen to have been operationally irrelevant. France, which shared a comparable ex-imperial reluctance to face facts, left NATO's integrated military command in 1966 and developed her own long-range submarine-launched missiles, intermediate-range and short-range land-launched missiles, and air-to-surface air-launched missiles with accompanying distinct deterrent doctrine and targeting plan. This may have been 'folie de grandeur', belied in practice by unacknowledged French dependence on NATO strategy and American nuclear know-how, but there was at any rate some substance to the claim that in France the question of 'independent' deterrence (dissuasion) and defence was a real one. In Britain it was not, and the continuing British refusal to argue defence and deterrence issues in a truly European context revealed, not only self-delusion and insularity, but ignorance of what the reality of Britain's defence commitments actually were.

3. Although in the 1950s and early 1960s Britain's nuclear force of Valiant, Victor and Vulcan bombers equipped with free-fall and stand-off nuclear weapons (like the Blue Steel missile) were semi-independent like French nuclear weapons today, the Polaris deal with the United States made Britain entirely dependent on American technology for strategic delivery systems. In addition, unlike France, Britain provided bases for American nuclear weapons (submarines and aircraft), and manned short-range missiles and artillery in Germany which fired American nuclear warheads kept under American control via the dual-key system. When

Britain wanted to acquire a sub-strategic air-to-surface missile she had to choose between dependence on American or French technology.

4. Christopher Coker, IEDS Occasional paper 34, 1988, pp. 16–20.

5. Mike Gapes, 'The Evolution of Labour's Defence and Security Policy', in Gordon Burt (ed.), *Alternative Defence Policy*, Croom Helm, 1988, p. 82: 'part of the problem was that a study group set up in 1981 had not completed its work at the time Mrs Thatcher called the 1983 General Election one year early'.

6. The first disadvantage was shown up on 25 May when, on a Sunday morning television interview, David Frost asked Neil Kinnock what he would do if the Russians were about to invade Britain. The reply failed to convince, ending with a reference to guerrilla warfare. The national press seized on this the next day, thus apparently giving substance to the Conservative Party poster of a British soldier with his hands up above the slogan 'Labour's Defence Policy'.

   The second disadvantage was demonstrated during Neil Kinnock's visit to Washington on 27 March 1987, when Ronald Reagan gave him less than the agreed half hour followed by a dismissive White House press briefing afterwards. This contrasted with a rapturous welcome for Margaret Thatcher one week later.

7. *Defence and Security for Britain*, NEC policy statement, 1984; *The Power to Defend our Country*, Labour Party policy statement as part of the 'Modern Britain in a Modern World' campaign, 1986.

   The British peace movement gained in professionalism and expertise during the 1980s, with CND expanding its theoretical range, European Nuclear Disarmament (END) acquiring an imposing reputation in Europe and building links with the democracy movements across the Iron Curtain, the Oxford Research Group (ORG) unravelling the intricacies of nuclear weapon decision-making worldwide, the British American Information Council (BASIC) tapping the vast information potential across the Atlantic, the Verification Technology Information Centre (VERTIC) becoming an acknowledged authority on all aspects of verification. The work of the Alternative Defence Commission familiarised British thinkers with European research into non-provocative defence, while university departments like the ADIU at Sussex and the School of Peace Studies at Bradford contributed expertise to match that found in the Whitehall ministries. Individual authors like Frank Blackaby and Robert Neild, both former directors of the Stockholm International Peace Research Institute (SIPRI), and Ken Booth of University College Wales integrated this material into a coherent alternative agenda. Organisations like Greenpeace helped to link the peace movement to other elements, particularly environmental, which went to make up the overall transformationist programme.

   The general reaction of the peace movement was disillusionment with the parochialism and limitations of British politics, with the Labour Party for failing to develop a vigorous alternative agenda, with the Conservative government for stifling independent debate, and with the media for letting them get away with it – a reaction with which the authors of this book sympathise.

8. See Labour's 1987 election manifesto based on the policy statements cited in n. 7.
9. NATO's dual track approach (modernisation and arms control) was an application of the 1967 Harmel principle. It represented an attempt to compromise between conservative rearmers (particularly in the United States) who rejected arms control, and disarmers who rejected modernisation. Britain was seen to lean one way and Germany and the Netherlands the other.
10. Apparently on the insistence of the West German and Dutch governments the idea of negotiation down to 'equal ceilings' in land-based SNF (short-range) missiles at some future date was included in NATO communiqués from June 1987. The prevailing opinion within the British defence establishment seems to have been that the INF Treaty had eliminated the wrong weapons. Had the longer-range Pershing II and Cruise missiles been kept, then the shorter range systems would perhaps have been expendable, but now their retention and modernisation were seen to be essential.
11. Throughout 1989 and into 1990 the British government was almost alone in continuing to insist on a 'firebreak' of short range nuclear weapons in Germany.
12. See Oliver Ramsbotham, *Modernising NATO's Nuclear Weapons*, Oxford Research Group, Macmillan, 1989, Chs 9, 11, 12; Scilla Elworthy, *Who Decides? Accountability and Nuclear Weapon Decision-Making In Britain*, Oxford Research Group, 1986; Scilla Elworthy, *In The Dark*, Oxford Research Group, 1989.
13. A Gallup poll conducted by the Institute for European Defence and Strategic Studies in June 1988 found that of 116 Conservative MPs questioned (a third of whom said that they specialised in defence) only 16 knew the name of the Secretary General of NATO and only 7 knew the name of the Supreme Allied Commander. Labour MPs fared only marginally better.
14. As the party of government Conservative Party policy was most carefully set out in Statements on the Defence Estimates and Ministry of Defence and Foreign Office policy papers.
15. The vigorous scrutiny to which United States presidential policy is subjected by Congress is well-known. The German system of parliamentary committees has been described, as well as the exchange of personnel between ministries and parliamentary parties. NATO nuclear weapon policy was openly discussed in the Dutch and Danish parliaments, with ministers answering substantial questions instead of evading them as in Britain (see example on pp 193–4 of Ramsbotham, *Modernizing NATO's Nuclear Weapons*).
16. See, in addition to separate policy statements by the two Alliance parties, the joint Defence and Disarmament report of June 1986.
17. Jean Lambert of the British Green Party is prominent in the Green Euro-MPs' policy coordinating bodies.
18. See the account in Colin Hughes and Patrick Wintour, *Labour Rebuilt*, Fourth Estate, 1990.

7 1990: The Debate that Wasn't

It was during 1990 that the new European agenda at last erupted into British politics. The Conservative government of Margaret Thatcher was overthrown among other things on the issue of Europe. The momentum of integration carried Britain inexorably into the exchange rate mechanism, and questions of economic and political union came to dominate the headlines. Yet one aspect of this process remained Cinderella-like in the background. Although inseparable from all the other elements, it was passed over. Because 'defence' was no longer seen to be a contentious issue, the whole security dimension was ignored. In the next chapter the spectrum of British party political opinion on security questions will be set out to show how in general it already mirrored the spread of opinion in other European countries such as Germany. But in Britain, for what can only be called cultural reasons, the political background was missing so that the embryonic debate remained unnoticed, unpublicised and undeveloped. For different reasons it suited the two main parties to play it down, the smaller parties were unable to generate interest and the whole subject was considered by the media to be too complicated, too technical or too unfamiliar to merit full analysis and coverage.

1 THE CONSERVATIVE PARTY

'I spoke to you first as leader of our party in 1975. I remember it so well. Freedom was in retreat; the countries of Eastern Europe seemed crushed for ever under the communist heel. But I said then that we were coming to a turning-point in our history. Few believed it, but that turning-point came in 1979, for we Conservatives were the pathfinders. We didn't know it at the time, but the torch we lit in

Britain which transformed our country, the torch of freedom that is now the symbol of our party, became the beacon that has shed its light across the Iron Curtain into the East. Today that beacon shines more strongly than at any time this century. You can see it in the faces of the young people from the communist countries who have reached the West. Like most young people the world over, they have resolved to make their own way, to achieve success by their own efforts, to live the life they choose as part of a free world. They are retelling the story of our history. We can't know the direction in which free nations in their future will progress, but this we do know and dare not forget: only those whose commitment to free enterprise and opportunity is a matter of conviction and not convenience have the necessary strength to sustain them. Only those who have shown the resolve to defend the freedom of the West can be trusted to safeguard it in the challenging, turbulent and unpredictable times that lie ahead.'[1]

This was how the situation was described by the Prime Minister in the autumn of 1989. A year later the same sentiments were expressed at the Conservative Party conference in October 1990 and projected to the country at large in a party political broadcast on 17 October. The sound-track to the broadcast was 'Land of Hope and Glory'. The brief film purported to thank Central and East European vistors for having accepted an invitation to the conference. In fact it used them to suggest that the Conservative government was responsible for the success of the 1989 revolutions and to discredit Labour Party socialism by associating it with the old communist regimes.

But there was no desire to involve wider discussion about the options that had been opened up as a result. Together with triumphalism about the past went a determination to suppress serious public debate about the future. The domestic political interests of the Conservative Party lay in trying to revive the old British agenda of the 1980s, not entering the uncharted waters of the European security debate of the 1990s. So it was that on 9 October the party chairman, Kenneth Baker, duly told the party conference that Labour had 'changed the rhetoric but not the reality' of its defence policy. He accused Labour of being prepared to leave Britain open to nuclear blackmail by abandoning the deterrent in exchange for minor cuts in Soviet forces. On 14 October in her closing speech at the conference the Prime Minister said that the prospect of Saddam Hussein getting nuclear weapons showed how misguided Labour unilateralism was.

But the rest was silence. Like any government, the Conservative government wanted to minimise unwelcome publicity in sensitive areas, keep control of the dissemination of information, make decisions in private and present policy in the most favourable light at times and places of its own choosing. To this end it would use whatever powers were available to it. In the defence field in Britain these powers were great. There were no coalition partners to worry about, no significant independent voices from within the Conservative Party, no involvement whatsoever of opposition parties, no dissemination of information beyond a narrow band of professionals sworn to secrecy, no media interest, no background knowledge in general through the country about the nature of European collective security arrangements and Britain's part in them. For a decade one party had been able to employ the resources of the Foreign Office and the Ministry of Defence to present its policy as 'multilateralist' as against the 'unilateralism' of Labour. The crucial passages in the annual *Statement on the Defence Estimates* (the most recent appearing in April 1990) were written, not by ministers, but by the most able senior civil servants, which prompted criticism of the politicisation of the civil service. For example, in March 1990 the Foreign Office and the Ministry of Defence produced an updated joint publicity pack for the general public called *Arms Control & Defence: The Vital Issues*. It passed over almost every issue analysed in Chapter 2, and concentrated its polemic instead on defending what it described as the government's 'multilateral approach' from the 'one-sided gestures' of 'unilateral arms control'.

In July an interim announcement was made on the 'options for change studies' prepared in the Ministry of Defence by the defence staff and the Office of Management and Budget. The outline programme was more radical than some had expected – certainly radical enough to invite criticism from those who thought it too bold as well as those who thought it too cautious. The point being made here, however, is that once again a handful of senior civil servants was conducting the operation behind closed doors as if 'defence' was still an apolitical matter, and commentators, habituated to this British tradition, were accepting it. The idea that conclusions about defence could only be derived from wider security judgements within a European context, and that these involved political questions which were already defined across the political spectrum in other European countries, seemed to have no takers. The wider political community was excluded. No attempt was made in public to compare possible alternatives, assess advantages and disadvantages and relate conclusions to coherent foreign policy priorities. The exercise was presented as a fait accompli, or rather as a minimalist interim report on a secret process which was still being worked out in detail away from the glare of publicity. There was a reference to 'discussions yet to come with the NATO authorities and with our allies', but experience suggested that these would be just as carefully shielded from the public gaze. In answer to the accusation that there was no sign that real 'options' had been considered at all, the name Alan Clark (minister for defence procurement) was mentioned and one or two bold suggestions were attributed to him. But, when the interim report was made public, everyone was assured that there had after all been no substantial quarrel. The British tradition does not allow differences of opinion within parties. They are treated as potential scandals rather than normal and healthy manifestations of political pluralism. It is all part of the two-party adversarial monopoly where alternatives are presented as starkly black and white and there is no room for variety within consensus of the kind found in other countries – such as Germany.[2]

In short, it is hardly a distortion to say that throughout 1990 the sum total of the Conservative Party contribution to public debate about the future of European and British security policy amounted to (a) an assertion that these are times of hope but also uncertainty so the government must maintain the robust defences which have brought us safely to where we are now, (b) an admission that changing circumstances do mean a certain amount of adaptation, (c) a claim that this is best left to the proper authorities to work out in secret with Britain's allies, and (d) an assurance that in due course we will all no doubt be told some of the details of what they have decided.

2 THE LABOUR PARTY

How does the record of the Labour Party compare?

Once again in principle the issues were described as being of the greatest importance. The sense of mission was just as intense, this time unequivocally aligned to the transformationist agenda:

'Only the Labour Party "can establish the principles of non-offensive defence and common security, not only at the top of the NATO agenda, but at the centre of Europe as well" and "rid Britain of nuclear weapons as part of a process that will move towards ridding our entire planet of nuclear weapons". "It is not only the victims of Thatcher's deceptions in Britain who need a Labour government. The prospect of a Labour government is a beacon of hope for millions of starving and oppressed people throughout the world."'[3]

But was this reflected in a real determination to generate serious public debate on these issues? During 1990 it was not.

In private Labour leaders expressed confidence that the security cards were now firmly in their hands. It was the Labour Party, not the Conservative government, which understood current European realities and had the policies to enable Britain to play a central role in the creation of a new European and global security order. The 1989 policy review paper *Meet the Challenge, Make the Change* had put it like this:

'Our overriding charge against the Tories is that they regard weapons, and especially nuclear weapons, as an end in themselves. Their foreign policy is often reactionary and negative. Within its context they tend to treat defence as a discrete issue, separate from and all too often uninfluenced by other highly relevant issues. Clausewitz said that "war is nothing more than the continuation of politics by other means". So, too, is peace. Defence cannot logically, usefully or constructively be considered except in the context of other world developments . . . For ten years the Tories have not talked about peace through negotiation because they do not believe in peace through negotiation. They are alone in NATO and the Warsaw Pact in being stuck hopelessly in the outdated and destructive language and thought-processes of the Cold War.'

Since then, the argument went on, events had borne out Labour's position. On the widening of the scope of conventional force reductions, the abandonment of a 'follow-on' to Lance, progress in the direction of a 'third zero', moves towards the scrapping of 'flexible response', and so on, the government had been forced to accept Labour recommendations. *Looking to the Future* summed up the situation:

'The present government, and Mrs Thatcher herself, have little understanding of the changes taking place. On issue after issue they stand alone.'

This broad critique was drawn from careful coordination in recent years with other European socialist/social democratic parties. As long ago as November 1986 the British Labour Party and what was described as its 'West German sister party', the SPD, had produced a lengthy joint policy statement covering the whole of the security field. Since then in the words of Labour's most experienced security policy researcher:

> 'Whereas in 1980 Labour and the SPD were a very long way apart on issues like their attitude to NATO's "double track" decision, now they are much closer and both recognise the need to reach common positions and further develop their growing relationship in the future.'[4]

Labour thinking was said to be in tune with the broad German SPD/FDP position as well as with the defence thinking of other NATO and non-NATO socialist governments such as those in Belgium, the Netherlands and Norway. In Britain Labour had won the June 1989 European elections, and since then the 45 Labour MEPs had been coordinating policy within the socialist/social democratic Parliamentary Group, which commanded a progressive majority in the European parliament. The claim here once again was that the Conservatives had 'stood on the sidelines' and 'the Conservative government has seemed determined to be alone, aloof and adrift from Europe'.[5]

Yet, despite all this, the top priority at home so far as security policy went was still judged to be damage limitation. Labour was seen to be vulnerable on 'defence' as understood in the 1980s, and conditions were not right for familiarising British voters with the new security agenda of the 1990s. Peter Mandelson's communications and campaigns directorate was said to have concluded that defence could lose votes but not win them. The target voter, the Midland car worker, would never understand the real defence debate. The media was too biassed. In addition large numbers of jobs in Labour constituencies depended on defence contracts. For Labour to become 'fire-proof' on defence, it would have to present itself as impeccably respectable and responsible – a tedious role for members of a radical party to play, but a necessary one. It was the strong opinion of some of Neil Kinnock's closest advisers that there was in any case no point in developing specific policies while the party was in opposition. First gain power, then use it. So no attempt was made to explain in detail what broad policy references to 'common security' and to a shared Euro-socialist security agenda meant.[6]

If the aim of the operation was to bury the defence debate, then the enterprise was partially successful. When the party's outline policy document *Looking to the Future* appeared in May 1990, the *Independent* listed the 'ten main points' on its front page. Nine of them were domestic. Only one was to do with the future of Europe and that was an item on British entry into the European Exchange Rate Mechanism. On the other hand, in the absence of a strong Labour lead in other directions, what media interest there was remained stuck in the 1980s rut. For example, Robin Oakley, interviewing Neil Kinnock on Labour's new agenda for *The Times* in September 1990 on the eve of the Labour Party conference, kept pressing only one question in the security field. It was a familiar one. Was Labour prepared to give up the British deterrent while others kept theirs? The entire European security debate was passed by.[7] By the end of 1990 the more moderate language adopted by the new Tory leadership and the cross-party consensus on the Gulf crisis in Parliament had further strengthened the general impression that there was now no significant difference between Labour Party and Conservative Party policy on security.

3 THE LIBERAL DEMOCRATS

Perhaps the most thoughtful policy papers produced in 1990 came from the Liberal Democrats. *Reshaping Europe*, appearing shortly before the party conference in September, covered the security field, and was intended to be read in conjunction with *A Europe for Democrats* on the development of the European Community and *Shared Earth* on sustainable world development. These documents claimed as traditional Liberal Democrat territory: devolution and democratic pluralism (including proportional representation and a Bill of Rights); full participation in the process of European integration; long-standing concern for the environment; investment in education and training in line with European practice. In marked contrast to Alliance policy papers from before the 1987 general election, there was now no criticism of Labour Party policy in the security field. Current Conservative government policy, however, was roundly condemned. The Government was seen to have been isolated, both at Strasbourg in December 1989:

'The European Council meeting in Strasbourg marked the point when the Prime Minister's self-imposed and fiercely maintained isolation from the dynamics of European integration reached its logical conclusion, which is to render Britain almost entirely irrelevant to the process';

and at the NATO summit in London in July 1990:

'Under the influence of President Bush NATO is now turning into an active proponent of demilitarisation. As is all too common at international gatherings, the British Prime Minister found herself substantially out of tune with the consensus . . . We welcome both its conclusions and her irrelevance.'

The emphasis, both in the policy papers and in the debate on 'European Affairs and Defence' at the party conference on 19 September 1990 (where the central motion recommended by the leadership was passed unamended) was on the need to evolve a common foreign, and therefore security, policy within Europe. Unlike the Conservative and Labour Parties, the Liberal Democrats openly stressed the need to 'set aside national sovereignty when necessary'[8] and to embrace 'international over national means of achieving security'.[9] The party was also more radical in demanding that security policy, both at national and international levels, should now be rethought from the ground up. Examples of this analysis will be given below. It remains to be seen whether British newspaper and television reporters take any more notice of these careful policy statements in the months ahead than they did of the equally careful 1989 policy statement *After the Cold War*.

4   THE GREEN PARTY

In contrast to the effectiveness of its contribution to heightening awareness of environmental issues since its founding in 1973, the British Green Party (originally the Ecology Party) was slower than many of its counterparts across the Channel to develop what it called the 'peace and defence' component of its security policy. A series of detailed draft proposals were formulated for the party conference in September 1990, however, and these, together with the debate on them, gave a good idea of the likely shape of future party policy in this area. It was perhaps harder for the Green Party than for other parties to formulate an official 'peace and defence' position, first, because of the general party aversion to policy being imposed from above, second, because the defence field was in any case one which a number of Green supporters found uncongenial in the first place. Or, rather, the pacifist wing of the party was averse to the 'militarist' overtones that were still seen to cling to concepts of common security and defensive defence when they were worked out in detail. Like other British opposition parties, the Green Party could draw on the impressive array of research expertise marshalled within the British peace movement, including full participation in every aspect of the new European debate. But lack of funds severely restricted the scope for thorough independent alternative policy research, a fundamental weakness in British politics. Some equivalent to the £1.5 million which the West German Greens earned in the 1979 European elections by winning a much smaller percentage of the vote than the British Greens won ten years later would have transformed the situation.

At the Green Party conference itself in the autumn of 1990 media interest in the security field was diverted from this programme by the denunciation of Western military intervention in the Gulf by a number of Green Party spokespersons.

5 SIGNS OF CHANGE

In 1990 British politics did not engage with the European security debate at all. This was symptomatic of a deeper malaise – a failure to come to terms with the fact that Britain no longer had an independent global role to play and that her destiny lay in Europe. Despite the fact that British defence had been dependent upon the United States and the cooperation of European partners for more than forty years, the implications of this revolution in foreign policy had still not been borne in upon the country at large. The Falklands Task Force and the dispatch of the Desert Rats to the Gulf fitted in with memories of previous imperial and colonial enterprises (despite the fact that the equipment sent came from Northern Norway and Germany respectively and had been procured as part of NATO strategic planning). The idea of an 'independent' deterrent revived memories of Britain standing on its own against the Armada or Napoleon's armies or Hitler's air assault. The unglamorous reality of the vast and complex multinational NATO command structure that Britain's nuclear and non-nuclear forces were actually committed to did not evoke a comparable response. Among the establishment élite the traditional rivalry with France often seemed stronger than the idea of shared security interests (this was for some the main reason why Britain must keep nuclear weapons). Conversely, the 'special relationship' with the United States, widely interpreted on the continent as clienthood, was more flatteringly thought of in Britain as partnership in world leadership (the fact that Britain's deterrent was entirely dependent upon American technology was brushed under the carpet). As for Europe, the reality of progressive economic and political integration, steadily advancing throughout the 1980s, had no historical echoes and so was not noticed. Belatedly in 1990 the danger of a loss of sovereignty through closer cooperation with European partners was suddenly proclaimed. The idea that failure to modernise British society along European lines had already led to a significant loss of sovereignty and would lead to a great deal more unless Britain became properly competitive, was not understood. Clinging to the assumption that the British parliament was a unique bastion of democracy which must on no account be sacrificed to continental bureaucracy, there was little close scrutiny of how it compared in its workings and effectiveness with what was going on elsewhere. The possibility that it might in some ways be less democratic and effective seemed not to be envisaged, as also the possibility that almost non-existent public provision for vigorous alternative policy research might be a serious weakness in a modern democracy.

NOTES

1. Margaret Thatcher, Conservative Party Conference, Blackpool, 13 October 1989.
2. The secrecy of the 'options for change' process was such that in response to the July interim statement by the Secretary of State for Defence, commentators could say little more than this:

   'Until we see the ultimate form of the firm commitments to change, fears must persist that the Ministry of Defence has skirted the edges of the problem, rather than recast the armed forces as decisively as is necessary. On the basis of today's statement, Britain will find itself spending not only a higher proportion of gross national product on defence than Germany with all its economic might, but also a larger cash sum. We may explain the figures by pointing to our nuclear deterrent and greater naval commitments. But a fundamental question must remain about the manner in which we deploy our limited national resources in the last years of the 20th century. The public, as well as the

Government, should consider and discuss this proposition in the months to come' (*Daily Telegraph* leader, 26 July 1990).

This interview with Alan Clark, the minister most often cited as an example of bold and innovative thinking, shows the sphinx-like discretion maintained by the British establishment. By the time 'ample time for debate' is allowed, government decision-making is a fait accompli and there is little left beyond a damage-limitation public relations exercise to protect its already adopted policy from undue public scrutiny (BBC Radio 4, 'Today' 31 May 1990, Media Transcription Service, ref. no. 757 [edited]):

PRESENTER: Is there a difference of opinion between you and Tom King, the Defence Secretary, about when and if and to what extent we should be cashing in the so-called 'peace dividend'?

ALAN CLARK: Absolutely not. Tom King is a personal friend and we are working very closely on this.

P: But is it true that you sent a set of recommendations to Mrs Thatcher and that he does not agree with that set of recommendations?

AC: It's true that I wrote a paper many months ago and that paper is secret. And it must remain secret.

P: Why?

AC: Well, because at this stage the Secretary of State is considering all the options and he has to cast his net very wide and in the fulness of time he will decide what he includes and what he rejects.

P: But did Mr King approve you sending that set of recommendations to Mrs Thatcher?

AC: Oh yes. The paper was circulated at the time on a very narrow basis – it went to the Prime Minister, the Treasury and the Foreign Office.

P: And what did the Defence Secretary think of it?

AC: Well, he had thoughts at the time and these thoughts have developed since. But you shouldn't ask one person to comment on the thoughts of another. We are working as a team.

P: If this debate were being conducted in public, there would be no misunderstanding. Why can it not be conducted in public?

AC: I don't think it's ready to be conducted in public yet, because in the very nature of things much of the material we are looking at is highly classified and you can't make decisions until you evaluate figures and forecasts and orders of battle and deployment which are very very secret. But in the fulness of time, when we decide the kind of recommendations we are going to put to colleagues in Government and to the House of Commons, there will be ample time for debate.

P: Let me ask you then about a few matters of perhaps broad principle. Should we be considering fewer frigates? Smaller British Army of the Rhine? Half the number of infantry battalions? Reducing our Trident forces?

AC: Well I wouldn't want to go into particular figures. And I would say that most of the figures allegedly quoted from my paper were inaccurate, which heartens me because it shows noone has actually read that paper except those to whom it was circulated. But certainly the broad headings you mention are being considered. They are all part of the input which Tom King has entitled 'options for change'.

3. Martin O'Neill and Gerald Kaufman, Labour Party Conference, Brighton, 2 October 1989.
4. Mike Gapes, 'The Evolution of Labour's Defence and Security Policy', in Gordon Burt (ed.), *Alternative Defence Policy*, Croom Helm, 1988, p. 90.
5. Labour National Executive Council Report, 8 September 1990, p. 40.
6. Colin Hughes and Patrick Wintour, *Labour Rebuilt*, Fourth Estate, 1990, and conversations with Gerald Kaufman, Martin O'Neill and Charles Clarke.
7. *The Times*, 17 September 1990.
8. Preamble to Liberal Democrat constitution.
9. *Reshaping Europe: Liberal Democrat Policies for East–West Relations*, Federal White Paper 3, used in final draft form, August 1990, p. 9.

8 Outline of the New British Security Debate

Despite the inhibitions against public discussion just noted, the outline of a new British security debate is already clearly visible. It is undeveloped and as yet virtually ignored in public, but is comparable in subject matter and range to the debate currently going on in other West European countries such as Germany. This is not surprising, since these countries share many if not most of the same security interests as Britain and have a broadly similar party political system. It is by its nature an international debate, both in terms of subject matter (it deals with policy areas which are in essence multi-national) and form (it is made up of a spectrum of opinion common throughout the Western democracies). As in Germany the root of the debate can be seen to be a dialogue between the 'realist' and 'trans-formationist' poles around which the political spectrum gravitates.

What follows are openly stated party political positions as of spring 1991, not the private opinions or intentions of party leaders. Keeping to this brief may forfeit subtlety, but has the merit of bringing out the dynamics of the public debate more clearly.[1]

1 THE THREAT TO SECURITY

Most of Britain's defence resources are still committed to NATO's central region and are shaped and structured for instant response and rapid reinforcement against massive surprise Soviet frontal attack. Ministry of Defence and Foreign Office statements make it clear that, despite recent changes, 'in looking at our defence requirements our primary concern is the military capability of the Soviet Union and its

156

allies'. The signature of a CFE agreement and its implementation over the next few years would eliminate 'the present superiority of the Warsaw Pact over NATO in conventional arms', but 'modernisation and improvement of Soviet forces has continued, particularly in their mobility and firepower' and the Soviet Union will remain a military superpower 'for the foreseeable future'. In a submission to the House of Commons Select Committee on Defence published in July 1990 the Secretary of State for Defence acknowledged that warning times were 'under examination', but cautioned that in terms of capabilities the equipment now being supplied to Soviet forces in East Germany was of higher quality and greater scale 'than it has ever been in their history'. The prospect of either a hard-line reaction in the Soviet Union or a slide towards anarchy underlines how important it is to maintain sound defence as an insurance policy. The shifting of equipment East of the Urals and from land to naval forces so as to evade CFE restrictions is seen to show how the Soviet military can pursue policies which seem to be at odds with the professed intentions of political leaders.[2]

In addition to the continuing Soviet threat, ministers have warned against uncertainty and danger elsewhere:

> 'To those who suggest that it's bound to come out all right, there is a two-word answer – Tiananmen Square' (October 1989); 'We have had Ceaucescu and Securitate, Azerbaijan, Lithuania . . . People now understand that there are still problems in the world and we do need to stick together' (March 1990); 'There is always and will always be evil in human nature and we never know where the next threat may come from – as the Iraqi invasion of Kuwait has shown in the last two days' (August 1990).[3]

In contrast to this emphasis on direct military threats to the West, both the Labour Party and the Liberal Democrats acknowledge continuing danger in Europe such as ethnic unrest in Eastern Europe and turmoil in the Soviet Union ('formidable hazards remain' and 'the situation contains dangers'), but stress that, whatever happens in the Soviet Union, 'there is now no realistic threat of invasion from the East' and 'the threat from a united Warsaw Pact no longer exists'. As a result, the Labour Party insists that 'the role of NATO must be fundamentally reassessed' and the Liberal Democrats maintain that the time has come to 'embark on the task of establishing a lasting peaceful order in Europe'.[4]

Beyond this, both parties see what might be called common or global threats, such as mutually aggressive military strategies, weapon proliferation, economic imbalances East/West and North/South and environmental hazards as the greatest dangers:

'It is obvious that the main threat to human survival comes from the thermonuclear weapons possessed by five countries. Another threat, less easy to counter through great power negotiation, comes from the proliferation of lower-grade nuclear weapons, now possessed by or within the capacity of far too many other countries in such regions as the Middle East, the Indian sub-continent, Southern Africa and South America.'[5]

'The arms race, tension in East-West relations, the threat to the world environment, imbalances in world trade, the sapping of the resources of developing countries by the developed world: all of these are or could be threats to the world's future.'[6]

For the Green Party:

'The division of the world into several armed camps is symptomatic of our failure to live peacefully with our neighbours, and of our false belief that conflict is inevitable and can be solved by violence. Green policies on international trade and foreign affairs are intended as a contribution towards a world of peace. The new era has a bitter lesson for us: if we are to survive we must unlearn the old glib solutions. The present environmental destruction threatens our common survival and can only be met effectively by common and cooperative responses. A new alliance is required – a global alliance of the forces of nature and spiritual strength of humankind . . . In the future, either peace will be our common security, or we perish together.'[7]

2   THE RESPONSE

The present British government is adamant that, although changing circumstances in Europe will have implications for force structures and deployment:

'The basic elements remain firm – the vital role of the Atlantic Alliance, and of the presence of United States forces in Europe as its military keystone; the need for nuclear weapons to help prevent war; the continuing value of a British contribution in Germany; and the importance of flexibility and versatility in our forces for roles beyond as well as within NATO . . . In a fundamentally uncertain world the need for collective security will remain.'[8]

The continuing importance of forward defence ('if you do not defend your frontiers in NATO where do you stand?')[9] and flexible response ('the best means of deterring war remains flexible response')[10] are also stressed, although in the light of the 1991 NATO review forward defence no longer implies massive deployment along what was the inner German border. As for flexible response, whatever the outcome of the review (and even if the term itself is dropped) the keeping open of the option of a first use of nuclear weapons and the retention of a capacity for graded conventional and nuclear response is considered essential.

The aim is to plan for smaller, better-equipped forces, with greater flexibility, mobility and all-round capability. Stationed forces in Germany will be halved, with more emphasis on the building of a strategic reserve division and the retention of air mobile and amphibious capabilities. There will be a reduction of 18 per cent in regular services manpower by the mid-1990s and a destroyer/frigate force of around 40 ships. But it is seen to be essential to maintain all-round quality in every department because defence professionalism can be easily built down but not nearly so easily built up again.[11] Major programmes like the European Fighter Aircraft, a new British main battle tank, a new nuclear air-to-surface missile, and so on, are considered essential, as is continued investment in research and development of new weapons systems of all kinds. Although inter-operability among NATO allies is important, neither multinational forces below, say, division level, nor role specialisation by nation is thought advisable. If Britain did hive off a particular skill and became dependent on another country to provide it, Britain's freedom of action would be undermined. In general, we face an uncertain future full of dangers and need to be prepared with all-round capabilities of every kind to meet them.[12]

The Labour Party begins from the premise that 'in the 1990s and beyond Britain must be properly defended'. There is no question of a future Labour government doing any less than past Labour govern-ments to see that this is so. But in view of the fact that the Warsaw Pact no longer exists as a military alliance and Soviet troops will probably be out of Eastern Europe by 1994, it is absurd to pretend that NATO strategy remains essentially unchanged. The reformulation of NATO strategy in 1991 is seen to be in line with long-standing Labour policy. 'Forward defence has gone' and 'flexible response based on nuclear weapons has collapsed'.[13] Instead, the signing of the CFE agreement in November 1990 opens the way to a fundamental restructuring of forces throughout Europe in line with 'the concept and the practice of "defensive defence", sometimes referred to as "non-provocative" or "non-offensive" defence'. In this way 'disarmament, properly negotiated and properly verified' would become 'an increasingly key element in the defence of Britain' and emphasis would shift to the principles of common security:

> 'In the 1930s Labour was the first party to urge collective security to prevent war and to urge defence planning when war became inevitable. For the 1990s Labour is the only party to insist that we adopt common security as the means to make peace inevitable.'[14]

A Labour government on taking office 'will immediately initiate the widest possible defence review that will look at our commitments worldwide and our ability to pay for them'.[15] Details cannot be determined before then, but for one experienced former Labour defence minister the European Fighter Aircraft is no longer needed, there is a question-mark over a new main battle tank likely to be inappropriate both in Europe and out-of-area, it would be better for Britain to concentrate on sea-air capabilities, and, in general:

> 'I hope that we are not going to drag into the 21st century the illusions of 19th century imperial grandeur which ruined us in the 20th century.'[16]

The Liberal Democrats are largely in agreement with the Labour Party, although contesting priority as advocates of the principle of common security and more thorough in following its implications through:

> 'A programme of common security is based on two commitments: international over national means of achieving security, and means that are peaceful over those that rely on the use or threatened use of force. It depends upon the acknowledgement that security is indivisible – the security of one nation cannot be bought at the expense of others. Its aim is to provide for a certainty of collective action to frustrate aggression in the international community by a law-breaker. It places particular emphasis on techniques such as crisis-management, confidence building measures, verification

arrangements and non-proliferation of armament technology. Clearly, a common security approach extends to all areas of policy that can lead to tension between nations, from economic policies to environmental issues. In terms of defence policy, a nation's security is not just a matter of strong defence: indeed, higher defence spending may even make a nation less secure, if growth of armaments fuel international tension and diversion of resources away from productive civilian investment causes economic weakness and internal dissatisfaction and instability . . . The Liberal-SDP Alliance was the first of the major UK parties to embrace this concept; we are pleased to say that it is now far more generally accepted.'[17]

The Liberal Democrats are forthright in advocating a range of measures which include the abandonment of NATO's 'deep strike' strategies in the interest of non-offensive defence, and the necessity to rethink defence requirements from the ground up within the context of pan-European negotiations:

'Future progress in disarmament should be based on the procedure known as "zero-basing". This means that the requirement for any given capability is assumed to be nil until proved otherwise, thus cutting the feet away from any approach which takes for granted that the starting point for analysis should be what exists already. In the case of armed forces, this requires that the need be reassessed against first principles. The question becomes not "how do we reduce forces currently in existence?", but "what justification is there for this level of armed forces?"'[18]

For the Green Party:

'In order to defend the UK against attack or invasion or any infringement of our rights under international law, the Green party has always believed in the necessity of an adequate defence force. Any defence policy has to ensure that acts of aggression will not be rewarded – either politically or economically – but the present UK policy of "offensive deterrence" is only one of the many options available. The Green Party will produce a defence strategy which is more credible, more stable and for which the consequences of failure would be less catastrophic. The Green party's defence policy is therefore based on five fundamental principles. Defence must be effective (unlike the insecurity created by the current "nuclear balance" system). Defence must be non-provocative. Defence must be legitimate (defence based on the mass-killing or threatened mass-killing of innocent non-combatants is contrary to established legal and moral traditions). Defence must be set in the context of a comprehensive strategy for disarmament and common security. Defence must be open and democratic and based on information available for public debate' [edited].[19]

3   THE FUTURE SECURITY ARCHITECTURE IN EUROPE

There is a range of opinion within the Conservative Party which seems to mirror that in the German CDU, although less clearly articulated. There are 'nationalists' and 'Atlanticists' as well as those who place more emphasis on the WEU and even hint at the possibility of a defence function for the European Community. But, until the resignation of Margaret Thatcher, the Government itself, in the person of the Prime Minister, was unremittingly Atlanticist:

'The defence of the West is not done in the European Community, it never has been. It is done in NATO . . . Is it really so difficult to sell people the truth, that NATO has kept the peace in Europe for over forty-five years, and that this is a longer period of peace than Europe has ever enjoyed? And therefore this system, which has kept the peace, which matters to us more than anything else, is the one which can go on keeping the peace, and will do?'[20]

The Western European Union is officially seen as the European pillar of the Atlantic Alliance, not an alternative to it, and CSCE as an addition to NATO, not a substitute. A permanent secretariat for CSCE is supported and it is a British suggestion that CSCE might evolve a conflict-resolution function. But, from a Thatcherite position, this is seen to have nothing to do with defence. Defence remains the preserve of NATO and NATO is 'the forum for our main transatlantic relationship between the United States, Canada and Europe'. The idea that 'we should enlarge that forum from a defence forum to a more political forum' is favoured (this might include some formal economic relationship between the United States and Europe), as is the possibility of developing 'out of area' roles for NATO and the WEU. The prospect of other Western, Central and Eastern European countries eventually joining the Alliance is not ruled out.[21] It is not clear how the change in the Conservative Party leadership will affect this, although it seems possible that it may lead to a steady convergence with the German CDU position.

The Labour Party also embraces a range of opinion, comparable to that in the German SPD but missing the background commitment to European integration – although this deficit is being rapidly made up by Labour MEPs within the wider socialist grouping in the European parliament. As long as NATO continues in existence 'the Labour Party is pledged and committed to membership of the Alliance'. But any idea of an 'out of area' role is rejected, and even in Europe the bloc system is regarded as outdated:

> 'We say "as long as NATO continues", because we look forward to a time when suspicion and tension between East and West will be sufficiently dispelled for both NATO and the Warsaw Pact to be dissolved.'[22]

In the meantime two reasons are given why NATO will be needed for the foreseeable future:

> 'First, we in the West need an organisation to negotiate, implement and verify disarmament agreements. Second, NATO's existence makes it unnecessary for the European Community to have any military role – something which Labour would implacably oppose.'[23]

Labour's stated reasons for opposing a defence function for the EC are that it would make the position of Eire difficult and expansion to include other neutral countries impossible, and that the Soviet Union would feel threatened if Eastern European countries joined.

Finally, although the Labour Party is still officially cautious on the prospects for a central security role for the CSCE ('All the countries of Europe now need a forum for regular discussion. A basis is provided by the Helsinki CSCE process'), many prominent members of the party are more enthusiastic:

> 'The CSCE should provide the framework for a new security system whose function will not be to protect Western Europe against invasion from the East – that threat has gone – but to police the whole of Europe against the possibility of armed conflicts arising particularly in some of the newly democratic countries. A new European security system would be a very good model for the UN as a whole. If Europe cannot produce a peace-keeping force now that it is united and democratic, then there is not much hope for the United Nations doing it.'[24]

In British politics at the moment it is left to the Liberal Democrats to place the main emphasis on the European Community in the security field. In the 1989 paper *After The Cold War* it was the WEU that was emphasised, but now:

'given the evolving integration of all other aspects of Community policy we believe that the European Community should develop a common security policy, with regular meetings of a Council of Defence Ministers and new responsibilities allocated to existing or new directorates-general of the Commission. This may require an amendment to the Treaty of Rome or the Single European Act.'

There is support for the idea of a common approach to defence procurement (saving some 20 per cent of weapons expenditure each year as a result), standardisation of military equipment, joint approaches to arms conversion and progressive integration of armed forces themselves.

But the European Community cannot guarantee the peace of Europe on its own. There is a need for a wider pan-European structure as well, and 'the obvious organisation to form the basis of this framework is CSCE'. The Helsinki Final Act should be broadened into a Treaty, there should be regular meetings at summit and ministerial levels, a secretariat and permanent agencies should be set up including provision for a peacekeeping force. 'This enhanced CSCE would be established as a regional body under the United Nations Charter and could in its turn cater for smaller groupings within it to deal with special problems and regions where this would be appropriate.'

As for NATO:

'although it is now changing its approach significantly, as shown by the London Summit in July 1990, it was still designed for a quite different purpose, is overloaded with bureaucracy and incorporates a specific and functional military command structure.'

Nevertheless, in view of current uncertainties and the difficulties involved in creating a new security framework, between the two structures of the European Community and the CSCE there will still be a transitional role for a changed NATO alliance. But 'assuming no major setbacks, we would be disappointed if NATO's existence was still proved necessary far into the next century'.[25]

The aims of the Green Party are:

'To secure the dissolution of both military alliances along with the withdrawal of all "foreign" military bases from Europe; to create in the place of NATO and the Warsaw Pact a pan-European political alliance designed to manage conflict within the European continent and to prevent the outbreak of war between member countries; and to bring about these changes in a manner designed to protect the stability of Europe, e.g. within a pan-European forum such as the Helsinki Conference on Cooperation and Security in Europe (CSCE).'[26]

4 THE ROLE OF NUCLEAR WEAPONS

Unless and until revised NATO strategy dictates otherwise, the British government still describes NATO's doctrine of flexible response as the operational context for Britain's nuclear weapon planning. The chief function of Britain's nuclear weapons is said to be to enhance the role of the Western deterrent in preventing war by complicating the thinking of Soviet planners. A second function, not officially admitted, is as a component in a possible European deterrent in case of American defection. A third function, particularly stressed in the run-up to a general election, is as a purely British weapon to protect the country standing on its own against the possibility of nuclear blackmail or attack – for example from a future nuclear-armed Gadaffi or Saddam Hussein. In this context it is described as an 'insurance policy'.[27]

Of these three functions, it is the first that has determined the configuration of present and planned British nuclear forces, which are structured almost entirely in terms of a perceived Soviet threat. In fact the actual processes which have produced and are producing these weapons are only loosely connected to the shifting rationales now being said to justify them.

'NATO members must take account of the military forces stationed in Europe, and continue to pursue a strategy that deters war of all kinds. The best means of doing this remains flexible response . . . Flexible response depends on conventional forces of sufficient size and quality to prevent an aggressor achieving a quick and easy conventional victory; second, on sub-strategic nuclear weapons which enhance deterrence by providing a range of nuclear options short of a strategic nuclear exchange; and, thirdly, strategic nuclear forces which remain the ultimate deterrent.'[28]

Britain's own strategic deterrent is to be provided from the mid-1990s by the new four-boat Trident force, and sub-strategic capabilities will be supplied by a new nuclear stand-off missile (TASM) for Britain's dual-capable Tornados (to be developed in collaboration with the United States and/or France and to be in operation by the end of the decade). A sub-strategic capability of this kind is said to be essential because:

> 'Strategic weapons alone, for all their awesome power, could not be morally tolerable, practically feasible or politically credible for every scenario.'[29]

These forces, representing Britain's contribution to NATO's 'appropriate mix of nuclear and conventional forces', are to be deployed within the context of a NATO strategy which keeps open the option of a first use of nuclear weapons in order to deter conventional as well as nuclear attack.[30] As such they are to be targeted (a) for 'selective theatre use' through NATO's Nuclear Operations Plan (NOP), and (b) for 'general nuclear response' through the American Single Integrated Operational Plan (SIOP).

All three opposition parties officially reject both NATO's flexible response strategy in general and Britain's planned sub-strategic air-to-surface missile (TASM) in particular (although Labour Party leaders now seem to be wavering on the latter)..

Of the three levels of response envisaged in flexible response, they reject the second level which keeps open the option of a first use of 'sub-strategic weapons' on the grounds that the initiation of nuclear use would 'risk a rapid escalation of nuclear war' (Liberal Democrat), 'precipitate a nuclear holocaust' (Labour) and threaten 'civilisation itself' (Green Party). The third level of response, the 'strategic nuclear exchange', is considered entirely irrational and immoral.

The Labour Party advocates multilateral negotiation down to zero as part of a fundamental reordering of the international security system. A Labour government 'will give the highest priority to achieving such progress'. It will work through the United Nations to secure a Comprehensive Test Ban Treaty and to strengthen the Non-Proliferation Treaty, arguing that it is only if all five current nuclear weapon states enter START-2 negotiations to eliminate the nuclear menace that the threat of further proliferation can be contained. The

Conservative scenario in which both Britain and, say, Iraq have nuclear weapons is rejected in favour of a scenario in which neither do.

In NATO the officially stated aim is to oppose the modernisation of short range nuclear weapons and TASM, to work for a third zero, to adopt a policy of no first use and to abandon flexible response. The reference to NATO's nuclear weapons as 'weapons of last resort' in the London Declaration of 6 July 1990 is taken as a sign that Alliance thinking is moving in Labour's direction and away from that of the Conservative government which insisted on adding 'there are no circumstances in which nuclear retaliation in response to military action might be discounted'.'[31]

According to published party policy, a Labour government would end the testing of British nuclear weapons, adopt a policy of no first use, scrap plans for the nuclear stand-off missile for Tornado (TASM) (saving 'up to £2 billion'), cancel the fourth Trident submarine, restrict the number of warheads on the remaining three and place all Britain's nuclear capabilities in START 2 negotiations with a view to 'ridding the world of nuclear weapons entirely'.[32]

The Liberal Democrats advocate a switch from flexible response, which is based on the idea that nuclear weapons can be used to deter non-nuclear attack, to minimum deterrence in which their only function is to deter others from using or threatening to use their nuclear weapons – for example 'rogue powers seeking to terrorise the world'. At global level the party urges all five nuclear weapon states to negotiate further reductions as part of an international regime to end the nuclear arms race and curb the dangers of proliferation:

'The most effective non-proliferation measure, however, would be the successful negotiation of a Comprehensive Test Ban Treaty. Britain, a depository state for the Partial Test Ban Treaty, should now call for a resumption of negotiations with all nuclear weapon states to conclude such a Treaty to outlaw all nuclear weapon tests.'

The party sees 'no military or political justification' for the deployment of any of NATO's sub-strategic systems including an American TASM. As for Britain's nuclear weapons, the four-boat Trident force must now be retained by Britain because cancellation would be too costly, but its missiles should not have more warheads than the present Polaris force, and (together with French nuclear weapons) it should be seen as 'an ultimate insurance against a loss of credibility of the US nuclear guarantee' for Britain as part of Western Europe. Beyond this, 'as far as UK holdings of free-fall bombs go, we see no argument whatsoever for their replacement by a British TASM'.[33]

The aim of the Green Party is 'immediate and unconditional nuclear disarmament'. To this end:

'The Green Party will decommission Britain's own nuclear weapons and insist on the removal of US nuclear bases. It also means the repudiation of a "nuclear umbrella" of any kind either for Britain itself or for Europe as a whole. No further research will take place into nuclear weapons and the export of nuclear technology will be stopped. Ships carrying nuclear weapons will be banned from British ports.'[34]

5   THE ALLOCATION OF RESOURCES

At the moment Britain devotes nearly 4 per cent of GDP to defence and half government R&D spending; 9000 companies are on the MOD's list of approved suppliers and about 11 per cent of British industrial production is defence related (a higher proportion than in 1979 because defence industries were protected from subsequent deindustrialisation); a million jobs are tied up in defence; the Ministry of Defence makes up a third of the civil service (over 170 000 employees); in 1989 Britain was (unusually) the third largest 'defence exporter'. The retention of top-class scientists, engineers and technologists is considered essential to maintain the quality of British defence research and sustain exports. In all, the defence budget of over £20 billion represents some 10 per cent of government spending.[35]

The present government is determined to maintain British defence capacity both for national security and economic reasons. The idea of a 'peace dividend' ('a phrase that we do not use') is seen to be illusory. There is the 'cost inflation' that afflicts defence spending (exacerbated by planning in cash), there is the need for a 'services dividend' to ensure proper conditions for service personnel, there are enhanced capabilities (such as air-lift) to be acquired, there are equipment deficiencies in quality, reliability and adequacy of spares to be made up, and so on.[36]

Planned reductions in manpower will be easily offset by all this:

'The defence capabilities of tomorrow will be very expensive and to start talking about a "peace dividend" is the typical language of opposition politics – always trying to spend the easy way and make the cheap promises. But that's not the role of government, the responsibility of government.'[37]

Having said this, according to some estimates treasury cuts already announced are likely to reduce defence spending in real terms by up to 25 per cent by the end of the decade.

As for the idea of a government-funded Arms Conversion or Arms Diversification agency:

'Government encouragement means taking money from the tax-payer to guide industry to perform some other function and we've completely rejected that. They're perfectly intelligent human beings and can make their own commercial decisons.'[38]

The Conservative government has now adopted the idea of a UN arms register. But no further measures are thought necessary to prevent arms manufacturers from making good lost markets in the developed world by stepping up sales to the Third World nor to restrict sales to regimes likely to use them for internal repression:

'Whatever the allegations about, say, Indonesian conduct in East Timor, or Israeli conduct on the West Bank or Indian conduct in Kashmir and so on, these remain essentially matters for the sovereign country concerned in relation to what it regards as an internal problem. Although they may be shocking and horrific to decent minded ¬eople who look at this, I would not regard them as being prohibiti\ , to the sale of strategic or tactical weapon systems which allow th؞se countries to defend their own sovereign independence.'[39]

Turning to the Labour Party, in 1989 and again in 1990 the leadership resisted conference calls to 'reduce defence spending to equal the average level of other West European countries' and transfer the proceeds to social services and economic regeneration in Britain. Although it is recognised that 'most people probably think that too much of the British GDP is being spent on defence', it is thought to be essential to review defence needs thoroughly before making any judgements. On the other hand, Britain spends a 'much higher proportion [of public R&D funds on defence] than our major competitors', and this should be adjusted.[40]

Above all, in contrast to the Conservative government's 'refusal to plan properly', a Labour government would establish a Defence Diversification Agency 'with the responsibility of assisting workers, communities and companies affected by changes in British defence policy. The Agency will offer expert technical and marketing advice, channel recommendations on grants and financial aid, help in civil research and assist companies to tender for public contracts.'[41]

On arms exports:

'a Labour government will immediately establish a code of conduct for the Defence Export Services Organisation and armaments manufacturers in Britain, stringently limiting the scope and scale of arms sales by Britain . . . We will refuse permission for arms sales to any country which might use them for internal repression or international aggression.'[42]

The Liberal Democrats are forthright about a 'peace dividend', which, it is claimed, if properly invested, could increase national GDP substantially by the end of the century. Germany and Japan, which are spending less on defence, are doing better economically:

'We call for a reduction of at least 50 per cent in UK defence expenditure phased in over the next ten years. This would represent a cut of about £1 billion a year from the current total of £20 billion.'[43]

The party favours a reduction in Ministry of Defence spending on military R&D, the setting up of an Arms Conversion Agency within the Department of Trade and Industry, and determined steps (i.e. closure of the Defence Export Services Organisation and a total embargo on arms sales to all countries deemed by the United Nations to be human rights violators) in conjunction with other major arms exporters to ensure that

'the progress of disarmament in Europe does not result in an increased flow of arms to the rest of the world – especially to unstable and aggressive governments.'[44]

The Green Party, in addition to measures to reduce military R&D and restrict arms sales,

'aims to achieve a 50 per cent reduction in the defence budget within five years . . . The resulting savings – a "peace dividend" of the same order of magnitude as North Sea Oil – will be shared between social, educational and health services, environmental protection, arms conversion and the relief of poverty and hunger in the Third World.'[45]

6 DECISION MAKING

The present British government sees nothing wrong with the existing system. Defence and security is perhaps the area of gravest government responsibility and it cannot be jeopardised by loose talk and a public bandying around of 'options'. The realities of threat assessment can only be properly made and responded to by those qualified to do so. Ministers know things that others do not; they must respond to capabilities not intentions; and they must make sure that allies are not embarrassed and misleading signals are not given to potential opponents in the middle of delicate disarmament talks. They are intimately responsible for maintaining the welfare and morale of those who are serving their country in the armed forces. Others, who are not responsible, can speculate freely, but

'I have to take the responsibility for the decisions. I have to take decisions and not back hunches.'[46]

As to the idea that the time has come for a full-scale public defence review, this is strongly resisted. It is thought better for the various interests represented by the FCO, the MoD, the Treasury and the Prime Minister's relevant Cabinet Committee to work it out in Whitehall in private. In this way concerted action with allied governments, coordinated where appropriate through NATO's Military Committee, High Level Task Force, etc., can go ahead smoothly.[47]

The opposition parties argue that this exaggerated paraphernalia of official secrecy is now quite unnecessary, as a comparison with the situation in other Western countries including the United States shows. For the Labour Party:

'During the last decade Britain has become an increasingly secretive society. The government has tried to stifle public debate and discussion . . . We are determined to make Britain a more open society with a government more open to democratic challenge. We will replace the Official Secrets Act with a Freedom of Information Act. This will be based on the principle that people have the right to know the basis on which government makes its decisions. The new definition of official secrecy will relate solely to matters which are a direct or potential threat to national security.'[48]

In the 1989 party conference Labour strongly advocated a proper public defence review:

'A Labour government on taking office will immediately initiate the widest possible defence review that will look at our commitments worldwide and our ability to pay for them.'

Events since then have not affected this.[49]

In general, Labour condemns the way 'defence' decisions tend to be weapons-led and are taken in isolation from wider foreign policy considerations. Strategy should guide weapon procurement, not vice versa. The barriers within and between current ministries need to be broken down so that broader policy priorities, economic and political as well as military, shape long-term force planning.

The Liberal Democrats are also sharply critical of the way defence decision making is monopolised by a small élite of senior civil servants and government ministers which denies relevant information to parliament:

'The current covert examination by the UK government in the Options For Change exercise is a typically inadequate and excessively secretive approach to the issue. The Government should, we believe, prove itself willing to think more imaginatively and openly, floating options for the future shape of UK armed forces for informed parliamentary and public debate. There is no need for one single all-embracing "Defence Review", because, as the last year has shown, events are likely to move so rapidly that the conclusions of any such Review would be rendered quickly out of date. Instead, British spending on defence should be kept continuously under review, and reductions implemented in a coherent and managed way.'[50]

For the Green Party

'Defence policy must be open and democratic and based on information available for public debate. Defence decisions should only be made after proper parliamentary debate based on the provision of the fullest possible information. Defence budgets must be published in such a way that parliamentarians can learn the costs of individual weapon systems at an early stage.'[51]

7 SUMMARY OF QUESTIONS ARISING

1. Although not well developed, the spectrum of party political assessment of threat does span the transformationist/realist divide. This is fundamental to what follows. It determines the overall priorities within which British policy is seen to be defined. Further questions concern assessments of particular British interests and responsibilities in relation to this. Fc⁻ example, what are the specific interests peculiar to Britain alone, what interests coincide with those of other European countries, and what interests can be said to be shared with the world community? In what ways do these overlapping interests and responsibiliti∪s clash? Where they do, which should prevail?

2. In the light of this what is the proper response? Confining attention to the defence component, how does a realist emphasis 'from within' on strong armed forces and deterrence (with a stress on modernisation) relate to a transformationist emphasis 'from above' on mutual reassurance and disarmament (with a stress on arms control)? Do existing references to 'forward defence', 'deep strike', 'flexible response' on one side, and to 'non-provocative defence' and 'common security' on the other still apply in the 1990s? If so, what are the implications for force planning? It not, what has replaced them? What is the scope for independent British action here, or must these strategies be worked out at alliance level? Should there now be planning for role specialisation? And multinational forces? Should British forces be structured, equipped and trained for traditional defence operations around the British Isles, residual commitments in Germany, policing or peace-keeping roles in Europe, future 'out of area' operations?

3. What is the significance of differing party views on an optimum future security framework for Europe? For example, what does it mean to say that NATO should become a 'more political forum'? Or that 'the European Community should develop a common security policy'? Or that 'the CSCE should provide the framework for a new security system'? Are these complementary or rival conceptions? And how do they relate to ideas about European integration, and to relations with the United States and the Soviet Union? Looking further afield, how should European countries contribute to security requirements in other parts of the world?

And how much can be expected of the United Nations in helping to control the arms race, settle disputes, encourage Third World development and protect the environment?

4. Why have the radically different party political views on the future role of nuclear weapons not been publicly argued out? Is a Comprehensive Test Ban Treaty the best way to halt proliferation? Why does one British party insist on retaining a first use option for NATO's nuclear weapons, and the others determine to abandon it? Can and should British and French nuclear weapons form an extended deterrent for Europe? What are the arguments for and against a British nuclear stand-off weapon in addition to Trident? This debate has not yet begun in Britain even though the government has already decided that it is essential and the opposition parties have officially rejected it.

5. What should the priorities in government expenditure be? Is it true that Britain spends more on defence than Germany? What are the pros and cons of present civil and military R&D funding in comparison with what goes on in other countries? What is the best way to manage the complex process of defence diversification? How can legitimate defence be strengthened through arms sales to other governments without fuelling repression and aggression? On all these issues there are important differences between the declared policies of British political parties, including differing assessments of existing statistics which need to be sorted out if realistic comparisons are to be made.

6. Why have 'options for the future shape of UK armed forces' not been offered for 'parliamentary and public debate'? Is defence planning too secretive? Is it too 'weapons-led'? Are protected markets one reason for the high cost inflation of defence equipment? Should defence decision-making be more open and more directly guided by broader strategic and foreign policy judgements? 'In general, does the rapidly changing security environment in Europe suggest that inherited decision-making structures and practices should themselves be adapted?'

Finally, it is time the policies of British political parties were compared with those in other European countries, particularly in those areas where Britain cannot act on its own. Only when this becomes habitual will British politics really have entered the mainstream of the European debate.

BOX 8.1   THE CASE OF THE TACTICAL AIR-TO-SURFACE MISSILE (TASM)

'Flexible response is the only strategic concept that makes sense for a defensive alliance in the nuclear age . . . For flexible response NATO has to maintain an effective nuclear armoury at several levels. Strategic weapons alone, for all their awesome power, could not be morally tolerable, practically feasible or politically credible for every scenario . . . The United Kingdom will continue to play a full part in this effort, and also to maintain the independent non-strategic contribution without which the value of our strategic force, which provides a separate second centre of nuclear decision-making in support of Alliance strategy, would be seriously incomplete. Our non-strategic contribution has since the 1960s rested on WE177 free-fall weapons [i.e. bombs], usable from various aircraft in various roles. For technical and operational reasons these cannot be relied upon beyond the 1990s . . . Procurement lead-times mean that initial decisions on modernisation – particularly on the choice of an air-launched missile to which warhead work at Aldermaston will be geared – must be taken before long.'[52]

A British TASM would be fired from the Tornado GR1, adding say 400 km to the plane's range of 2000 km so that it could reach Leningrad, Moscow and Libya from the UK (and Iraq from Cyprus), with variable yields between 10 kilotons (just under the yield of the Hiroshima bomb) and 300 kilotons. It could attack 'cities, airfields, ports, barracks, troop concentrations, industrial facilities, research centres, power stations, large ships or groups of ships'.[53] It could not be expected to come into service before 2000 and would last on more than two decades into the next century.

Although it would be possible for Britain to develop an all-British missile (like Blue Steel in the 1960s), it is likely that costs would be too high, so the alternatives are reduced to American missiles with British warheads (like the Short Range Attack Missile Tactical or SRAM-T), or French missiles either already in existence like the 300 km Air-Sol à Moyenne Portée (ASMP) or to be developed like the longer range Air-Sol Longue Portée

(ASLP). Likely overall costs would vary with choice of system but estimates range up to £1 billion and above.[54]

The question of a British TASM should be distinguished from the separate question of whether an American TASM (probably SRAM-T), due to be deployed in Europe from about the middle of the decade, would be fitted to American F-15E and F-111 planes based in Britain. This is the issue that divides the German parties, with the SPD and it seems the FDP opposing basing in Germany and the CDU recommending that the decision should be postponed.

As has been seen the Labour Party, Liberal Democrats and Green Party all oppose both a British TASM and an American TASM deployed in Europe as part of NATO, although Labour leaders seem to be wavering on the former under pressure from France, the United States and the British establishment, and, on the latter, concede that if NATO allies do want an American TASM, then 'we would accept our responsibilities as an alliance member'.

What is at issue in this controversy? The answer is that conclusions about TASM are derived from answers given to the other questions which go to make up the wider dimensions of the European debate. Assessments of threat are linked to judgements about response. In this way complex areas of debate are generated, for example across the use/deterrence watershed analysed with reference to flexible response in Chapter 2, or between conceptions of collective alliance security and common security, or between strategies of deep strike and non-offensive defence, or between principles of unilateral modernisation and multilateral arms control. This is what defines the context for the TASM debate, and TASM in turn is perhaps the critical issue in it, summing up as it now does the whole legacy of flexible response and through it extended deterrence itself.[55]

When it comes to institutions, once again TASM is a catalyst. There is the Atlanticist emphasis on a wide NATO basing of American TASM in which the British TASM is subsumed as a 'second centre of nuclear decision-making'. There is the Euro-statist emphasis on British-French cooperation in which TASM is seen as a component of a European deterrent 'with ASLP as an initial nuclear deterrent and Trident [UK] plus M5 [France] submarine launched ballistic missiles as the ultimate resort'.[56]

Finally there is the nationalist emphasis on an independent British deterrent in case all else fails. Critics challenge each of these models. The Atlanticist conception is said to founder on likely resistence to US basing in Germany, the Benelux countries and France. The Euro-statist conception to lack substance in the absence of any equivalent of NATO's Nuclear Planning Group. The nationalist conception to be chimerical in view of British dependence either on American or French technology.

In addition there are strenuous objections on grounds of cost to a British TASM;[57] and complaints that the whole issue has been unhealthily shielded from proper parliamentary scrutiny.[58]

In box 2.3 in Chapter 2 it was concluded that 'it will be the question of the air-to-surface missile which will be the catalyst in forcing the evolution of nuclear deterrent thinking in Europe in the 1990s'. Without it NATO's nuclear strategy as envisaged in UK doctrine can hardly survive. And the value of Britain's new Trident force 'would be seriously incomplete'. Since the Conservative, Labour and Liberal Democrat Parties all now agree about the retention of at least three Trident submarines this is an entirely new field of debate. All three main opposition parties (as well as the SNP and Plaid Cymru) officially reject the idea of a British TASM. So this is a head-on clash in precisely the area of policy that obsessed British commentators to the exclusion of everything else in the 1980s. Yet even here there has been almost no public discussion.

8   BRITAIN, GERMANY AND THE FUTURE OF EUROPE

Reviewing Geoffrey Smith's book, *Thatcher and Reagan*, for *The Times* in December 1990, John Campbell made this judgement on the special understanding between the two leaders:

'The cost for Britain was that the world role she was able to play at Reagan's side revived yet again the post-imperial illusions that have cursed this country since 1945, prolonging the delusive Atlantic orientation at the expense of Europe. Reality returned as soon as

Bush took over: his first visitor was not Mrs Thatcher but Helmut Kohl. Eventually it was the determination of her Cabinet colleagues that Europe must take priority that brought about her downfall. The Reagan/Thatcher relationship was indeed "special": it was a unique chapter that will not be repeated, and will surely be seen historically as an aberration.'[59]

In 1990 Soviet–German 'new thinking' seemed to be confirmed by the peaceful revolutions in Central and Eastern Europe, by Soviet acquiescence in the unification of Germany, by the signing of the CFE agreement and the Paris charter, by Soviet abandonment of its Iraqi ally and the new unanimity in the United Nations security council. French–German pressure in the direction of West European integration seemed unstoppable, with Britain being forced to enter the Exchange Rate Mechanism and finding herself in a minority of one on the prospects for economic and monetary union. Margaret Thatcher looked all at once old-fashioned, Helmut Kohl the man of the future. The change of leadership in Britain was greeted with jubilation by Tory Euro-MPs. The new British prime minister immediately agreed with the German chancellor that, just as Labour Euro-MPs sat with the Social Democrats, so Conservative Euro-MPs should now sit with the Christian Democrats in the European Parliament, not in a separate bloc as before.[60] It appeared inevitable that British policy would be drawn closer to that of Germany.

Yet the course of history never runs smoothly. In the early weeks of 1991 all of this seemed suddenly to be thrown into reverse. First there was what was happening in the Soviet Union. Faced with the undermining of the central ground in Soviet politics by economic failure and nationalist separatism, Mikhail Gorbachev had apparently reverted to his Leninist instincts and sided with the conservatives. All the gains of Perestroika seemed threatened. British criticisms of German policy revived. The Germans were accused of being weak on Soviet repression in the Baltic states because of the presence of Soviet troops in Germany and the need to ratify the unification treaties. And then there was the Gulf war. Here the Germans were portrayed in Britain and the United States as selfish weaklings, ready to accept forty years of protection through NATO but unwilling to pay up when allies in turn needed support in the Gulf. Britain and the United States were fighting the battle for freedom and democracy in the world on behalf of the international community; Germany was making money and reaping the reward. The idea of the 'special relationship' as the cornerstone of the great Atlantic alliance was mightily revived. Earlier talk of a new American–German 'partnership in leadership' was discarded. Another victim as seen through the eyes of a number of commentators in Britain was the Franco-German vision of a united Europe. All talk of political union, and in particular of foreign policy, security and defence union, was seen to have been delusory if not hypocritical. Ill-conceived solo French diplomatic initiatives and supine European failure to provide unified support for the Gulf war were said plainly to reveal the sham that this had been.[61]

What is the upshot of this? Britain is pulled in two directions: West across the Atlantic in foreign policy; East across the Channel in economic policy. In foreign policy continuing ex-imperial traditions enable Britain, when acting with the United States, to take the lead on a global scale in a way that Germany still cannot. There is public support for such policies in Britain of a kind not found in Germany. In terms of economic policy, however, British culture and society have hardly begun to catch up with what has been happening on the continent. There is as yet little awareness of the depth of change in practices and attitudes needed for Britain to achieve European standards. On the world stage Germany is an economic giant but a political pygmy, Britain in comparison a political giant but an economic pygmy. Few Germans or French understand the British conception of Atlanticism as a great alliance for freedom and democracy in the world. They do not share the imperial Whig tradition. It is too moralistic and Anglo-Saxon for French realism, and too nationalistic and militaristic for German internationalism. The 'special relationship' is seen as clienthood. But for their part few Britons understand the deep post-war German commitment to the principle of the peaceful resolution of conflict, expressed through the great enterprises of building European unity through Westpolitik and overcoming the division of Europe through Ostpolitik. If Germany is wealthy today, it is the result of hard work and sacrifice, not something to be resented, say the Germans, who feel that they have generously funded and are generously funding both of these enormous projects. The Gulf war was seen to be 'out of area' for European countries, and, as the 250 000 strong peace demonstration in Bonn on 26 January 1991 showed, many Germans, while sharing a determination to get Iraq out of Kuwait, believed that this should have been done by non-violent means. Opinion on the political right in Germany strongly disagrees and regrets Germany's failure to play a more determined role in support of the coalition. But there still seems to be a consensus that the lesson to be learned is not that European political union is an illusion, but, on the contrary, that it must be speeded up.

There can be no doubt that Britain's future lies in Europe. No matter what the geographical and historical differences, highlighted as they were during the Gulf crisis, as members of the same integrated Alliance (NATO) and the same economic and political community (the EC), Britain and Germany now share the same fundamental security interests. Each can no doubt learn from the other. Germany, perhaps, needs to acquire a global perspective to complement Britain's, Britain to gain a European consciousness like Germany's. Above all there is a need to escape from projected and often conflicting national stereotypes such as those that surfaced in Britain during the period of German unification and the Gulf war. This book shows that beneath these crude and unhelpful generalisations there is a comparable spread of party political opinion in the two countries about most of the main security issues of the day. It is just not true that 'Britain' thinks one way and 'Germany' another. The book also shows why these similarities and contrasts now need to be properly articulated and understood within the context of the new pan-European security debate as both countries combine in the great common enterprise of shaping the new Europe upon which their joint destinies depend.

And beneath this again lies the realist/transformationist debate common to all countries with an interest in European security. Part IV highlights the historic significance of the debate. Realist instincts inherited from the past must somehow be reconciled with aspirations for a 'new Europe', indeed a 'new world order', which look ahead to a transformationist future. The crux of this tremendous dilemma is well presented in the last of the three United Nations commissions set up during the 1980s to explore the developmental, security and environmental challenges facing humankind:

> 'The earth is one but the world is not. We all depend on one biosphere for sustaining our lives. Yet each community, each country, strives for survival and prosperity with little regard for its impact on others.'[62]

The same applies to most other aspects of security in the nuclear age.

Yet, for politico-historical reasons, the transformationist pole of the debate is not yet centrally articulated in Britain as it is in a number of other European countries. Despite a potentially large reservoir of support, the barriers to political divergence and alternative policy formulation in Westminster remain high and in Whitehall almost insuperable. The same unspoken traditions which block economic innovation and social change at home insulate British culture from European trends abroad. So the embryonic British party political debate remains undeveloped and stunted. It is time that this changed.

NOTES

1. There have also been many thoughtful non-party policy recommendations, such as Ken Booth's proposed three-stage programme from 'constructive engagement' 1985–2000, to the medium-term goal of 'a legitimate international order' 2000–15, to the long-term goal of 'stable peace' thereafter: 'Steps Towards Stable Peace In Europe: A Theory And Practice Of Coexistence', *International Affairs*, vol. 66, no 1, 1990. Compare with a German equivalent: Dieter Senghaas, *Europe 2000. Ein Friedensplan*, Suhrkamp Verlag, 1990.
2. Quotations in this paragraph are taken from *Arms Control & Defence: the Vital Issues*, FCO/MoD, March 1990, and *Statement on the Defence Estimates*, vol. 1, HMSO, April 1990. 'The figures that have been given to me for Soviet performance in 1989 are striking. We believe that the USSR completed ten submarines, six major surface ships, 50 bombers, 600 fighters, at least 1700 tanks and 450 ballistic missiles. Soviet tank production, even at half the previous level, is still more than double the annual output of NATO', Tom King, 'Defence And Security in a Time of Change', *RUSI Journal*, Summer 1990.
3. Respectively: John Major, BBC 2; Tom King, Defence Select Committee evidence; Margaret Thatcher, ITN, Media Transcription Service.
4. *Looking to the Future*, Labour Party, Walworth Road, 1990, p. 46; *Reshaping Europe*, pp. 3, 6.
5. *Meet the Challenge, Make the Change*, Labour Party Policy Review, Walworth Road, 1989, pp. 87–8.
6. *Reshaping Europe*, p. 8.
7. *Peace and Defence*, Green Party draft working paper, August 1990, p. 104, PD 101–3.
8. *Statement on the Defence Estimates*, 1990.
9. Tom King, evidence to the House of Commons Select Committee on Defence, *Defence Implications of Recent Events*, July 1990, p. 6.
10. *Arms Control and Defence: The Vital Issues*.
11. Tom King, Statement to the House of Commons, 25 July 1990.
12. Tom King, *Defence Implications of Recent Events*.
13. *Looking to the Future*. p. 46.
14. *Meet the Challenge, Make the Change*, p. 85.

15. Labour Party Conference Report, 1989, p. 33.
16. Denis Healey, *Defence Implications of Recent Events*, p. 76.
17. *Reshaping Europe*, p. 9.
18. Ibid., p. 25.
19. *Peace and Defence*, pp. 104–5.
20. BBC 1, 'Panorama', 27 November 1989; TV am, 10 June 1990, Media Transcription Service.
21. TV am, 10 June 1990. An out of area role for NATO was demanded by Tom King at the North Atlantic Assembly Session, 28 November 1990, *Daily Telegraph*, 29 November 1990. An out of area role for the Western European Union was suggested by Douglas Hurd in the shape of a rapid reaction force which could intervene in conflicts outside Europe in a speech in Berlin, 10 December 1990, *The Times*, 17 December 1990.
22. *Meet the Challenge, Make the Change*, p. 85.
23. *Looking to the Future*, p. 46.
24. Denis Healey, *Defence Implications of Recent Events*, p. 74.
25. For this and previous paragraphs see *Reshaping Europe*, pp. 12–15.
26. *Peace and Defence*, p. 110.
27. Tom King: 'It's like a fire insurance: you have to maintain a policy not just when you think your house is going to burn down, but have it there just against the risk that it might happen', BBC 1, 'Question Time', 7 June 1990.
28. *Statement on the Defence Estimates* 1990.
29. *Statement on the Defence Estimates* 1989.
30. Tom King, Statement to the House of Commons, 25 July 1990.
31. For Labour Party policy on the stationing of American TASM in Britain, see box 8.1.
32. For this and previous paragraphs see *Meet the Challenge, Make the Change*, pp. 86–8.
33. *Reshaping Europe*, pp. 20–31.
34. *Peace and Defence*, pp. 105–7.
35. The Chancellor of the Exchequer's 1990 Autumn Statement announced anticipated figures for the percentage of GDP devoted to defence for 1991/2, 1992/3 and 1993/4 as 3.8 per cent, 3.6 per cent and 3.4 per cent respectively.
36. Tom King, Defence Implications of Recent Events, pp. 9–10.
37. Michael Heseltine, Channel 4 News, 29 January 1990, Media Transcription Service.
38. Alan Clark, BBC 2 Television 'Open Space - Death on Delivery', 3 July 1990, Media Transcription Service.
39. Ibid. See also Timothy Sainsbury, *Arms Transfers and Conventional Arms Control: An Ethical Approach*, Council for Christian Approaches to Defence and Disarmament, 9 November 1988.
40. *Looking to the Future*, p. 47. See also *UK Military R&D*, Council for Science and Society, Working Party Report, Oxford University Press, 1986.
41. Ibid.
42. *Meet the Challenge, Make the Change*, p. 88.
43. *Reshaping Europe*, p. 28.

44. Ibid. See also Russell Johnston, *Curbing the Arms Trade*, Council for Arms Control, Bulletin 48, February 1990.
45. *Peace and Defence*, p. 108.
46. Tom King, *Defence Implications of Recent Events*, p. 4.
47. Ibid., p. 6.
48. *Looking to the Future*, p. 40.
49. Confirmed by letter, December 1990.
50. *Reshaping Europe*, p. 28.
51. *Peace and Defence*, p. 105.
52. This passage is taken from the 1989 *Statement on the Defence Estimates*, HMSO, pp. 11–12. Written by a senior civil servant, it is formally cited as the 'United Kingdom nuclear doctrine' and reprinted in full as such in the Secretary-General of the United Nations' report, *Comprehensive Study on Nuclear Weapons*, UN General Assembly, 18 September 1990, A/45/373.
    Crucial elements are:

a. that the Soviet Union 'still has much larger forces in most categories' and 'its strategic situation is not the same as the West's';
b. that nuclear weapons contribute essentially to NATO's central defence aim of 'removing the option of war permanently from the East/West scene';
c. that this is why an option of first use must be kept open, and, in the words added at British insistence to the July 1990 NATO London Declaration, it must be made plain that 'there are no circumstances in which nuclear retaliation in response to military action might be discounted'. Britain's nuclear weapons do not have the sole function of deterring an opponent's use or threatened use of his own nuclear weapons;
d. that sub-strategic systems like TASM are needed to support strategic systems like Trident because otherwise the INF Treaty would 'leave a hole in the middle of NATO's ability to respond flexibly'. It is important not to abandon the operational roles and strategies associated with the weapons removed by the INF Treaty;
e. that 'nuclear weapons are not mere symbols; like other weapons they can deter only by evident capability for effective use', which is why it is essential to continue to modernise and improve them;
f. that if it came to use the aim could not be 'military victory in the classical sense' but 'to deny an aggressor swift success and to show him that he has underrated the defender's resolve and must, for his own survival, back off' (this could be seen as an approximation to French doctrine);
g. that this is in no way incompatible with arms-control commitments, but that new technology of this kind can assist 'deeper understanding on both sides of the minimum imperatives of mutually assured security';
h. that the main function of Britain's non-strategic nuclear weapons, above all TASM, is, therefore, to provide essential support for the future strategic Trident force as part of NATO strategy.

53. Duncan Lennox, *Tactical Air to Surface Missiles: The Key Issues*, International Security Information Service, ISIS Briefing no. 15, November 1990. See also Richard Ware, *The Modernisation of British Theatre Nuclear Forces*, House of Commons Library Background Paper No. 225, 5 April 1989.
54. The American alternatives at the end of 1990 were: AGM-131 SRAM 2 or SRAM-T, or AQM-127 Supersonic Low Altitude Target (SLAT) developed by the US navy. The existing French ASMP is thought to have too short a range for UK requirements, but France does not need the newer ASLP as soon as Britain.
55. It seems hardly an exaggeration to say that without TASM there could be no flexible response. Sea-launched systems such as American Sea-Launched Cruise missiles could not fulfil the same operational roles, and would not have the important political function of widespread basing. There are objections to each of the components in the MoD rationale outlined in note 52:

   a. that the Soviet threat is now no longer sufficient to justify such a capability (Soviet equivalent missiles are not usually cited as a reason for British counter-deployment);
   b. that in the new circumstances conventional defences are quite adequate to deter conventional attack, particularly if there is a coordinated move to non-provocative defence on both sides;
   c. that NATO doctrine of 'ensuring that there are no circumstances in which nuclear retaliation in response to military action might be discounted' while maintaining that 'in the transformed Europe they will be able to adopt a new NATO strategy making nuclear weapons truly weapons of last resort' is incoherent, and TASM can in any case not be a weapon of last resort because it would be based at airfields vulnerable to attack;
   d. that the whole idea of a 'seamless robe' of graduated response is flawed, based as it is on the delusion that there can be a 'discriminate' and 'politically controlled use' of nuclear weapons;
   e. that to see nuclear weapons as being 'like other weapons' in only deterring through 'evident capacity for use' betrays the fatal logic whereby the search for the chimera of credibility in conditions of mutual deployment drives strategists to the operational lunacy of deliberately planning for initiation and intra-war escalation;
   f. that the idea that nuclear weapons could be used 'to deny an aggressor swift success, and to show him that he . . . must . . . back off' ignores the fact that he also has nuclear weapons and is almost certain to use them in turn. It is based on untested, contradictory and irresponsible assumptions about rationality in conditions of intense crisis. The notion that, nuclear deterrence having failed, nuclear weapons could be used unilaterally to restore deterrence, indeed to achieve compellence in inducing an aggressor to withdraw, is incoherent;
   g. that a deployment of TASM towards the end of the decade to last well on into the next century would damage arms control prospects, not enhance them, and would be seen as a violation of the spirit of the

INF Treaty; it would also be harmful in the context of non-proliferation;

h. that the whole idea that Britain's sub-strategic nuclear weapons are needed to make the strategic Trident deterrent viable is a gratuitous new argument not heard at all during two previous General Elections when Trident on its own was the issue; and the idea that British strategic and sub-strategic weapons are needed as a 'second centre of nuclear decision-making in support of Alliance strategy' is a rationalisation not taken seriously elsewhere.

56. Philip Sabin, quoted in *Jane's Defence Weekly*, 22 December 1990, p. 1270.

On 22 October 1990 the French Prime Minister, Michel Rocard, addressing the French Institute of Higher Defence Studies, said that British-French nuclear cooperation, with particular reference to ASLP, would 'have considerable significance' for European security because American and European interests were not always 'identical', *Daily Telegraph*, 23 October 1990.

57. 'If we do not cooperate with the French, will we pay for the project ourselves, and, if so, where will the £3 billion come from?', Martin O'Neill, debate on the Defence Estimates, 18 June 1990, *Hansard*, col. 699.

58. Scilla Elworthy, *In The Dark*, Oxford Research Group, Oxford, 1989.

59. *The Times Saturday Review*, 22 December 1990.

60. *The European*, 20 December 1990.

61 Such were the sentiments expressed in a radio interview by Alan Clark, Minister for defence procurement, 24 January 1991.

62. *Our Common Future*, (the Brundtland commission), 1987, Oxford University Press. The reports of the other two commissions, chaired by Willy Brandt and Olof Palme respectively, are published as *North–South: A Program for Survival*, 1980, MIT Press, and *Common Security: A Blueprint for Survival*, 1982, Pan Books.

Part IV
Conclusion

9   Beyond Deterrence

What is the significance of the new European security debate? In this book the analysis presented in Part I has been illustrated with reference to Germany and Britain. But it is a debate which involves all the countries represented in the CSCE process. It is in the fullest sense a pan-European debate. It concerns not only relations between the CSCE countries, but the role that they can and should play, individually and collectively, in the world at large. As has been seen, it is a broad and complex debate, varying from country to country, party to party and interest group to interest group. Yet, as the German and British examples have illustrated, beneath the complexity two main poles to the debate can be discerned – a realist 'view from within' and a transformationist 'view from above'. It is time to relate these poles to the international situation we now find ourselves in, because it is through this relationship that the full significance of the debate is seen.

1   ENDINGS AND BEGINNINGS

There is a widespread feeling that a momentous turning-point in human history has now been reached. It is an apprehension shared, not only by radicals and idealists, but also by pragmatists and many of those in positions of political power. The dates 9 November 1989 and 2 August 1990 are seen to define a new context for global politics. The talk is of endings and beginnings. The end of the Soviet Empire, of Stalinism, of superpower bipolarity, of the bloc system, of the Cold War, even of history itself. The beginning of the post Cold War world, of the threat of rising nationalist, ethnic and religious tensions, of mounting environmental dangers, of the first North–South conflict, but at the same time of the hope of creating a truly global collective security system, of a revived role for the United Nations, of a new World Order.

For the Soviet President and the Indian Prime Minister:

'At this moment, more than at any previous time in recent history, mankind has the prospect of building a new structure of cooperation and brotherhood among nations and peoples.'[1]

For the US Secretary of State:

'I think that we stand at a critical juncture in history. The Iraqi invasion of Kuwait is one of the defining moments of a new era, a new era full of promise, but also one that is replete with new challenges.'[2]

For the British Foreign Secretary:

'This is a defining moment in history. How we act now will define, will shape, the future . . . I am more hopeful than before that the international community, through the United Nations, is equal to the tasks. The new world order must succeed in getting Iraq out of Kuwait, otherwise it will be stillborn and no one will take it seriously. But once that is done – and I am sure it will be – then this new order, in its different shapes and guises, will grow. I believe it will flourish, I believe it will consolidate.'[3]

What happened in Europe in the autumn of 1989 is seen to have opened the door to a possible new era in international relations. What happened in the Gulf is seen to have threatened to close it again. In the terminology introduced in Chapter 1, the former seemed to point to the possibility of a future age of mutually assured security, the latter to represent a perpetuation of the age of war. Crucial to both was the question whether the UN/CSCE principle of border inviolability could now become a universally recognised priority effectively guaranteed by the international community.

What was extraordinary here was not Iraq's invasion of Kuwait. That had historically been a normal way for states to behave. For centuries the militarily powerful had found pretexts for expanding at the expense of the militarily weak. Power had flowed like water. Wessex defeated Mercia and Northumbria to create England. Britain defeated France to create an English-speaking United States. The United States defeated Mexico to absorb Texas. The Falkland Islands were British rather than Argentine because British naval power had been greater in 1832 (and again a hundred and fifty years later). The borders of Iraq and Kuwait had been decided by occupying colonial powers, as had the existence of Israel. Since the early modern period coercive power had increasingly come to be concentrated in emergent sovereign states able to pacify the area within their own borders and direct their military potential outwards. In relations between states the ultimate sanction of policy was war. So, having spent on average 32 per cent of Iraqi GNP during the 1980s on building armed forces to make himself the most powerful military ruler in the region, Saddam Hussein was behaving in traditional manner when he proceeded to use these forces, first to attack Iran, then to invade Kuwait. Historically it was normal to suppose that military power could be projected across international borders to political advantage in this way.

What was extraordinary was the situation in Europe. Former inveterate enemies like France and Germany had transformed relations between themselves to the point where war was simply unthinkable. Here an era of mutually assured security had already arrived. And now the remarkable behaviour of the Soviet Union in accepting the defection of Central and Eastern European allies, even though it had the military power to prevent this and could have done so without fear of Western intervention, seemed to herald the possibility that the

---

BOX 9.1   RELATIVE MILITARY STRENGTHS OF IRAQ AND THE SOVIET UNION IN 1990[5]

	Iraq	*Soviet Union*
Total Armed Forces:		
active	1 000 000	4 258 000
reserve	850 000	5 560 000
Main Battle Tanks	5 500	53 350
Artillery	3 700	40 000
Armed Helicopters	160	2 000
Combat Aircraft	500	4 600

These figures do not include categories like naval strength or nuclear capabilities, where Iraq has little or nothing.

BOX 9.2   TWO HUNDRED YEARS OF WAR AND
PEACE IN EUROPE[6]

The characteristic political units in the later stages of the age of
great power war in Europe were nation states. In the age of
deterrence it was blocs. In a future age of mutually assured
security might it be some form of 'common' or 'collective'
system (the distinction no longer being meaningful)? Or will
there be a relapse to independent national defence forces?
Previous periods of relative peace in Europe eventually broke
down. Will the same happen again?

1760s to 1790s	peace
1790s to 1815	Napoleonic wars
1815 to 1854	peace
1854 to 1871	Bismarck's wars
1871 to 1914	peace
1914 to 1918	First World War
1918 to 1939	peace
1939 to 1945	Second World War
1945 to ????	peace

In each inter-war period a structure of temporarily stable
relations was erected which for a while succeeded in maintaining peace. From 1815 it was the Congress of Vienna system.
From 1871 it was the Concert of Europe. From 1918 it was the
'collective security' of the League of Nations. On each occasion
a revisionist power arose which refused to tolerate its position in
the status quo or its exclusion by the dominant powers. Since
1945 stable relations have been defined in terms of the two
blocs. Now that the bloc system has collapsed can a new system
be created, this time to ensure a final and definitive end to inter-
state war in Europe?

same might be achieved in the rest of Europe. It was the British
Secretary of State for Defence's annual *Statement on the Defence
Estimates*, not a peace movement proposal, that described the future in
Europe in terms of the joint creation of a system of 'mutually assured

security' in which 'the total neutralisation of war becomes so sure, accepted and permanent that, even when interests may differ widely, nations of East and West can conduct their business together by means in which the thought of armed conflict simply plays no part.'[4]

A comparison of the relative military strengths of Iraq and the Soviet Union underlines this point. It was the country with ten times the conventional military strength of the other which felt unable to use that strength even to shore up its position in its own sphere of influence, whereas the smaller country was uninhibited about using its armed forces in traditional ways. Paradoxically from an historical point of view, the mutual inhibition against war, characteristic of the deterrent age, so far operated at great power level, not below.

Those who spoke in this way of 'a critical juncture in history' or 'one of the defining moments of a new era' were in effect presenting a stark alternative to the world community: the upholding of the United Nations/CSCE principle of border inviolability down one path; the continuation of cross-border war down the other. The first (adumbrated in Europe) pointed to a possible future global collective security system; the second (exemplified in the Gulf) threatened a disastrous perpetuation of the age of war. Would the European experience be extended to other regions, for example through the setting up of a Conference on Security and Cooperation in the Middle East (CSCME), or, in view of mounting uncertainties in Eastern Europe and the Soviet Union, would the tradition of interstate war as exemplified in the Gulf spread back to areas that had apparently moved beyond it?

No doubt in terms of probable outcome the two alternatives were overdrawn. Developments were likely to be patchy and interpretations of them controversial. Yet in general terms the analysis stands. The principle of border inviolability was clear-cut and the question whether or not it could now be made universally and permanently effective was an historic challenge which confronted the international community as a whole. The threatened further spread of nuclear weapon and missile technologies made it an urgent one.

2 THE AGE OF DETERRENCE AND THE NEW SECURITY DEBATE

The choice between perpetuation of the age of war and passage to a future era of mutually assured security defined the significance both of current security relations between the great powers and of international controversy about them. It is time to relate the two together.

In Chapter 1 the intermediate 'age of mutual deterrence' at great power level was defined as a transition period between what all CSCE leaders said they hoped was a past age of great power war and what they all hoped would be a future age of mutually assured security. (It should be remembered that this so far applied only to relations between the great powers. As the Iraqi invasion of Kuwait and the Gulf war showed, it did not yet apply elsewhere).[7]

It will be worth re-emphasising some of the paradoxical features of this hybrid era. In the pre-1945 age of great power war political purpose and military strategy could coincide at all force levels. The predominant function of armed forces, whether offensive or defensive, was to win wars. Hitler could conquer France. The allies could overthrow Hitler. Military strength at maximum force levels could be mutually used to serve rational political ends. In a future age of mutually assured security political purpose and military strategy could again be reconciled. In such a period, when relations between the great powers might resemble those between, say, France and Germany or the United States and Canada today, the predominant function of armed forces would be little more than internal policing and external multinational peacekeeping.

But in the transitional age of mutual deterrence the great powers could no longer rationally use maximum force against each other as they had in the past during the centuries of great power war – and yet, unlike the possible future age of mutually assured security, were nevertheless compelled to plan to do so.

As a result, for the first time in history, political purpose no longer coincided with military strategy at this level. No rational goal would be compatible with a mutual use of maximum force. Even in defence mutual use would mean mutual destruction. The rationale for maximum force deployment changed from physical defence to psychological deterrence. The idea was to work on enemy perceptions so that defence would not be necessary. The predominant function of great power armed forces was now said to be the paradoxical one of preventing their own use. This rift between the overriding political priority of deterrence and continuing military planning for defence should deterrence fail bedevilled strategic thinking. As indicated in Chapter 1, each was both dependent upon, yet contradicted by the other. Effective deterrence meant mutual perception of the irrationality of physical use. Yet without a credible threat of physical use there

BOX 9.3 PARADOXES OF MUTUAL DETERRENCE AT
STRATEGIC LEVEL[8]

In 1988 Steven Kull recorded this interview with 'a prominent
pro-defense US senator'.

Q Do you feel we need to have a war-fighting strategy or war-
fighting capability?

A Yeah. Deterrence is creating that uncertainty and doubt in
the adversary's mind. Our goal is to be the mirror image of
what we perceive to be their doctrine and their force
posture.

Q Why?

A It comes back to deterrence. I think they have to perceive
that we are prepared just as they are. That our goal is to
prevail. The whole purpose of their nuclear weapons is to
make us think 'hey, we've got to stay away from that stuff
'cos we can't lick 'em'.

Q Do you think we can lick 'em?

A No, and I don't think they can lick us. I agree it's a self-
defeating goddam thing. But I think this is one of their
illusions that they believe.

Q So what you're saying is that we've got to act as if we've got
that illusion too?

A Right (*laughter*).

Q But you don't really believe we can prevail in a war?

A I agree with you. It's senseless. I mean, what is there that's
going to be left that really has any value or that is
recognisable to us or to them? I mean, I'm not sure there
is anything of value in what will remain.

Q But we should do what we can to develop the hardware that
makes it look as though we are getting ready to fight a war
in which we think we could prevail? Because that's going to
have the right psychological effect on them? Is that right?

A As crazy as it sounds, I think so. I think so.

Q How do you know the Soviets are not doing the same thing?

A I don't (*surprised laughter*). I don't. But if that's all it is, it
sure is a waste of GNP on both sides.

would be no deterrence. Other tensions of the age of mutual deterrence flowed from this: the progressive infection of sub-strategic levels through the paradox that deterrence demands credibility but credibility undermines deterrence; the contradictory attempts to reconcile imperatives of unilateral modernisation and multilateral arms control; the pulling apart of flexible response doctrine between 'deterrent' criteria of 'first use' and 'defence' criteria of 'last resort'; the fact that in order to render particular weapons operationally obsolete an unparalleled number and variety of such weapons had been and were being operationally deployed; the buckling of moral thinking under pressure from conflicting priorities of maximising deterrence and minimising damage should deterrence fail.

In short, the ambiguities inherent in strategic and moral thinking in the age of mutual deterrence betrayed its hybrid nature. It looked both ways. Political deterrent purposes looked ahead to the possibility of a mutually secure future such as would exist if deterrence were guaranteed to be successful. But military strategic planning still necessarily looked back to the age of war in case deterrence failed.

And this is where the nature of the era of mutual deterrence at great power level links with the new security debate. The two poles to the debate, realist and transformationist, accurately reflect the contradictory aspects of this transitional period. The realist preoccupation with existing structures of power mirrors the fact that strategic forces are still controlled by defence establishments inherited from the age of great power war. Present and future political leaders can indeed still use and abuse these increasingly lethal capabilities in traditional ways. The transformationist concern with the implications of mutuality, on the other hand, accurately acknowledges the new conditions of mutual vulnerability, opportunity and threat in the nuclear age. This is indeed the agenda that must be universally adopted if international security is to be permanently assured.

It is this linkage between the nature of the international security debate and the critical transition period the world community is going through that constitutes the central theme of this book.

Before pursuing the linkage further, it is important to emphasise the fact that continuing disagreement, deep and at times bitter though it is, is now being conducted within the general constraint of overarching agreement. This is an unprecedented state of affairs which projects a preferred overall direction to the evolution of global society, and thereby a decisive weighting to the debate.

3 THE CENTRAL AGREEMENT

Adversarial party politics of the British kind tends to obscure the significance of broad consensus. Yet in the security field in Europe there is undoubtedly central agreement now about a number of fundamental principles, embodied in the Helsinki process and expressed in general terms in the 1975 Final Act and the November 1990 Paris Charter. Leaders of all CSCE countries agree with Mikhail Gorbachev's 1991 new year message to the American people:

> 'The most important thing now, at this crucial period of history, is firmly to understand that the nations of the world may achieve progress and security for all, and consequently for themselves, only through common efforts, cooperation and acknowledgement of interdependence of interests.'

Foremost among the conditioning constraints within which this progress is to be achieved is universal acceptance of the 'thesis of the priority of the all-human value of peace over all others to which different people are attached'. Although the prevention of inter-state war in Europe can only be made permanent by deep long-term integration in the direction of shared democratic practices, economic interests and cultural values, this process in turn can only be furthered in an international environment made safe from the threat of war. It is a hallmark of the deterrent age that this is now generally accepted in Europe. Both proponents and critics of nuclear deterrent policy, for example, agree that the avoidance of full-scale war between the great powers is now an overriding political, if not moral, priority which eclipses sectional interest. They disagree about how this is to be achieved, not that it should be. They would all rather the present situation persisted than that a Third World War were precipitated in an effort to change it. If 'deterrence' is understood to mean mutual inhibition against full-scale war between the great powers, and 'pacifism' to mean the conviction that the consequences of war of this kind would be likely to dwarf any conceivable politically significant gain, then all now believe in deterrence and all are in that sense pacifists. Some critics of current policy may be reluctant to be labelled advocates of deterrence in this way, and some supporters of current policy may be reluctant to be called pacifists. If so, then this perhaps shows once again that the participants in the debate are more used to concentrating on what divides them than on what they share.

The agreement extends beyond relations between the great powers to the world community as a whole. Once again, although there were passionate feelings about whether war in the Gulf over the Iraqi invasion of Kuwait was justified, both sides to the debate in Europe concurred in upholding the principle of border inviolability. Those who advocated war if no other means could be found to eject the Iraqis, claimed to do so on the grounds that it was Iraq that had initiated the use of war as an instrument of policy and that only such action would demonstrate the determination of the international community that this could now no longer be tolerated. It would be a war to end war.

The same applies in terms of broad generalisation and declaratory policy to other features of the current situation. A number of features of the transformationist agenda set out by Mikhail Gorbachev were echoed in her 5 August 1990 speech at Aspen, Colorado, for example, by Margaret Thatcher, regarded by many as the embodiment of anti-transformationist views. She said that she embraced the enterprise of 'shaping a new global community'. She described 'the first and most exalted' priority as 'the creation of a world in which democracy and the rule of law are extended far and wide'. In Europe she suggested a 'European Magna Carta' to enshrine citizens' rights throughout the continent. These can be interpreted as traditional Atlanticist aims. But she offered Western help to run key sectors of the Soviet economy, emphasised the need to avoid protectionism which would harm developing countries and spoke of the importance of assisting them. Above all she proclaimed that 'our ability to come together to stop or limit damage to the world's environment will be the greatest test of how far we can act as a world community' and emphasised the importance of the United Nations, taking comfort from the fact that 'the five permanent members of the Security Council have acquired authority in recent times by working together'. Acknowledging realist scepticism ('some would say all this is a triumph of hope over experience') she concluded in transformationist vein, urging her audience not to be 'hypnotised by the past' because otherwise there would be no prospect of shaping a better future.

What are we to make of this central agreement? Is it only rhetorical? Perhaps no more substantial than habitual appeals to abstract concepts like 'freedom' and 'justice' by those who thereby accuse each other of violating them? Does this not usually happen when there are deep clashes of interest or principle? No doubt it does. But in this case it seems to be more than that. The declared priority of avoiding great power war, for example, now common to all European governments and political parties, is not the lip-service paid in the past to 'peace' by those who were in fact planning to violate it. It undoubtedly represents a hard-headed appreciation of what the British annual Statement on the Defence Estimates calls 'objective military fact'. As such, it is unprecedented. In every era up to and including the Second World War it was widely assumed that maximum use of force at great power level was not only an ultimate sanction of policy, but in many cases an early and acceptable expedient. Now this is no longer the case. There is genuine agreement in hoping that the age of great power war is over in Europe and that a future era of mutually assured security may come.

4 CONTINUING DISAGREEMENT

Yet despite the fact that in the broadest terms there can now be said to be agreement about long-term goals, the continuing disagreement about means is profound. The dispute involves almost every aspect of how the present situation has come about, how it should be consolidated and how the shared long-term aim should be realised. Nationalist, statist and Atlanticist conceptions on one side, and liberal, socialist and radical views on the other, compete to analyse current reality, define priorities and gain the political power to implement preferred policies. The debate reaches out to embrace the whole of politics.

From one perspective the universalist language of President Bush announcing a 'New Atlanticism' in Brussels in December 1989 is interpreted as Western triumphalism. 'Freedom', 'liberty' and 'peace' are seen to be coded words concealing an ambition to secure the permanent hegemony of Atlanticist interests:

'Our transatlantic partnership can create the architecture of a new Europe and a new Atlanticism, where self-determination and individual freedom everywhere replace coercion and tyranny. Where economic liberty, everywhere, replaces economic controls and stagnation, and where lasting peace is reinforced everywhere by common respect for the rights of man.'

From the other perspective the universalist language of President Gorbachev in his October 1989 address in the Finlandia palace is interpreted as a traditional Soviet attempt to dissolve NATO, denuclearise Europe and remove American troops from Europe:

> 'Peace envisages a general agreement between states that no problems, past or present, can be solved with the help of weapons. If this is so, armaments should be reduced to the level of sensible defensive sufficiency, while power politics, hegemony and interference in the internal affairs of other states should be renounced. Phenomena like the presence of troops on foreign territories, military alliances and vast areas kept off limits, which are so habitual but are incompatible with the peaceful period, should be phased out.'

The Soviet concern that a revival of nationalist and separatist movements in Europe 'could undermine the creation of all-European structures and hamper the building of a common home' is seen to reflect determination to crush the Baltic independence movements.[9]

To an extraordinary degree transformationist and realist perspectives interpret and reinterpret the situation in incompatible ways. Each identifies its own position with the way things are (it is a description) and the opposed position with the way the other wants them to be (it is a projection of motive and conditioning). Since what the other says is wrong, individual and social psychology must be invoked to explain why the other nevertheless says (and believes) it. Each sees its own arguments as reasons, the other's as rationalisations. Each cites as 'facts' what serves to support the preferred conclusion – whether it is assessments of Soviet conventional strength during the Cold War, judgements about the efficacy and robustness of nuclear deterrence, or predictions of likely war-damage in the 1990–1 Gulf crisis. Each denies responsibility for what are generally agreed to be bad developments, and claims credit for what are generally agreed to be good ones (like the INF Treaty or the overthrow of the communist East European regimes in 1989).[10]

From one pole the 'reasonable' realists who occupy positions of power are seen to stand in the way of the creation of a new Europe:

> 'Throughout my life, whenever I was thinking about public affairs, about civic, political and moral matters, there was always some reasonable person who sooner or later started very reasonably to point out, in the name of reason, that I too should be reasonable, should cast aside my eccentric ideas, and finally accept that nothing can change for the better because the world is divided once and for

all into two worlds. Both these half worlds are content with this division and neither wants to change anything. Naturally I was far from being the only one to disregard this wise advice and continue to do what I considered to be right. There were many of us in my country, Czechoslovakia. We were not afraid of being fools, we went on thinking about how to make the world a better place and we did not hide our thoughts. We dreamt of a Europe without barbed wires, high walls, artificially divided nations and gigantic stock-piles of weapons, of a Europe discarding "blocs", of a European policy based on the respect of man and his rights, of politics unsubordinated to transient and particular interests. Yes, we dreamt of a Europe that would be a friendly community of independent nations and democratic states.

At that time my friend Jiři Dienstbier (now Deputy Prime Minister and Minister of Foreign Affairs) was working as a stoker and wrote a book called *Dreaming of Europe*. "What sense is there in a stoker writing utopian notions of the future when he can't exert the tiniest influence on this future and can only bring further harassment upon himself?" asked the friends of reason, shaking their wise heads. And then a strange thing happened. Time suddenly accelerated and what otherwise took a year suddenly happened in an hour, everything started to change at surprising speed, the impossible suddenly became possible and the dream became reality. The stoker's dream became the daily routine of the Minister of Foreign Affairs. And the advocates of reason have now divided into three groups. The first are quietly waiting for some bad things to happen which will serve them as yet another argument in support of their nihilistic ideology. The second are looking for ways to push the dreamers out of government positions and replace them again by "reasonable" pragmatists. And the third are loudly proclaiming that at last what they have always known would happen has come to pass.'[11]

From the other pole, the transformationist 'dreamers' are seen to be, not only fools, but self-opinionated meddlers, fortunately in most cases irrelevant, but, if allowed any influence in public affairs, dangerous. It is only the Western realists who understand the brute facts of the situation and have the strength and moral courage to respond accordingly:

'Platoons of peace-people, intoxicated with the prospect of some kind of social dividend consequent upon the perceived liquidation of the East–West confrontation, are proclaiming triumphantly, much as though they were directly responsible for the entire phenomenon, that we really are witnessing, not only the failure of communism, but also the end of the Cold War, not to mention the demise of history itself. This extrusion of earnest platitudes by the progressive *nomenklatura* prompts the morose reflection that it would indeed be pleasant to be as sure of anything as they seem to be of everything. It may not be entirely inopportune to express some of the uncertainties which now assail those who prefer for the moment to remain at the coalface, resisting the temptation to throw away their shovels and join the manifestations of unrestrained joy at the pithead.'[12]

Beneath the formal civilities of public debate there often lurk the more primitive instincts of mutual contempt.

5 TWO ASYMMETRIES

In the last two sections the situation has been described in terms of symmetry of belief. First, an overarching central agreement. Second, a continuing disagreement that revolves around the realist and transformationist poles. The idea has been that the two poles represent genuine perceptions of aspects of reality in the transitional deterrent age, the realist pole acknowledging inherited traditions and structures of power, the transformationist pole recognising the long-term implications of mutual vulnerability. But, in saying this, two fundamental asymmetries between the two poles are revealed, and it is with these that the argument in this book now ends.

6 REALIST REALITY: RELATIONS OF POWER

The first asymmetry is constituted by the fact that the assumptions, attitudes and beliefs which cluster around the realist pole are still dominant in traditional centres of power, whereas transformationist assumptions, attitudes and beliefs are not. This asymmetry favours the realist pole.

In Central and Eastern Europe, for example, a number of transformationist politicians, drawing popularity and prestige from their role in the overthrow of the old regimes, came to occupy positions of influence and power within national defence establishments in the months that followed. The example of Vaclav Havel and Jiři Dienstbier in Czechoslovakia has just been given. But, as Vaclav Havel himself noted, 'reasonable' pragmatists in the realist tradition immediately started looking for ways to drive them out of office. Others found their own radicalism tested if not dissipated under pressure from competing national and international pressures against a background of mounting economic problems. It was difficult to maintain a 'view from above' while at the same time being responsible for what were at times overwhelming demands 'from within' discrete power structures. Mikhail Gorbachev found it increasingly difficult to sustain the integrity of the Soviet state and maintain the impetus and energy of his 'new thinking' in international affairs.

One of the most poignant examples was what happened in East Germany. The revolution of 1989 had represented the quite unexpected triumph of transformationist peace and democracy protesters like Bärbel Bohlei of Neues Forum, who had risked persecution, insecurity and imprisonment during the 1980s at a time when none of the pragmatic realists expected the regime to fall. As the peaceful crowds of protesters grew during the autumn of 1989, she suddenly became a celebrity, her flat in East Berlin, previously ignored, all at once the focus of world attention. Batteries of reporters camped outside to hear what she and her fellow protesters had to say. The pragmatists were caught by surprise. It represented the apotheosis of the radical dream – a spontaneous and unified grassroots movement uncontaminated by party politics. Yet the moment it became plain that the old regime was doomed, the pragmatists rushed to reoccupy the vacuum of power. East German politicians, who had until that moment been accommodating their careers to the old dispensation, immediately began mapping out their own futures in terms of the new one. West German politicians hurried to the East to make sure that their own party interests would be served in the imminent elections. Bärbel Bohlei, and others like her, were elbowed aside. During the brief interlude before and after the March 1990 East German elections there were radical transformationists like Rainer Eppelmann (defence and disarmament minister) in positions of influence. Professionals in the Western defence establishments treated them with disdain, likening it to 'the vicar taking over the ministry of defence' and predicting (accurately) that they would be 'eaten alive' after unification. In the December 1990 federal elections the East German experiment was swallowed up.[13]

It is hard to exaggerate the strength of the pull to the realist pole exerted by the fact of inherited structures of political power. To those who have experience of the arms trade and the way it is linked to the most ruthless political forces, for example, transformationist talk of shared interests and common security seems irrelevant. The brute existence of tanks, planes, missiles and the whole parapernalia of modern war-fighting capabilities is undeniable. They are still controlled by largely autonomous governments in a multipolar international state system still at the mercy of unregenerate political forces. In the Soviet Union, for example, the manifest economic failure of the Brezhnev 'years of stagnation' made the initial impulse of the Andropov/Gorbachev reforms irresistible. The transformationist foreign policy programme which revolutionised international affairs during the second half of the 1980s sacrificed vested Soviet defence establishment interests in order to cut loose from the dead weight that was seen to be dragging the country to ultimate ruin. But accelerating economic decline and disintegration at home in turn discredited Perestroika and allowed the vested interests to stage a recovery. In the security field Soviet realists pointed to the Western refusal to reciprocate the visionary international programme of the Soviet leadership and determined to arrest what they saw as the asymmetrical surrender of Soviet interests. Western planners pointed in turn to this gathering threat to justify a perpetuation of mirrored realist policies. Beneath the level of rhetoric large scale military research and development in conventional, nuclear, chemical and biological weaponry was vigorously pressed forward. In the face of mounting uncertainty, security instincts in separate countries and alliances dictated continuing reliance on a complete panoply of all possible means of coercion and the indefinite retention of full political control over them. 1991 opened in sombre vein. It was difficult to see how transformationist thinking could ever make headway in the face of the mutually reinforcing realist tradition entrenched in positions of power.

7   TRANSFORMATIONIST REALITY: THE ARROW OF HISTORY

The second asymmetry, however, militates in favour of the transformationist pole. It is derived from the transitional nature of the age of mutual deterrence at great power level and from the central agreement that the long-term direction of historical evolution must be away from the age of war and towards the definitive and permanent achievement of an era of mutually assured security. This is the arrow of history. It is not romanticism or wishful thinking that dictates as much. It is generated in the first place by the logic of great power rivalry at maximum force levels in the deterrent age – the critical arena for realists themselves – and then translated down to condition the nature of relations between states in general. The priorities in Europe now are widely recognised to be ones which can no longer, even in theory, be controlled by single nations or alliances acting unilaterally. The minimisation of the risk of accidental war, the buttressing of crisis stability, the mutual interest in terminating conflict early should deterrence fail, even the scope for significant reductions in cost, are now necessarily trans-national and trans-alliance concerns. National security is seen in the end to depend upon reciprocal success in ensuring that the overarching common interest in restraint from full-scale war is properly reinforced. This places the main emphasis for the first time on areas which have only been peripheral in traditional defence strategy: confidence-building, tension-reduction and the whole enterprise of international cooperation. Because mutual deterrence is mutual perception, reassurance of the other becomes an essential component in each party's own defence arrangements. Arms-control and disarmament becomes, not a narrow interface between competing power-blocs, but one aspect of a joint search for common security.

Looking beyond the military dimension, the political implications are even more important. So far deterrent restraint at great power level has been imposed on an otherwise unregenerate world order made up of what have traditionally been predatory and warring states. Economic, social, political and ideological forces, which in previous ages have erupted into the most violent convulsions of history, have been capped, not dispersed. Not only disparate interests, but incompatible conceptions of justice are still in conflict. If the UN/CSCE ideal of peaceful coexistence is indeed to have priority over all other values, then a way must somehow be found of accommodating these forces permanently beneath the absolute constraints of border inviolability. But the borders themselves are historical products. The whole international system as it exists today is a legacy from the centuries when great power war was endemic. Present frontiers have been carved out, regimes established, dominant interests imposed within this context. The nature of political structures of all kinds bears testimony to the fact that national identities were built at a time when the ultimate sanction of policy was the use of maximum force. The whistle has been blown at an arbitrary point leaving the powerful in possession of the field. If these underlying problems are not seriously addressed, then mutual deterrence from war at great power level remains an artificial constraint behind which dangerous political tensions can build, perhaps to the point where they threaten to sweep away deterrence itself. In this way it is the logic of mutual deterrence that forces the world community to look beyond deterrence.[14]

BOX 9.4   CONFLICT RESOLUTION AND DETERRENCE[15]

If mutual deterrence is successful, then incipient inter-state conflicts of all kinds have to be resolved below the threshold of war. That is why realists as well as transformationists now place increasing emphasis on the complex and extraordinarily demanding art of conflict prevention and resolution. The aim is not just peace-keeping, it is nothing less than peace-making.[16]

The UN Charter calls on member states to 'settle their international disputes by peaceful means in such a manner that international peace and security, and justice, are not endangered'. The Final Act of the CSCE incorporated a similar declaration:

'The participating states . . . will use such means as negotiation, enquiry mediation, conciliation, arbitration and judicial settlement or other peaceful means of their own choice including any settlement procedure agreed to in advance of disputes to which they are parties. In the event of failure to reach a solution by any of the above peaceful means, the parties to a dispute will continue to seek a mutually agreed way to settle the dispute peacefully.'

Realists and transformationists agree that it is desirable to institutionalise new political means to settle European conflicts short of war, and that it would be preferable if all states moved from military to non-military procedures for conducting their disputes. In November 1990 a Conflict Prevention Centre (CPC) was created by the CSCE countries at the Paris meeting and has started to operate from offices in the Hoffburg Palace, Vienna. Its current mandate is to implement confidence and security-building mechanisms (CSBMs) – not to conciliate or settle political conflicts. It has become a home for the original Soviet proposal for a risk reduction centre. The British government proposed in 1990 that the CSCE should take on a role towards conflicts in Europe similar to that of ACAS in industrial conflicts – it could 'play a mediating role in disputes between member states', said Mrs Thatcher. Chancellor Kohl spoke of the CSCE's role as a 'European conflict centre' to 'settle potential military conflicts', and President Bush said that 'we should consider whether new CSCE mechanisms can help mediate and settle disputes in Europe'. The CSCE summit in Paris in 1990 agreed to further develop such mechanisms.

Traditionally it has been taken for granted that most conflicts are 'zero-sum' contests of power in which one side wins and the other loses. Exponents of conflict resolution, however, see many if not most conflicts as positive-sum situations in which parties have shared as well as conflicting interests. They stress negotiation and mediation procedures through which parties can perceive their conflict as a shared predicament. By using a problem-solving approach parties may both be able to reach mutually satisfactory outcomes which respect their interests and needs. On the other hand if they pursue conflict through arms, they are both likely to suffer costly losses.

Half of the difficulty of settling conflicts is not the settlement of the substantive issues (though that is difficult), but the setting up of a process whereby parties can air grievances, and explore the issues which divide them. There is, of course, a deep problem in terms of relations of power here, when, as in the case of Israeli occupation of the West Bank or Iraqi occupation of Kuwait, one party already enjoys possession of what is in dispute. A third party or an agency outside the conflict may help to facilitate such a process. President Carter played this role in relation to the Arab–Israeli conflict, and the UN Secretary General frequently plays it in relation to other conflicts.

BOX 9.5   NUCLEAR WEAPONS AND INTERNATIONAL LAW[17]

The tension between inherited realist traditions and the transformationist challenge to them is well illustrated by attempts to bring nuclear weapon possession and use within the ambit of international law. The failure of attempts to reach agreement on outlawing use and thereby possession shows how the asymmetry of power favours a realist position. On the other hand the bilateral and multilateral agreements which now govern aspects of deployment suggest that in the long run the logic of mutual vulnerability favours the transformationist approach. The interplay between the two represents the response of the world community to the nuclear challenge.

International law and use

There have been numerous attempts since 1961 in the General Assembly of the United Nations to outlaw the use of nuclear weapons and thereby to outlaw the preparations for possible use inherent in production and deployment. So far these attempts have failed. Current nuclear weapon powers like Britain, France and the United States refuse to recognise the premises on which such claims are based. They consider deterrence essential to security and impossible without the option of use. In answer to those who condemn use as a violation of existing treaty provisions or international customary law, they deny that there are such norms or rules which specifically govern the use of nuclear weapons and assert that such use is therefore governed by the general rules of war. Principles of proportion and discrimination apply to all weapons and not just to nuclear weapons. In addition, declarations of non-use are seen to be ineffective and 'no substitute for concrete measures of arms control or disarmament.'[18]

Behind such arguing lies the brute fact of possession. Nuclear devices were first conceived and used as instruments of war and have since been developed within the traditional defence establishments of the great powers and deployed by their armed forces without regard to considerations of international law. As a number of studies have shown, this process has been instinctive. Most systems evolved first and were rationalised afterwards. Questions of legitimacy simply have not arisen.[19]

So at the moment there is an apparently unbridgeable gulf between the thinking of those who want to outlaw the use of nuclear weapons by present nuclear weapon countries, and the thinking of officials and planners in those countries brought up to find such interference unwarranted, dangerous and misconceived. It is a disagreement that extends to include the scope and nature of international law itself:

'Law simply does not deal with questions of ultimate power – power that comes close to the sources of sovereignty.'[20]

Since it is the latter who occupy the positions of power, it may seem that the attempt by the former to outlaw nuclear weapons use (and thereby possession) is still a folorn one: 'states, including the nuclear powers, have not agreed upon a single explicit set of rules governing the use or non-use of nuclear weapons.'[21]

International law and deployment

While international attempts to outlaw use and preparations for use have so far failed, however, the logic of mutual vulnerability inherent in the nuclear age has forced a slow but steady expansion of bilateral and multilateral agreements to restrict deployment. The paradoxical reciprocity of mutual deterrence, unplanned by any one nation or alliance, has forced an unexpected concomitant reciprocity at precisely the point of greatest mutual risk. Even the most hard-headed statesmen have been driven to formalise this logic, for example bilaterally in the ABM, SALT and INF Treaties, and multilaterally in the Partial Test Ban and Non-Proliferation Treaties.[22]

During the next few years this may well begin to converge with the kind of efforts being made through the United Nations to bring nuclear weapons under the umbrella of international law referred to above. For example, to the extent that the threat of nuclear weapon proliferation increases and the monopoly of deterrent power so far enjoyed by a handful of countries is

eroded, so their own increased vulnerability may force concessions to international law in this area. It is not clear yet whether
the 1995 renegotiation of the Non-Proliferation Treaty will
involve such concessions (for example in the direction of
demands for a Comprehensive Test Ban Treaty as a quid pro
quo). But it seems plain that ad hoc bilateral and multilateral
agreements will one way or another eventually have to be
universalised and underpinned by generally accepted principle.
This would seem quite typical of the way in which international
law has in fact evolved – a process of continual definition
through mutual accommodation between principle and *force
majeure*.

Behind these considerations lies this deep question:

'Is [international law] to be seen as a progressive instrument
of change, as a means of furthering the interests of peoples
rather than governments, as something antithetical to the
Hobbesian world of brute force, as a means of outlawing war
and the weapons of war? Or is it to be seen as a practical
means of devising modest and limited adjustments between
conflicting interests of great powers, who are the principal
agents of its creation?.'[23]

The first of these alternatives is transformationist, the second
realist. Asymmetry of power favours the realist interpretation.
But the evolution of the world community towards the preferred
goal of mutually assured security, if it is ever to come about, in
the long run favours the vision of the transformationist.

In addition to the fact that mutual great power deterrence in itself
forces policy-makers to search for the resolution of conflict below the
threshold of war, there is the further fact that the political conditions
within which such deterrence has been defined in the past are now
rapidly passing away. However complicated the intricacies of deterrent
theory that preoccupied strategists during the Cold War, they were
posited on unusually simple political premises: superpower hegemony
and bloc-to-bloc confrontation across a clearly defined and mutually
accepted border; stable goverment on either side; no desperate

incompatibility of needs; militarisation of relations which drastically reduced political complexity. None of these conditions is likely to apply in future. The world is becoming multipolar and therefore politically more confused. Already the Soviet Union is plunging towards possibly violent disintegration. What if the giant populations of China or India go the same way? Increasingly sophisticated weaponry is being made available to unstable governments and sub-national groups. There are already ten developing countries with more than 1000 main battle tanks each, and seven with more than 500 combat aircraft. This is likely to be swollen by a 'cascade' of surplus weapons from Europe. By the end of the century perhaps ten or more countries will have a ballistic missile capacity capable of projecting warheads thousands of miles. A number are on the verge of going nuclear. Classic deterrent theory has assumed an opportunist aggressor. What happens in conditions where the motive is need rather than opportunism and where the roles of challenger and defender are part of what is at issue? In a politically unstable world deterrent restraints might well themselves be used by unscrupulous or desperate regimes in a potentially lethal game of bluff and counter-bluff for high political stakes. If Hitler had had nuclear weapons as well as France and Britain, would this have stopped him marching into the Rhineland? Would a Saddam Hussein who has been undeterred by the prospect of destruction at the hands of an international alliance led by a super-power, be restrained by a nuclear threat if he himself was able to mount a nuclear counter-threat?

So it is that rapid political change combined with evolving weapon technologies challenges the complacency of deterrence theory in its classic realist guise. Conflicting interests will indeed remain. So will unregenerate human nature. The powerful will not want to compromise with the dispossessed. The rich will not want to concern themselves with the poor. The present generation will not want to bother with the next. Against a background of exploding population growth and deprivation violent nationalist, ethnic and religious movements will clash, providing ample scope for fanaticism and dictatorship. These realist features of the international scene will no doubt persist. But what is the conclusion to be drawn from all this? Whatever happens in the short term, confirming as it may the realist scenario, in the long term it has to be the transformationist agenda that prevails in centres of power. The arrow of history points in that direction – or else in a direction that none of us would like to contemplate.

It is in the middle term that this historic transition must be effected – as all at once seemed possible in Europe in the early months of 1990. During the relatively painless unification of Germany, despite all its attendant fears, the realist and transformationist insights seemed to find a proper accommodation: realist caution not precluding undoubted progress in a transformationist direction. Keeping a firm hold on both aspects of the deterrent age, realist and transformationist, the agreed purpose, at any rate rhetorically, seemed to be safely and steadily to transfer weight to the latter. It appeared during those months that most governments in Europe believed that this might be done through cooperation, thus breaking the fatal realist double-bind of never being able to move because the other might take advantage. Looking beyond the first phase of the Conventional Forces in Europe negotiations, even cautious planners were able to envisage qualitatively different security arrangements once these agreements had been implemented. And, in true tansformationist style, the whole concept of security began to widen and deepen to take in shared political, economic, environmental and cultural dimensions. The armed blocs would either dissolve (WTO) or become progressively more 'political' (NATO) as deterrent weaponry was steadily marginalised. Reductions and peace dividends would come about, if not through willing abnegation by defence establishments, then through cut-backs imposed by treasuries under pressure from non-military priorities at a time when there seemed no need to maintain such extravagant forces.

Have these hopes proved illusory? Was the dynamic figure of Mikhail Gorbachev, who so cavalierly broke the realist rules in the early heady days of Perestroika, underneath it all a realist? As the grim conservative backlash gathers strength in the Soviet Union, will the events of 1989 be shown not to have been such a turning-point after all? Or will the conservatives in turn become discredited by the unmanageable nightmare of the Soviet economy, and a process of disintegration, if not reform, continue? Time will tell. But let the last word be with the man who, no matter what happens, and however misguided and unsuccessful at home, was the central figure in an extraordinary transformation of European politics abroad, a foreshadowing of what must, if not just yet, then one day come about:

'We are all passengers aboard one ship, the Earth, and we must not allow it to be wrecked. There will be no second Noah's Ark.'[24]

BOX 9.6   CHARTER OF PARIS FOR A NEW EUROPE

Opening statement adopted by all 34 CSCE countries at the summit meeting in Paris 21 November 1990.

A New Era of Democracy, Peace and Unity

We, the Heads of State or Government of the States participating in the Conference on Security and Co-operation in Europe, have assembled in Paris at a time of profound change and historic expectations. The era of confrontation and division of Europe has ended. We declare that henceforth our relations will be founded on respect and co-operation.

Europe is liberating itself from the legacy of the past. The courage of men and women, the strength of the will of the peoples and the power of the ideas of the Helsinki Final Act have opened a new era of democracy, peace and unity in Europe.

Ours is a time for fulfilling the hopes and expectations our peoples have cherished for decades: steadfast commitment to democracy based on human rights and fundamental freedoms; prosperity through economic liberty and social justice; and equal security for all our countries.

The Ten Principles of the Final Act will guide us towards this ambitious future, just as they have lighted our way towards better relations for the past fifteen years. Full implementation of all CSCE commitments must form the basis for the initiatives we are now taking to enable our nations to live in accordance with their aspirations.

Human Rights, Democracy and Rule of Law

We undertake to build, consolidate and strengthen democracy as the only system of government of our nations. In this endeavour, we will abide by the following:

– Human rights and fundamental freedoms are the birthright of all human beings, are inalienable and are guaranteed by law. Their protection and promotion is the first responsibility of government. Respect for them is an essential safeguard against an over-mighty State. Their observance and full exercise are the foundation of freedom, justice and peace.

 – Democratic government is based on the will of the people, expressed regularly through free and fair elections. Democracy has as its foundation respect for the human person and the rule of law. Democracy is the best safeguard of freedom and expression, tolerance of all groups of society, and equality of opportunity for each person.

 – Democracy, with its representative and pluralist character, entails accountability to the electorate, the obligation of public authorities to comply with the law and justice administered impartially. No one will be above the law.

We affirm that, without discrimination,

every individual has the right to:

 – freedom of thought, conscience and religion or belief,
 – freedom of expression,
 – freedom of association and peaceful assembly,
 – freedom of movement;

no one will be:

 – subject to arbitrary arrest or detention;
 – subject to torture or other cruel, inhuman or degrading treatment, or punishment;

everyone also has the right:

 – to know and act upon his rights,
 – to participate in free and fair elections,
 – to fair and public trial if charged with an offence,
 – to own property alone or in association and to exercise individual enterprise,
 – to enjoy his economic, social and cultural rights.

We affirm that the ethnic, cultural, linguistic and religious identity of national minorities will be protected and that persons belonging to national minorities will have the right freely to express, preserve and develop that identity without any discrimination and in full equality before the law.

We will ensure that everyone will enjoy recourse to effective remedies, national or international, against any violation of his rights.

Full respect for these precepts is the bedrock on which we will seek to construct the new Europe.

Our states will co-operate and support each other with the aim of making democratic gains irreversible.

Economic Liberty and Responsibility

Economic liberty, social justice and environmental responsibility are indispensable for prosperity.

The free will of the individual, exercised in democracy and protected by the rule of law, forms the necessary basis for successful economic and social development. We will promote economic activity which respects and upholds human dignity.

Freedom and political pluralism are necessary elements in our common objective of developing market economies towards sustainable economic growth, prosperity, social justice, expanding employment and efficient use of economic resources. The success of the transition to market economy by countries making efforts to this effect is important and in the interest of us all. It will enable us to share a higher level of prosperity which is our common objective. We will co-operate to this end.

Preservation of the environment is a shared responsibility of all our nations. While supporting national and regional efforts in this field, we must look to the pressing need for joint action on a wider scale.

Friendly Relations among Participating States

Now that the new era is dawning in Europe, we are determined to expand and strengthen friendly relations and co-operation among the States of Europe, the United States of America and Canada, and to promote friendship among our peoples.

To uphold and promote democracy, peace and unity in Europe, we solemnly pledge our full commitment to the Ten Principles of the Helsinki Final Act. We affirm the continuing validity of the Ten Principles and our determination to put them into practice. All the Principles apply equally and unreservedly, each of them being interpreted taking into account the others. They form the basis of our relations.

In accordance with our obligations under the Charter of the United Nations and commitments under the Helsinki Final Act, we renew our pledge to refrain from the threat or use of force against the territorial integrity or political independence of any State, or from acting in any other manner inconsistent with the principles or purposes of those documents. We recall that non-compliance with obligations under the Charter of the United Nations constitutes a violation of international law.

We reaffirm our commitment to settle disputes by peaceful means. We decide to develop mechanisms for the prevention and resolution of conflicts among the participating States.

With the ending of the division of Europe, we will strive for a new quality in our security relations while fully respecting each other's freedom of choice in that respect. Security is indivisible and the security of every participating State is inseparably linked to that of all others. We therefore pledge to co-operate in strengthening confidence and security among us and in promoting arms control and disarmament.

We welcome the Joint Declaration of Twenty-Two States on the improvement of their relations.

Our relations will rest on our common adherence to democratic values and to human rights and fundamental freedoms. We are convinced that in order to strengthen peace and security among our States, the advancement of democracy, and respect for and effective exercise of human rights, are indispensable. We reaffirm the equal rights of peoples and their right to self determination in conformity with the Charter of the United Nations and with the relvant norms of international law, including those relating to territorial integrity of States.

We are determined to enhance political consultation and to widen co-operation to solve economic, social, environmental, cultural and humanitarian problems. This common resolve and our growing interdependence will help to overcome the mistrust of decades, to increase stability and to build a united Europe.

We want Europe to be a source of peace, open to dialogue and to co-operation with other countries, welcoming exchanges and involved in the search for common responses to the challenges of the future.

Security

Friendly relations among us will benefit from the consolidation of democracy and improved security.

We welcome the signature of the Treaty on Conventional Armed Forces in Europe by twenty-two participating States, which will lead to lower levels of armed forces. We endorse the adoption of a substantial new set of Confidence- and Security-Building Measures which will lead to increased transparency and confidence among all participating States. These are important steps towards enhanced stability and security in Europe.

The unprecedented reduction in armed forces resulting from the Treaty on Conventional Armed Forces in Europe, together with new approaches to security and co-operation within the CSCE process, will lead to a new perception of security in Europe and a new dimension in our relations. In this context we fully recognize the freedom of States to choose their own security arrangements.

Unity

Europe whole and free is calling for a new beginning. We invite our peoples to join in this great endeavour.

We note with great satisfaction the Treaty on the Final Settlement with respect to Germany signed in Moscow on 12 September 1990 and sincerely welcome the fact that the German people have united to become one State in accordance with the principles of the Final Act of the Conference on Security and Co-operation in Europe and in full accord with their neighbours. The establishment of the national unity of Germany is an important contribution to a just and lasting order of peace for a united, democratic Europe aware of its responsibility for stability, peace and co-operation.

The participation of both North American and European States is a fundamental characteristic of the CSCE; it underlies its past achievements and is essential to the future of the CSCE process. An abiding adherence to shared values and our common heritage are the ties which bind us together. With all the rich diversity of our nations, we are united in our commitment to expand our co-operation in all fields. The challenges confronting us can only be met by common action, co-operation and solidarity.

The CSCE and the World

The destiny of our nations is linked to that of all other nations. We support fully the United Nations and the enhancement of its role in promoting international peace, security and justice. We reaffirm our commitment to the principles and purposes of the United Nations as enshrined in the Charter and condemn all violations of these principles. We recognize with satisfaction the growing role of the United Nations in world affairs and its increasing effectiveness, fostered by the improvement in relations among our States.

Aware of the dire needs of a great part of the world, we commit ourselves to solidarity with all other countries. Therefore, we issue a call from Paris today to all the nations of the world. We stand ready to join with any and all States in common efforts to protect and advance the community of fundamental human rights.

NOTES

1. Soviet-Indian statement, signed Moscow, 23 July 1990, *Soviet News*, no. 6536.
2. James Baker, testimony to Congress, broadcast BBC 1, Breakfast News, 5 September 1990, Media Transcription Service, ref. no. 948.
3. Douglas Hurd, address to the United Nations, broadcast BBC 2, 'Newsnight', 26 September 1990, Media Transcription Service, ref. no. 998.
4. *Statement on the Defence Estimates*, 1989, vol. 1, HMSO, May 1989.
5. *The Military Balance, 1990–1*, International Institute for Strategic Studies, London.
6. F. H. Hinsley, *Power and the Pursuit of Peace*, Cambridge University Press, 1979.
7. Some may not be happy with the description 'age of mutual deterrence' because the word 'deterrence' suggests that it is nuclear weapons that

have kept the peace in Europe for the past 45 years. Others may not be happy because the word 'mutual' suggests that the West has had to be deterred just as much as the Soviet Union. If those at both poles of the debate are equally unhappy in this way, it may be as well to preserve the description and ask each to accept that neither unwelcome overtone is necessarily intended. The term 'deterrence' is important because it sums up the crucial shift in declaratory strategy (particularly in the West) away from the hitherto dominant idea of war-fighting defence at maximum force levels. The term 'mutual' is equally important because it encapsulates what is problematic about such a declared strategy (together with what backs it up) when it is mutually applied.

It is, in fact, difficult to determine what counts as deterrent success in the first place. Out of 54 examples of politico-military crises looked at in one study, for example (P. Huth and B. Russett, 'What Makes Deterrence Work?', *World Politics*, 36, July 1984, pp. 496–526), 31 were classed as deterrent successes and 23 as deterrent failures. R.N. Lebow and J.G. Stein, however, report in When Does Deterrence Succeed and How Do We Know?, Canadian Institute for International Peace and Security, February 1990, that on reviewing the same 54 cases they rejected 37 as having had nothing to do with deterrence, 4 as compellence rather than deterrence and another 4 as ambiguous. Of the remaining 9 cases, 3 were classed as deterrent successes and 7 as failures (one was compound). But not one of the 3 cases cited as 'successes' by Lebow and Stein was included among the 31 'successes' listed by Huth and Russett.

8. Steven Kull, *Minds At War*, Basic Books, 1989.
9. *Soviet News*, no. 6559, 2 January 1991.
10. For example, the claim that the INF Treaty was the result of NATO's steadfastness in deploying Pershing 2 and Ground Launched Cruise Missiles was countered by the claim that it was, on the contrary, the result of Mikhail Gorbachev's calling NATO's bluff by accepting the disingenuous zero option.
11. Vaclav Havel, address to the Parliamentary Assembly of the Council of Europe, *Ceteka Daily News and Press Survey*, 10 May 1990.
12. Alun Chalfont, *Encounter*, September 1990.
13. Comments by British Ministry of Defence official at the visit of the East German deputy defence and disarmament minister, Frank Marcinek, to Britain, May 1990.
14. Those who have spent time trying to formulate general principles of human rights and human justice usually say that disputes over what is perceived as an injustice can only be solved rationally and satisfactorily if there is some sort of agreement about what counts as just in the first place:

> 'Being designed to reconcile by reason, justification proceeds from what all parties to the discussion hold in common. Ideally, to justify a conception of justice to someone is to give him a proof of its principles from premises that we both accept, these principles in turn having consequences that match our considered judgements' (John Rawls, *A Theory of Justice*, Oxford University Press, 1972) pp. 580–1.

But, as events in the Middle East, Iran and China suggest, the ideological divide may be so fundamental that no such agreement is possible. Even then, if recourse to war is indeed to be ruled out, they are nevertheless forced to find some common basis on which, if not actually to settle their disputes, at least to prevent them from escalating to a dangerous level. Something along these lines is suggested in Stuart Hampshire's concept of 'minimum procedural justice', *Innocence and Experience*, Allen Lane, the Penguin Press, 1990.

15.   There is a large and growing literature on conflict resolution. See, for example, John Burton, *Conflict: Resolution and Provention*, Macmillan, 1990; John Burton and Frank Dukes, *Conflict: Practices in Management, Settlement and Resolution*, Macmillan, 1990; C. R. Mitchell, *The Structure of International Conflict*, Macmillan, 1981; Martin Patchen, *Resolving Disputes Between Nations: Coercion or Conciliation*, Duke University Press, 1988; Dean Pruitt and Jeffrey Rubin, *Social Conflict: Escalation, Stalemate and Settlement*, Random House, 1986; C. Mitchell and K. Webb (eds) *New Approaches to International Mediation*, Greenwood Press, 1988; S. Touval and I. W. Zartman (eds) *International Mediation in Theory and Practice*, Westview Press, 1985; Adam Curle, *In the Middle: Non-Official Mediation in Violent Situations*, Berg, 1986.

16.   On peace-keeping, see Alan James, *Peacekeeping in International Politics*, Macmillan, 1990.

17.   The Institute for Law and Peace (INLAP), set up in 1987, has devoted itself to the task of promoting 'respect for the universal right of non-combatants to seek protection by law from indiscriminate attack, mass destruction and preparations and threats to kill'. Its members maintain that current nuclear strategies are illegal.

18.   See Sydney Bailey, *War and Conscience In The Nuclear Age*, Macmillan 1987, pp. 117–19; and Burns Weston, 'Nuclear Weapons Versus International Law: Contextual Reassessment', *McGill Law Journal*, vol. 28, no. 3, July 1983.

In addition to international customary law, there is international conventional law including: the Hague Convention IV 1907 ('the territory of neutral powers shall be inviolable'), the Geneva Protocol 1925 ('the use in war' of all 'poisonous gases, substances and devices' is outlawed), the Prevention of Genocide Convention 1948, the Geneva Conventions 1949, the Human Rights Conventions 1948, 1966, etc. Protocol I 1977: Additional to the Geneva Conventions of 12 August 1949 and relating to the protection of victims of international armed conflicts (Ch. II, Art. 51, Sections 4, 5):

'4.   Indiscriminate attacks are prohibited. Indiscriminate attacks are:

(a)   those which are not directed at a specific military objective;
(b)   those which employ a method or means of combat which cannot be directed at a specific military objective;
or (c)   those which employ a method or means of combat the effects of which cannot be limited as required by this protocol;

5.   Among others, the following types of attacks are to be considered as indiscriminate:

(a)   an attack by bombardment by any methods or means which treats as a single military objective a number of clearly separated and distinct military objectives located in a city, town, village or other area containing a similar concentration of civilians or civilian objects;

and (b) an attack which may be expected to cause incidental loss of civilian life, injury to civilians, damage to civilian objects, or a combination thereof, which would be excessive in relation to the concrete and direct military advantage anticipated.'

Note the 'Stockholm Declaration' sent by Ingvar Carlsson, Prime Minister of Sweden, to Robert McNamara, 1 March 1988: 'A handful of nations have acquired the capability of destroying not only one another, but all others as well. No nation has the right to use such instruments of war. And what thus is morally wrong should also be explicitly prohibited by international law.'

Robert McNamara replied: 'I had expressed a similar thought to Olof Palme a year or two before he died and urged him to press the Palme Commission to issue a similar statement. Do not the superpowers and their allies have a responsibility to other nations to assure them that they will not be adversely affected if nuclear weapons are used? Should not such an assurance be subject to "verification"?', *Pugwash Newsletter*, no. 25, 4 May 1988.

19.   For example, Margaret Gowing, *Independence and Deterrence, Britain and Atomic Energy 1945–1952*, vol. 1, Macmillan, 1974.

20.   Dean Acheson, apropos the Cuba missile crisis, *Proceedings of the American Society of International Law*, 1963, p. 14. Quoted in 23.

21.   Adam Roberts and Richard Guelff (eds) *Documents on the Laws of War*, Oxford, 2nd edn, 1989, p. 18.

22.   This can be illustrated in terms of the relationship between unilateral modernisation and multilateral arms control, the former predominant during the age of war, the latter increasingly prominent under pressure from the logic of mutual deterrence. For example, Submarine Launched Ballistic Missiles (SLBM) and Multiple Independently Targeted Re-entry Vehicles (MIRV) both emerged through the traditional process of competitive unilateral modernisation from within the defence establishments of the great powers. But, once mutually deployed, mutual vulnerability dictated very different judgements on them in terms of multilateral arms control. Submarine launched missiles were thought to be good, because, as invulnerable second strike systems, they were seen to reinforce stability, whereas multiple warheads were thought to be bad because they threatened to undermine it. Yet no one had planned this. If submarine launched missiles did enhance stability when mutually deployed, it was only because the vigorous competitive efforts being made on both sides unilaterally to achieve a breakthrough in anti-submarine warfare had so far failed.

On a Comprehensive Test Ban Treaty note: 'Most countries in the world consider that an early end to nuclear testing by all states in all environments would be an essential step towards preventing the qualita-

tive improvement and the development of new nuclear weapons and
would also contribute to the goal of non-proliferation. Most nuclear
weapon states consider that their reliance on nuclear weapons for their
security requires their continued testing and do not agree that a
Comprehensive Test Ban is an urgent necessity', Secretary-General of
the United Nations' report, *A Comprehensive Study On Nuclear Weapons*,
18 September 1990, A/45/373, p. 136.

23. Adam Roberts, 'Law, Lawyers And Nuclear Weapons', *Review of
    International Studies*, vol. 16, no. 1, January 1990, p. 84.

24. Mikhail Gorbachev, *Perestroika: New Thinking For Our Country And The
    World*, Collins, London, 1988, p. 12.

Bibliography

Chapters 1 and 2

Agrell, W. (1987) 'Offensive versus Defensive: Military Strategy and Alternative Defence', *Journal of Peace Research*, vol. 24, no. 1.

Alternative Defence Commission (1983) *Defence without the Bomb* (London, Taylor & Francis).

Alternative Defence Commission (1987) *The Politics of Alternative Defence* (London, Paladin).

Arbatov, Alexei (1989) 'How Much Defence is Sufficient?', *International Affairs*, April 1989.

Arkin, William and Fieldhouse, Richard (1985) *Nuclear Battlefields* (Cambridge, Mass., Ballinger).

Ball, Desmond (1987) *Controlling Theatre Nuclear War* (Canberra, Strategic and Defence Studies Centre, Australian National University).

Bellamy, C. (1987) *The Future of Land Warfare* (London, Croom Helm).

Bluth, C. (1990) *New Thinking in Soviet Military Policy* (London, Pinter/RIIA).

Bogdanov, R. and Kortunov, A. (1989) *On the Balance of Power* (Moscow, Soviet Peace Committee).

Booth, Ken (1979) Strategy and Ethnocentrism (London, Croom Helm).

Booth, Ken (1990) 'Steps towards Stable Peace in Europe: a Theory and Practice of Coexistence', *International Affairs*, vol. 66, no. 1.

Boserup, Anders and Neild, Robert (eds) (1990) *The Foundations of Defensive Defence* (London, Macmillan).

Booth, Ken (ed.) (1991) *New Thinking about Strategy and International Security* (London, Harper/Collins).

Bracken, Paul (1983) *The Command and Control of Nuclear Weapons* (New Haven, Yale University Press).

Bundy, McGeorge (1989) *Danger and Survival: Choices about the Bomb in the First Fifty Years* (New York, Random House).

Buzan, B. (1987) 'Common Security, Non-Provocative Defence and the Future of Western Europe', *Review of International Studies*, vol. 13).

Carter, A., Steinbruner J. and Zracket, C. (eds) (1987) *Managing Nuclear Operations* (Washington, DC, Brookings Institution)

Chalmers, M., Stevenson, D. and Moller, B. (1990) *Alternative Conventional Defence Structures and Conventional Arms Control in Europe* (Mosbach, AFES–PRESS).

Coats, Dan (1990) 'US Defense Policy and the Emerging European Security Environment', *Strategic Review*, Winter 1990.

Dahrendorf, Ralf (1990) *Reflections on the Revolution in Europe* (London, Chatto & Windus).

Dean, Jonathan (1988) *Watershed in Europe: Dismantling the East–West Military Confrontation* (Lexington, Lexington Books)

Dean, Jonathan (1989) *Meeting Gorbachev's Challenge* (London, Macmillan).

Dewitt, David (1987) *Nuclear Non-Proliferation and Global Security* (London, Croom Helm).

Donnelly, Christopher (1988) *The Red Banner: The Soviet Military System in Peace and War* (London, Jane's).

Donnelly, Christopher (1990) 'The Development of Soviet Military Policy in the 1990s', *RUSI Journal*, Spring 1990.

Etzold, Thomas (1990) 'The Strategic Environment of the Twenty-First Century: Alternative Futures for Strategic Planners', *Strategic Review*, Spring 1990.

Finnis, John, Boyle, Joseph and Grisez, Germain (1987) *Nuclear Deterrence, Morality and Realism* (Oxford, Clarendon Press).

Forsberg, Randall (1987) *Non-Provocative Defence: a New Approach to Arms Control* (Brookline, Mass., Institute for Defense and Disarmament Studies).

Freedman, Lawrence (1986) *The Price of Peace: Living with the Nuclear Dilemma* (London, Firethorn).

Freedman, Lawrence (1989) *The Evolution of Nuclear Strategy* (London, Macmillan, 2nd edn).

Fukuyama, Francis (1989) 'The End of History', *The National Interest*, no. 16.

Galtung, Johan (1984) 'Transarmament: from Offensive to Defensive Defence', *Journal of Peace Research*, vol. 21, no. 2.

Gartoff, Raymond (1985) *Detente and Confrontation: American-Soviet Relations from Nixon to Reagan* (Washington, DC, Brookings Institution).

Gates, David (1987) *Non-Offensive Defence: A Strategic Contradiction?* (London, Institute for European Defence and Strategic Studies).

Gorbachev, Mikhail (1987) *Perestroika; New Thinking for Our Country and the World* (London, Collins).

Halliday, Fred (1983) *The Making of the Second Cold War* (London, Verso).

Harle, Vilho and Sivonen, Pekka (eds) (1989) *Europe in Transition* (London, Frances Pinter).

Higgins, Ronald (1978) *The Seventh Enemy: the Human Factor in the Global Crisis* (London, Hodder & Stoughton).

Howard, Michael (1976) *War in European History* (Oxford, OUP).

Howard, Michael (1983) *The Causes of Wars* (London, Unwin).

Hunter, Robert (1990) 'The Future of European Security', *Washington Quarterly*, Autumn 1990.

Joffe, J. (1987) *The Limited Partnership: Europe, the United States and the Burden of Alliance* (Cambridge, Mass., Ballinger).

Johansen, R.C. (1989) *The New Global Context for Security: a Strategic Overview* (University of Notre Dame, Institute for Peace Studies).

Kaldor, Mary (1982) *The Baroque Arsenal* (London, Andre Deutsch).

Kaldor, M., Holden, G. and Falk R. (eds) (1989) *The New Detente: Rethinking East–West Relations* (London, Verso).

Kennedy, Paul (1988) *The Rise and Fall of the Great Powers* (London, Unwin Hyman).

Krauss, M. (1986) *How NATO Weakens the West* (New York, Simon and Schuster).

Layne, Christopher (1989) 'Superpower Disengagement', *Foreign Policy*, Winter 1989/90.

Legge, J. (1983) *Theatre Nuclear Weapons and the NATO Strategy of Flexible Response* (Santa Monica, RAND Corporation).

Light, Margot (1988) *The Soviet Theory of International Relations* (London, Harvester).

Luard, E. (1986) *War in International Society* (London, Tauris).

Luard, E. (1988) *Conflict and Peace in the Modern International System* (London, Macmillan).

McCauley, Martin (1990) *Gorbachev and Perestroika* (London, Macmillan).

MccGwire, Michael (1986) 'Deterrence: the Problem – not the Solution', *International Affairs*, vol. 62, no. 1.

MccGwire, Michael (1988) 'A Mutual Security Regime for Europe?', *International Affairs*, vol. 64, no. 3.

MccGwire, Michael (1991) *Perestroika and Soviet National Security* (Washington, DC, the Brookings Institution).

McLean, Scilla (ed.) (1986) *How Nuclear Weapons Decisions Are Made* (London, Macmillan).

McNamara, Robert (1987) *Blundering into Disaster: Surviving the First Century of the Nuclear Age* (New York, Pantheon).

Malcolm, N. (1989) 'The Common European Home and Soviet European Policy', *International Affairs*, vol. 65, no. 4.

Mearsheimer, John (1990) 'Back to the Future: Instability in Europe After the Cold War', *International Security*, Summer 1990.

Medvedev, Z. (1983) *Andropov: His Life and Death* (Oxford, Blackwell).

Medvedev, Z. (1986) *Gorbachev* (Oxford, Blackwell).

Miall, Hugh (1987) *Nuclear Weapons: Who's in Charge?* (London, Macmillan).

Military Balance 1990–1991 (London, Brassey's for IISS).

Molnar, Thomas (1989) 'Recentralizing Europe', *National Review*, November 1990.

Mueller, John (1989) 'A New Concert of Europe', *Foreign Policy*, Winter 1989/90.

Neild, Robert (1990) *An Essay on Strategy* (London, Macmillan).

New Europe (1990) (Cambridge, Granta/Penguin).

Nolan, Janne E. (1991) 'US Nuclear Strategy After the Cold War: Who Decides?', *Massachusetts Technology Review*, MIT, January 1991.

Osgood, Charles (1962) *Neither War Nor Surrender* (University of Illinois Press).

Palmer, John (1988) *Europe Without America? The Crisis in Atlantic Relations* (Oxford, OUP).

Paul, Derek (ed.) *Defending Europe – Options for Security* (Philadelphia, Taylor & Francis).

Phillips, R. and Sands, J. (1988) 'Reasonable Sufficiency and Soviet Conventional Force', *International Security*, vol. 13, no. 2.

Prins, Gwyn (1984) *The Choice: Nuclear Weapons Versus Security* (London, Chatto & Windus).

Pugh, M. and Williams, P. (eds) (1990) *Superpower Politics: Change in the United States and the Soviet Union* (Manchester, Manchester University Press).

Ramsbotham, Oliver (1987) *Choices: Nuclear and Non-Nuclear Defence Options* (London, Brassey's).

Ramsbotham, Oliver (1989) *Modernizing NATO's Nuclear Weapons* (London, Macmillan).

Reid, B. H. and Dewar, M. (eds) *Military Strategy in a Changing Europe: Towards the Twenty-First Century* (London: Brassey's).

Schell, Jonathan (1982) *The Fate of the Earth* (London, Picador).

Shenfield, Stephen (1987) *The Nuclear Predicament: Explorations in Soviet Ideology* (London, Routledge & Kegan Paul).

Shenfield, Stephen (1989) *Minimum Nuclear Deterrence: the Debate Among Soviet Civilian Analysts* (Providence RI, Center for Foreign Policy Development, Brown University).

Sherwood, Elizabeth (1990) *Allies in Crisis: Meeting Global Challenges to Western Security* (London, Yale University Press).

Simpson, John (1989) *Nuclear Non-Proliferation: 1990, a Crucial Year?* (London, Council for Arms Control).

SIPRI Yearbook (1990) *World Armaments and Disarmament* (Oxford, Clarendon Press).

Sivard, Ruth L. (1990) *World Military and Social Expenditures* (Washington, World Priorities Inc.).

Smith, Dan (1989) *Pressure: How America Runs NATO* (London, Bloomsbury).

Spector, Leonard (1990) *Nuclear Ambitions: the Spread of Nuclear Weapons 1989-1990* (Boulder, Colorado, Westview Press).

Steele, J. (1984) *The Limits of Soviet Power* (London, Penguin).

Stromseth, Jane E. (1988) *The Origins of Flexible Response* (London, Macmillan).

Unterseher, Lutz (1989) *The Spider and the Web: the Case for a Pragmatic Defence Alternative* (Bonn, SAS).

Unterseher, Lutz (1990) *The Conventional Land Defence in Central Europe – Force Structure, Emerging Technology and Military Stability* (Mosbach, AFES–PRESS).

Utgoff, Victor (1990) *The Challenge of Chemical Weapons* (London, Macmillan).

Van Evera, Stephen (1990) 'Primed for Peace: Europe After the Cold War', *International Security*, Winter 1990/1.

Vayrynen, Raimo (ed.) (1985) *Policies for Common Security* (Stockholm, SIPRI).

Venn, F. (1986) *Oil Diplomacy in the Twentieth Century* (London, Macmillan).

Wæver, O., Lemaitre, P. and Tromer, E. (eds) (1989) *European Polyphony: Perspectives Beyond East-West Confrontation* (London, Macmillan).

Wallop, Malcolm (1990) 'A View from Capitol Hill. Beyond 1992: A European Lesson from German Politics', *Strategic Review*, Spring 1990.

Warner, Martin and Crip, Roger (eds) (1990) *Terrorism, Protest and Power* (Aldershot, Edward Elgar).

Webber, Philip (1990) *New Defence Strategies for the 1990s: from Confrontation to Coexistence* (London, Macmillan).

Wessell, Nils (ed.) (1991) *The New Europe: Revolution in East–West Relations* (New York, The Academy of Political Science).

Windass, Stan (ed.) (1985) *Avoiding Nuclear War: Common Security as a Strategy for the Defence of the West* (London, Brassey's).

Chapter 3

Allison, Graham, Albert Carnesdale and Joseph Nye (eds) (1985) *Hawks, Doves and Owls: an Agenda for Avoiding Nuclear War* (New York, W. W. Norton).

Allott, Philip (1990) *Eunomia* (Oxford, Oxford University Press).

Amin, S. (1977) *Imperialism and Unequal Development* (Sussex, Harvester).

Aron, Raymond (1966) *Peace and War: a Theory of International Relations* (Garden City, New York, Doubleday).

Axelrod, Robert (1984) *The Evolution of Cooperation* (New York, Basic books).

Bok, Sissela (1989) *A Strategy for Peace* (New York, Pantheon).

Brewer, Anthony (1990) *Marxist Theories of Imperialism* (London, Routledge).

Bull, Hedley (1977) *The Anarchical Society: a Study of Order in World Politics* (New York, Columbia University Press).

Bull, Hedley, Benedict Kingsbury and Adam Roberts (eds) (1990) *Hugo Grotius and International Relations* (Oxford, Oxford University Press).

Burton, John (1972) *World Society* (Cambridge, Cambridge University Press).

Carr E.H. (1940) *The Twenty Years' Crisis* (London, Macmillan).

Carver, Michael (1982) *A Policy for Peace* (London, Faber).

Clausewitz, Karl Maria von (1976 ed.) *On War* (ed. and tr. Michael Howard and Peter Paret, Princeton, NJ, Princeton University Press).

Coate, Roger and Rosati, Jerel (1988) *The Power of Human Needs in World Society* (Lynne Reinner Publishers).

Donelan, Michael (1990) *Elements of International Political Theory* (Oxford, Oxford University Press).

Falk, Richard (1989) *The Promise of World Order* (Brighton, Wheatsheaf).

Galtung, Johan (1984) *There Are Alternatives: Four Roads to Peace and Security* (Nottingham, Spokesman Books).

Gorbachev, Mikhail (1987) *For a Nuclear-Free World: Speeches and Statements by the General Secretary of the CPSU Central Committee on Nuclear Disarmament Problems* (Moscow, Novosti).

Grotius, Hugo (1925 ed.) *On the Law of War and Peace* (Indianapolis, Bobbs-Merrill).

Howard, Michael (1978) *War and the Liberal Conscience* (Oxford, Oxford University Press).

Johnson, James Turner (1987) *The Quest for Peace: Three Moral Traditions in Western Cultural History* (Princeton, Princeton University Press).

Kaldor, Mary (1990) *The Imaginary War: Understanding the East–West Conflict* (Oxford, Blackwell).

Keane, John (1988) *Civil Society and the State: New European Perspectives* (London, Verso).

Kennan, George (1985) 'Morality and Foreign Policy', *Foreign Affairs*, Winter 1985/6.

Keohane, Robert (1984) *After Hegemony: Cooperation and Discord in the World Political Economy* (Princeton, NJ, Princeton University Press).

Keohane, Robert (ed.) (1986) *Neo-Realism and its Critics* (Cambridge, Cambridge University Press).

Keohane, Robert and Nye, Joseph (1977) *Power and Interdependence: World Politics in Transition* (Boston, Little, Brown & Co.).

Keohane, Robert and Nye, Joseph (1987) 'Power and Interdependence Revisited', *International Organization*, vol. 41, no. 4.

Kim, S. (1984) *The Quest for a Just World Order* (Boulder, Colorado, Westview).

Konrad, George (1984) *Antipolitics* (London, Quartet).

Krasner, Stephen (1981) 'Transforming International Regimes: What the Third World Wants and Why', *International Studies Quarterly*, no. 25.

Krasner, Stephen (1985) *Structural Conflict: the Third World v. Global Liberalism* (Berkeley, University of California Press).

Little, R. and McKinley, R. (1986) *Global Problems and World Order* (London, Frances Pinter).

Machiavelli, Niccolo (1975) *The Prince* (Rev. ed., Penguin).

Miller, J. and Vincent, R. (1990) *Order and Violence: Hedley Bull and International Relations* (Oxford, Oxford University Press).

Miller, Lynn (1990) *Global Order: Values and Power in International Politics* (London, Westview).

Morgenthau, Hans (1973) *Politics Among Nations: the Struggle for Power and Peace* (New York, Alfred Knopf).

Niebuhr, Reinhold (1960) *Moral Man and Immoral Society* (New York, Scribner).

Onze, Kenneth (ed.) (1986) *Cooperation under Anarchy* (Princeton University Press).

Ornstein, Robert and Ehrlich, Paul (1989) *New World, New Mind* (London, Methuen).

Paret, Peter (ed.) (1986) *Makers of Modern Strategy from Machiavelli to the Nuclear Age* (Princeton, NJ, Princeton University Press).

Reiss, Hans (ed.) (1970) *Kant's Political Writings* (Cambridge, Cambridge University Press).

Rogers, Paul (ed.) (1976) *Future Resources and World Development* (London, Plenum).

Rosenau, James (1991) *Governance without Government in International Society* (Cambridge, Cambridge University Press).

Sanders, D. (1986) *Lawmaking and Cooperation in International Politics: the Idealist Case Reexamined* (London, Macmillan).

Smith, Dan and Thompson, Edward (1987) *Prospectus for a Habitable Planet* (London, Penguin).

Smoke, Richard and Harman, Willis (1987) *Paths to Peace* (Boulder, Colorado, Westview).

Smoke, R., and Kortunov, A. (1991) *Mutual Security? A New Approach to Soviet–American Relations* (London, Macmillan).

Taylor, T. (ed.) (1978) *Approaches and Theory in International Relations* (London, Longman).

Thompson, Edward (1982) *Exterminism and the Cold War* (London, New Left Books).

Vasquez, J. (1983) *The Power of Power Politics* (London, Pinter).

Von Laue, T. (1987) *The World Revolution of Westernization: The Twentieth Century in Global Perspective* (New York, Oxford University Press).

Waltz, K. N. (1959) *Man, the State and War* (New York, Columbia University Press).

Waltz, K. N. (1979) *Theory of International Politics* (London, Addison-Wesley).

Wallerstein, I. (1979) *The Capitalist World Economy* (Cambridge, Cambridge University Press).

Wallerstein, I. (1984) *The Politics of the World Economy, the States, the Movements and the Civilizations* (Cambridge, Cambridge University Press).

Chapters 4 and 5

Ardagl, John (1987) *Germany and the Germans: An Anatomy of Society Today* (New York, Harper & Row).

Bark, Dennis and Gress, David (1989) *A History of West Germany vol. 1, from Shadow to Substance 1945–1963 vol. 2; Democracy and Discontent 1963–1988* (Oxford, Blackwell).

Behme, Klaus von (1982) *The Political System of the Federal Republic* (New York, St. Martin's Press).

Binder, David (1975) *The Other German: Willy Brandt's Life and Times* (Washington, DC, New Republic).

Bogdanov, V. (ed.) (1983) *Coalition Government in Western Europe* (London, Heinemann).

Boutwell, Jeffrey (1990) *The German Nuclear Dilemma* (London, Brassey's).

Brandt, Willy (1976) *Begegnungen und Einsichten* (Hamburg, Hoffman und Campe Verlag).

Calleo, David (1978) *The German Problem Reconsidered: Germany and the World Order: 1870 to the Present* (Cambridge, Cambridge University Press).

Campbell, Edwina (1989) *Germany's Past & Europe's Future* (London, Pergamon-Brassey).

Coffey, J. (1985) *Deterrence and Arms Control: American and West German Perspectives on INF* (Denver, Colorado, University of Denver Press).

Cooney, James *et al.* (eds) (1984) *The Federal Republic of Germany and the United States: Changing Political, Social and Economic Relations* (Boulder, Colorado, Wheatsheaf).

Czempiel, Ernst-Otto (1990) 'Die Modernosierung der Atlantischen Gemeinschaft', *Europa Archiv*, April 1990.

Dalton, Russell (1989) *Politics in West Germany* (Boston, Scott Foresman).

Dennis, Mike (1988) *German Democratic Republic: Politics, Economics and Society* (London, Frances Pinter).

Dregger, Alfred (1989) 'Eine Strategie fur die Zukunft', *Europäische Wehrkunde/WWR*, December 1989.

Genscher, Hans-Dietrich (1990) 'Die Deutsche Vereinigung als Beitrag zur europäischen Stabilität', speech to WEU assembly, *Bulletin der Bundesregierung*, 27 March 1990.

Genscher, Hans-Dietrich (1990) 'Die neue europäische Friedensordnung', *Europa Archiv*, August 1990.

Gress, David (1985) *Peace and Survival: West Germany, the Peace Movement and European Security* (Stanford, California, Hoover Institution).

Griffith, William (1978) *The Ostpolitik of the Federal Republic of Germany* (Cambridge, Mass., MIT Press).

Gutjahr, Lothar (1990) 'Konservative Reaktionen auf das Ende von Jalta', *Hamburger Beitrage Heft 47*.

Hamm, Manfred (1990) 'A View from Germany. Transatlantic Relations and the Future of European Security', *Strategic Review*, Spring 1990.

Hanrieder, Wolfram (1989) *Germany, America, Europe: Forty Years of German Foreign Policy* (New Haven, Conn., Yale University Press).

Hoffmann, Stanley (1990) 'Reflections on the "German Question"', *Survival*, July/August 1990.

Hülsberg, Werner (1988) *The German Greens* (London, Verso).

James, Harold (1989) *A German Identity 1770–1990* (London, Weidenfeld & Nicolson).

Jesse, Eckhard (1990) *Elections: the Federal Republic of Germany in Comparison* (Oxford, Berg).

Kaiser, Carl-Christian (1988) *The German Bundestag* (Bonn, Bundestag Public Relations Division).

Katzenstein, Peter (1987) *Policy and Politics in West Germany* (Philadelphia, Temple University Press).

Kelleher, C. M. (1975) *Germany and the Politics of Nuclear Weapons* (New York, Columbia University Press).

Kirchner, E. (ed.) (1988) *Liberal Parties in Western Europe* (Cambridge, Cambridge University Press).

Kirchner, E. (1990) 'Genscher and What Lies Behind Genscherism', *West European Politics*, vol. 13, no. 2.

Kohl, Helmut (1990) 'Die Deutsche Frage und die europäische Verantwortung', *Bulletin der Bundesregierung*, 19 January 1990.

Kolinsky, Eva (1984) *Parties, Opposition and Society in West Germany* (London, Pinter).

Krauthammer, Charles (1990) 'The German Revival', *The New Republic*, 26 March 1990.

Langguth, Gerd (1986) *The Green Factor in German Politics: From Protest Movement to Political Party* (Boulder, Colorado, Westview).

Lees, J. and Shaw, M. (eds) *Committees in Legislatures* (London, Martin Robertson).

Monnet, Jean (1978) *Memoirs* (Doubleday).
Parkin, Sara (1989) *Green Parties: an International Guide* (London, Heretic Books).
Pridham, Geoffrey (1975) *Christian Democracy in West Germany* (New York, St. Martin's Press).
Rohe, Karl (ed.) (1989) *Elections, Parties and Political Traditions in Germany 1867–1987* (Oxford, Berg).
Rose, R. and Suleiman, E. (eds) (1980) *Presidents and Prime Ministers* (American Institute for Public Policy Research).
Saalfeld, Thomas (1990) 'The West German Bundestag after Forty Years: the Role of Parliament in a "Parliamentary Democracy"', *West European Politics*, vol. 13, no. 3.
Schmidt, Helmut (1985) *A Grand Strategy for the West* (New Haven, Yale University Press).
Schweitzer, C. *et al.* (eds) (1984) *Politics and Government in the Federal Republic of Germany* (Oxford, Berg).
Senghaas, Dieter (1990) *Europe 2000. Ein Friedenplan* (Suhrkamp Verlag).
Steinke, Rudolf and Vale, Michael (eds) (1983) *Germany Debates Defence: The NATO Alliance at a Crossroads* (New York, M.E. Sharpe).
Stoltenberg, Gerhard (1989) 'Perspektiven europäischer Sicherheit und trans-atlantischer Partnerschaft', *Bulletin der Bundesregierung*, 12 October 1989.
Stoltenberg, Gerhard (1990) 'A United Germany in Europe', *NATO's Sixteen Nations*, April 1990.
Szabo, Stephen (ed.) (1990) *The Bundeswehr and Western Security* (London, Macmillan).
Szabo, Stephen (1990) *The Changing Politics of German Security* (London, Frances Pinter).
Tilford, Roger (ed.) (1975) *The Ostpolitik and Political Change in Germany* (Lexington, Mass., Lexington Books).
Voigt, Karsten (1989) 'Germany After the Wall', *World Policy Journal*, Winter 1989/90.
Voigt, Karsten (1990) 'Eine europäische Friedensordnung ohne den Ungeist des Nationalismus', *Europäische Wehrkunde/WWR*, March 1990).
Windsor, Philip (1981) *Germany and the Western Alliance* (London, IISS).
Wolffsohn, Michael (1986) *West Germany's Foreign Policy in the Era of Brandt and Schmidt 1969–1982* (Frankfurt-am-Main, Lang).
Wörner, Manfred (1991) 'The Atlantic Alliance in the New Era', *NATO Review*, vol. 39, no. 1, February 1991.

Chapters 6, 7 and 8

Baylis, John (ed.) (1983) *Alternative Approaches to British Defence Policy* (London, Macmillan).
Baylis, John (1989) *British Defence Policy* (London, Macmillan).
Booth, Ken and Baylis, John (1989) *Britain, NATO and Nuclear Weapons* (London, Macmillan).
Burt, Gordon (ed.) (1988) *Alternative Defence Policy* (London, Croom Helm).
Byrd, P. (ed.) (1988) *British Foreign Policy Under Thatcher* (Oxford, Philip Allen/St. Martin's Press).

Campbell, Duncan (1984) *The Unsinkable Aircraft Carrier: American Military Power in Britain* (London, Michael Joseph).

Chalmers, Malcolm (1985) *Paying for Defence* (London, Pluto).

Clarke, Michael and Hague, Rod (eds) (1990) *European Defence Cooperation – America, Britain and NATO*, Fulbright Paper 7, Manchester, Manchester University Press.

Cmnd (1980) *Britain's Strategic Nuclear Force: the Choice of System to Replace Polaris* (London, HMSO).

Dillon, G. (1983) *Dependence and Deterrence* (Aldershot, Gower).

Dunne, Paul and Smith, Ron (1990) 'The Peace Dividend and the UK Economy', *Cambridge Econometrics*, Spring Report.

Elworthy, Scilla (1986) *Who Decides? Accountability and Nuclear Weapon Decision-Making in Britain* (Oxford Research Group).

Freedman, Lawrence (1980) *Britain and Nuclear Weapons* (London, Macmillan).

Gardner, Richard (1980) *Sterling–Dollar Diplomacy in Current Perspective* (New York, Columbia State University).

Gowing, Margaret (1964) *Britain and Atomic Energy 1939–1945* (London, Macmillan).

Gowing, Margaret (1974) *Independence and Deterrence: Britain and Atomic Energy 1945–1952* (London, Macmillan, 2 Vols.).

Gregory, Shaun (1990) 'French Nuclear Command and Control', *Defence Analysis*, vol. 6, no. 1.

Groom, A.J.R. (1974) *British Thinking about Nuclear Weapons* (London, Frances Pinter).

Hamwee, J., Miall H. and Elworthy, S. (1990) 'The Assumptions of British Nuclear Weapons Decision-Makers', *Journal for Peace Research*, vol. 27, no. 4.

Hennessy, Peter (1989) *Cabinet* (Oxford, Blackwell).

Hoffman, Mark (ed.) (1990) *UK Arms Control in the 1990s* (Manchester, Manchester University Press).

Howard, Michael (1972) *The Continental Commitment* (London, Temple Smith).

Howarth, Jolyon and Chilton, Patricia (eds) (1984) *Defence and Dissent in Contemporary France* (London, Croom Helm).

Hughes, Colin and Wintour, Patrick (1990) *Labour Rebuilt* (London, Fourth Estate).

Jensen, Eric and Fisher, Thomas (eds) (1990) *The United Kingdom – the United States* (London, Macmillan).

Johnson, Peter (1985) *Neutrality: A Policy for Britain* (London, Temple Smith).

Jones, Peter and Reece, Gordon (1990) *British Public Attitudes to Nuclear Defence* (London, Macmillan).

Kaiser, Karl and Morgan, Roger (eds) (1971) *Britain and West Germany: Changing Societies and the Future of Foreign Policy* (Oxford University Press).

Kaiser, Karl and Roper, John (1988) *British–German Defence Cooperation – Partners within the Alliance* (London, Jane's/RIIA).

Louis, William and Bull, Hedley (eds) (1986) *The 'Special Relationship', Anglo-American Relations Since 1945* (Oxford, Clarendon Press).
McMahon, Jeff (1981) *British Nuclear Weapons, For and Against* (London, Junction Books).
Malone, Peter (1984) *The British Nuclear Deterrent* (London, Croom Helm).
Marsh, Catherine and Fraser, Colin (eds) (1989) *Public Opinion and Nuclear Weapons* (London, Macmillan).
Owen, David *et al.* (1979) *Britain and the United States: Four Views to Mark the Silver Jubilee* (London, Heinemann).
Parkin, Sara (1989) *Green Parties* (London, Heretic Books).
Pierre, A. *Nuclear Politics: The British Experience with an Independent Strategic Force* (Oxford, Oxford University Press).
Richelson, Jeffrey and Ball, Desmond (1985) *The Ties that Bind* (Boston, Allen & Unwin).
Roper, John (ed.) (1985) *The Future of British Defence Policy* (London, Gower).
Rothwell, Victor (1982) *Britain and the Cold War* (London, Jonathan Cape).
Sanders, David (1990) *Losing an Empire, Finding a Role: British Foreign Policy Since 1945* (London, Macmillan).
Simpson, John (1984) *The Independent Nuclear State: the United States, Britain and the Military Atom* (London, Macmillan).
Smith, Dan (1980) *The Defence of the Realm in the 1980s* (London, Croom Helm).
Smith, M., Smith, S. and White, B. (eds) (1988) *British Foreign Policy* (London, Unwin Hayman).
Tatchell, Peter (1985) *Democratic Defence* (London, GMP Publishers).
Taylor, Peter (1990) *Britain and the Cold War: 1945 as Geopolitical Transition* (London, Frances Pinter).
Tugendhat, Christopher and Wallace, William (1988) *Options for British Foreign Policy in the 1990s* (London, Routledge/RIIA)
Ullman, Richard (1989) 'The Covert French Connection', Foreign Policy, Summer 1989.
Watt, David (1984) *Succeeding John Bull: America in Britain's Place* (Cambridge, Cambridge University Press).
Yost, David (1989) *France's Deterrent Posture and Security in Europe: Capabilities and Doctrine* (London, IISS Adelphi Paper 194).

Chapter 9

Azar, E. (1990) *The Management of Protracted Social Conflict: Theory and Cases* (Aldershot, Dartmouth).
Bailey, Sydney (1987) *War and Conscience in the Nuclear Age* (London, Macmillan).
Ball, Desmond and J. Richelson (eds) (1986) *Strategic Nuclear Targeting* (New York, Ithaca, Cornell University Press)
Bello, Walden (1990) *Brave New Third World: Strategies for Survival in the Global Economy* (London, Earthscan).

Blake, N. and Pole, K. (1983) *Dangers of Deterrence: Philosophers on Nuclear Strategy* (London, Routledge & Kegan Paul).

Blake, N. and Pole, K. (1984) *Objections to Nuclear Defence* (London, Routledge & Kegan Paul).

Boyle, Francis (1985) *World Politics and International Law* (Durham, North Carolina, Duke University Press).

Bundy, McGeorge (1988) *Danger and Survival: Choices about the Bomb in the First Fifty Years* (New York, Random House).

Burton, John (1990) *Conflict: Resolution and Provention* (London, Macmillan).

Burton, John and Dukes, Frank (1990) *Conflict: Practices in Management, Settlement and Resolution* (London, Macmillan).

Galtung, Johan (1989) *Solving Conflicts: a Peace Research Perspective* (Honolulu, University of Hawaii Press).

Halperin, Morton (1987) *Nuclear Fallacy: Dispelling the Myth of Nuclear Strategy* (Cambridge, Mass., Ballinger).

Hampshire, Stuart (1990) *Innocence and Experience* (London, Penguin).

Hinsley, F. (1963) *Power and the Pursuit of Peace* (Cambridge, Cambridge University Press).

Huth, P. and Russett, B. (1984) 'What Makes Deterrence Work?', *World Politics*, vol. 36, July 1984.

Independent Commission on International Development Issues (Brandt Commission) (1980) *North–South: A Programme for Survival* (London, Pan).

Independent Commission on Disarmament and Security Issues (Palme Commission) (1982) *Common Security: A Programme for Disarmament* (London, Pan).

Independent Commission on Environment and Development (Brundtland Commission) (1987) *Our Common Future* (Oxford, Oxford University Press).

James, Alan (1990) *Peacekeeping in International Politics* (London, Macmillan).

Kennan, George (1983) *The Nuclear Delusion* (New York, Pantheon).

Kull, Steven (1989) *Minds at War* (London, Basic Books).

Lebow, R. and Stein, J. (1987) 'Beyond Deterrence', *Journal of Social Issues*, vol. 43, no. 4.

Lebow, R. and Stein, J. (1990) *When Does Deterrence Succeed and How Do We Know?* (Canadian Institute for International Peace and Security, February 1990).

Maclean, Douglas (ed.) (1984) *The Security Gamble: Deterrence Dilemmas in the Nuclear Age* (Totowa, New Jersey, Rowman & Allenheld).

Mayall, J. (1990) *Nationalism and International Society* (Cambridge, Cambridge University Press).

Miall, Hugh (1991) *The Peacemakers* (London, Macmillan).

Mitchell, C. R. (1981) *The Structure of International Conflict* (London, Macmillan).

Mitchell, C. R. and Webb, K. (1981) *New Approaches to International Mediation* (New York, Greenwood).

North, Robert (1990) *War, Peace, Survival: Global Politics and Conceptual Synthesis* (London, Westview).

Patchen, M. (1988) *Resolving Disputes between Nations: Coercion or Conciliation?* (Duke University Press).

Powell, Robert (1990) *Nuclear Deterrence: the Search for Credibility* (Cambridge, Cambridge University Press).

Rapoport, A. (1989) *The Origins of Violence: Approaches to the Study of Conflict* (New York, Paragon House).

Rawls, John (1972) *A Theory of Justice* (Oxford, Oxford University Press).

Roberts, Adam (1990) 'Law, Lawyers and Nuclear Weapons', *Review of International Studies*, vol. 16, no. 1.

Sandole, O. and Sandole-Staroste, I. (eds) (1987) *Conflict Management and Problem-Solving: Interpersonal and International Applications* (London, Frances Pinter).

Tetlock, Philip *et al.* (1989) *Behaviour, Society and Nuclear War* (Oxford, Oxford University Press).

United Nations, Secretary-General's Report (1990) *A Comprehensive Study on Nuclear Weapons* (Report A/45/373,18 September).

United Nations General Assembly (1991) *Draft Handbook on Peaceful Settlement of Disputes Between States* (Special Committee on the Charter of the UN and the Strengthening of the Role of the Organization).

Urquart, B. (1989) 'The United Nations System and the Future', *International Affairs*, vol. 65, no. 2.

Woito, R. (1982) *To End War: A New Approach to International Conflict* (New York, Pilgrim Press).

Young, O. R. (1989) *International Cooperation: Building Regimes for Natural Resources and the Environment* (Ithaca, Cornell University Press).

Zacher, M. (1979) *International Conflict and Collective Security* (New York, Praeger).

Index